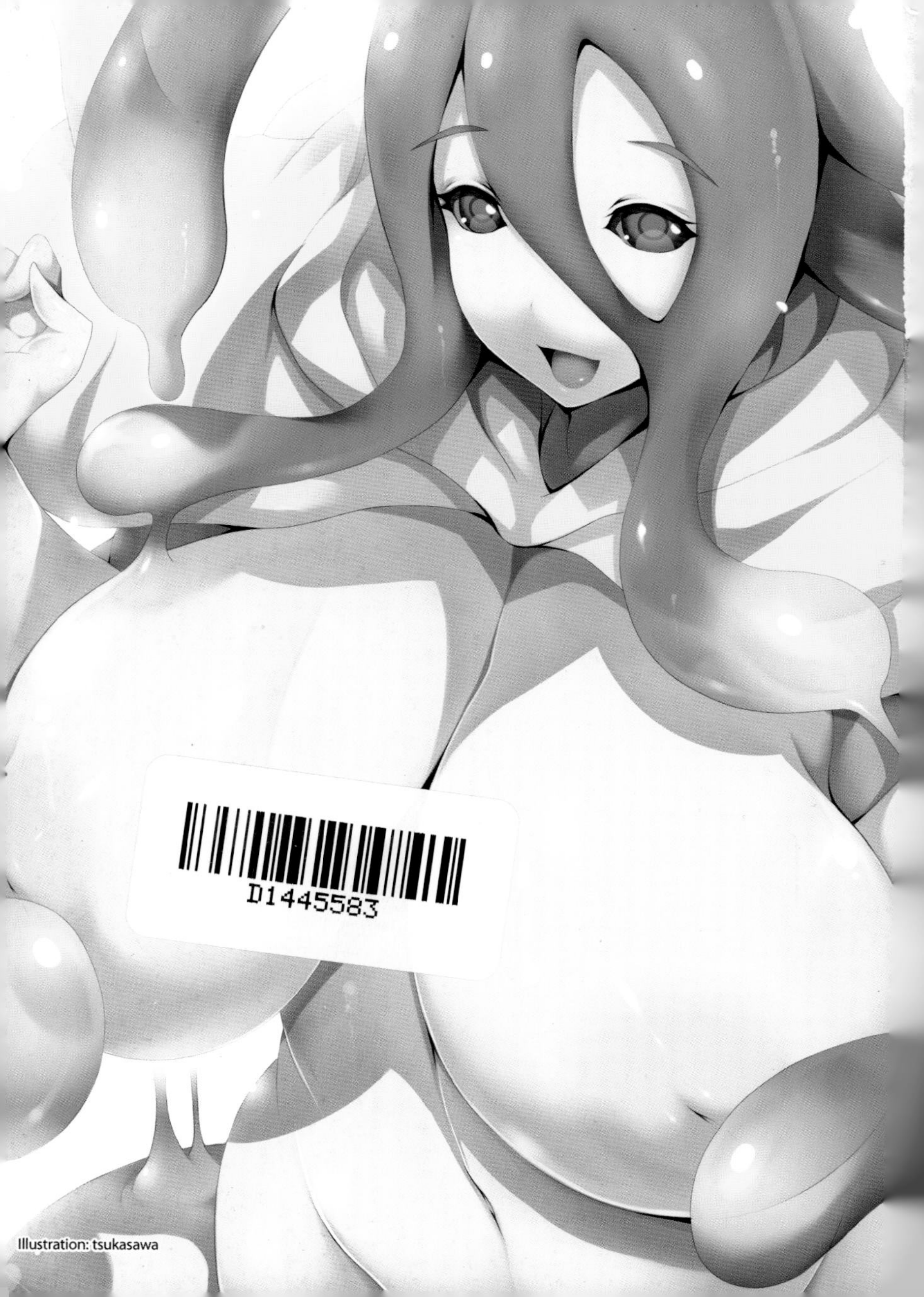

Illustration: tsukasawa

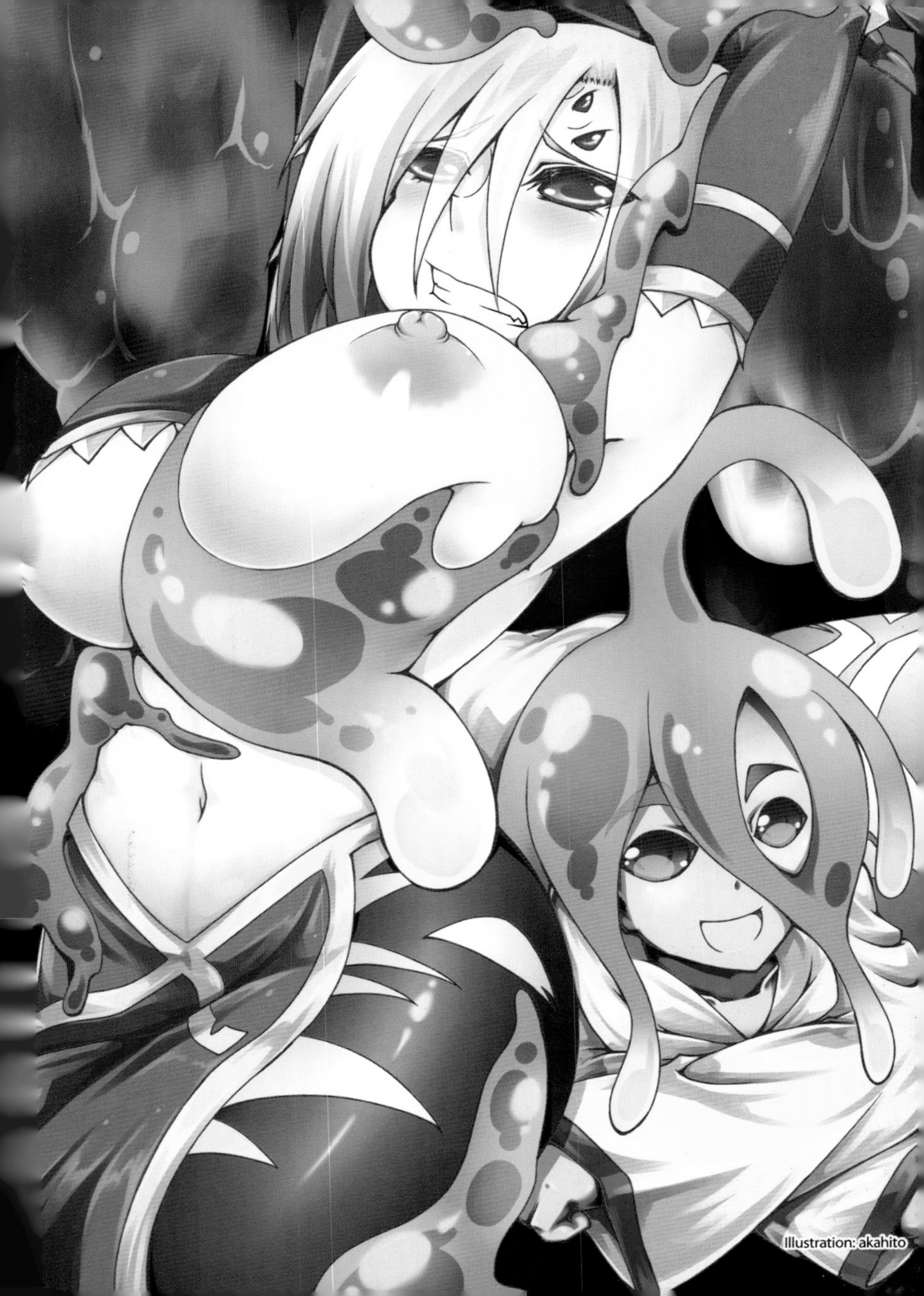

Illustration: akahito

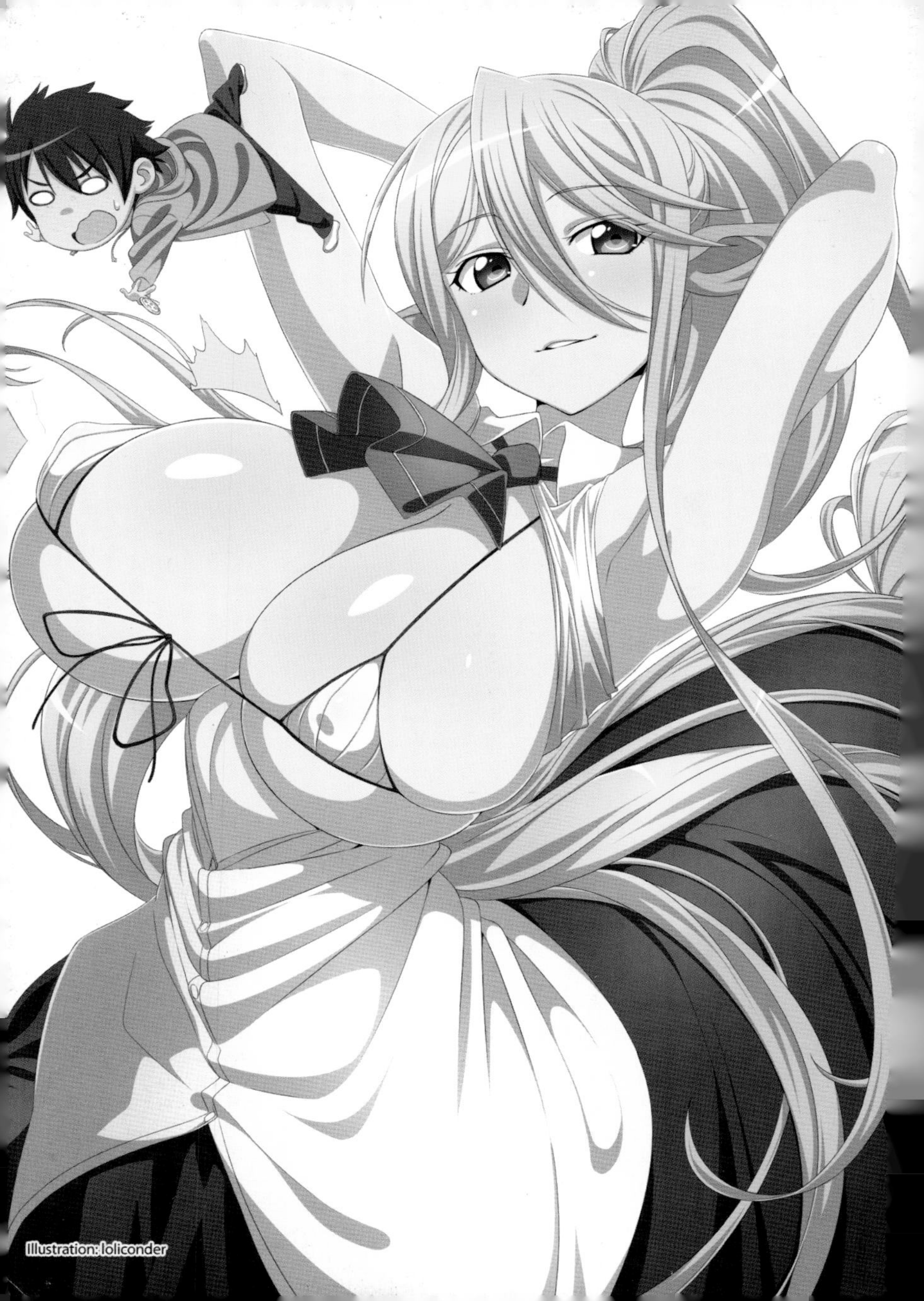

Illustration: loliconder

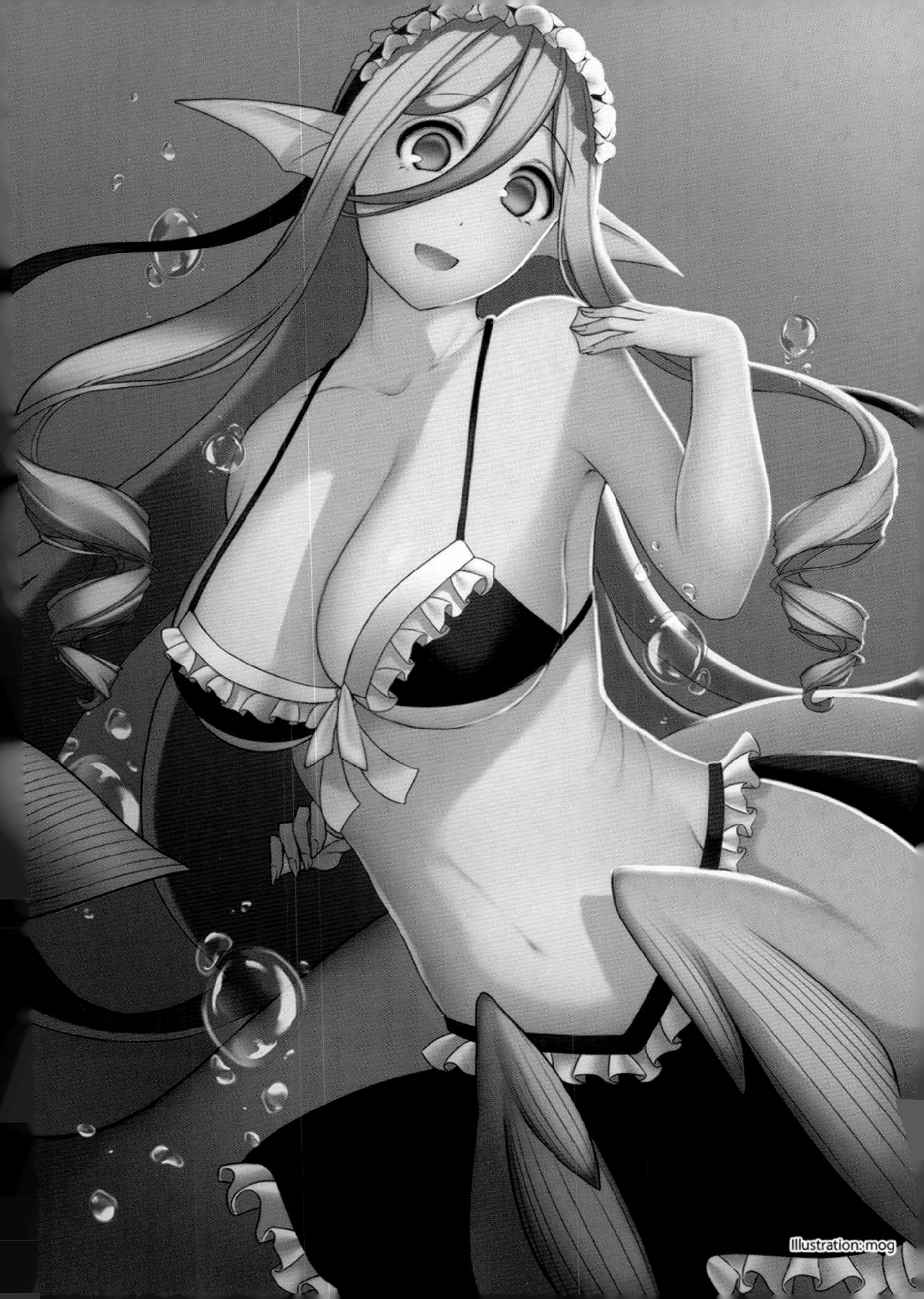
Illustration: mog

Tio & Horror Movies

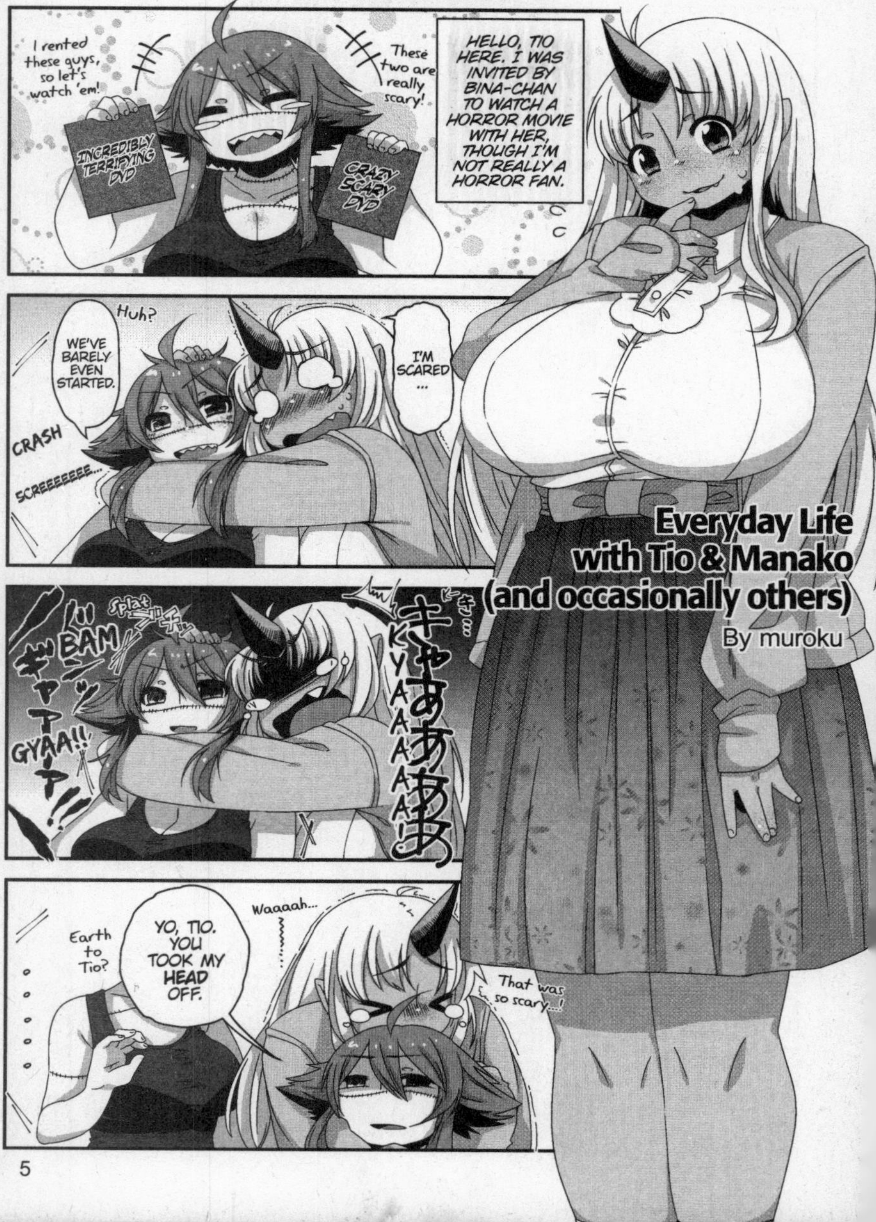
Everyday Life with Tio & Manako (and occasionally others)
By muroku
HELLO, TIO HERE. I WAS INVITED BY BINA-CHAN TO WATCH A HORROR MOVIE WITH HER, THOUGH I'M NOT REALLY A HORROR FAN.
These two are really scary!
CRAZY SCARY DVD
INCREDIBLY TERRIFYING DVD
I rented these guys, so let's watch 'em!
I'M SCARED ...
Huh?
WE'VE BARELY EVEN STARTED.
CRASH
SCREEEEEEEE...
KYAAAAAA!
Splat
BAM
GYAA!!
That was so scary...!
Waaaah...
YO, TIO. YOU TOOK MY HEAD OFF.
Earth to Tio?

Meet Tio

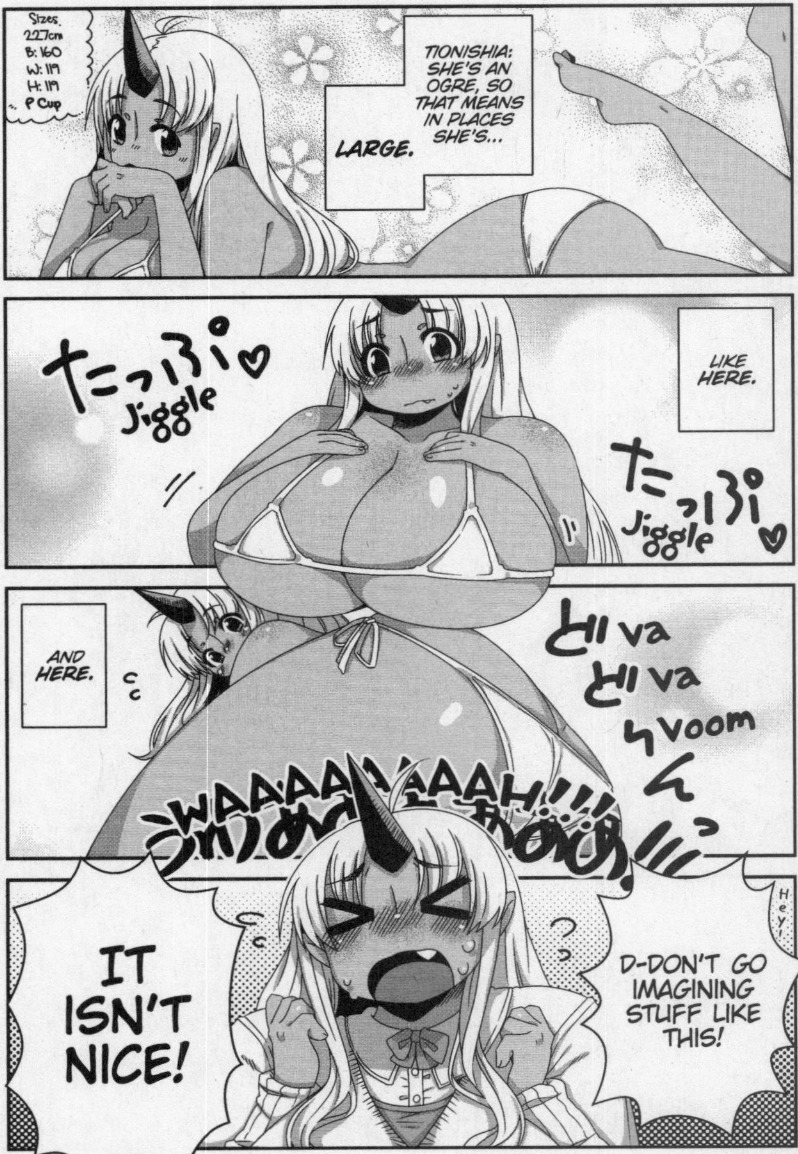

TIONISHIA: SHE'S AN OGRE, SO THAT MEANS IN PLACES SHE'S...
LARGE.
Sizes. 227cm B: 160 W: 119 H: 119 P Cup
LIKE HERE.
たっぷ♥ Jiggle
たっぷ Jiggle ♥
AND HERE.
どい va どい va
ぅ voom
ん
WAAAAAAAAAH!!!!
Hey!
D-DON'T GO IMAGINING STUFF LIKE THIS!
IT ISN'T NICE!

Tio & Elevators

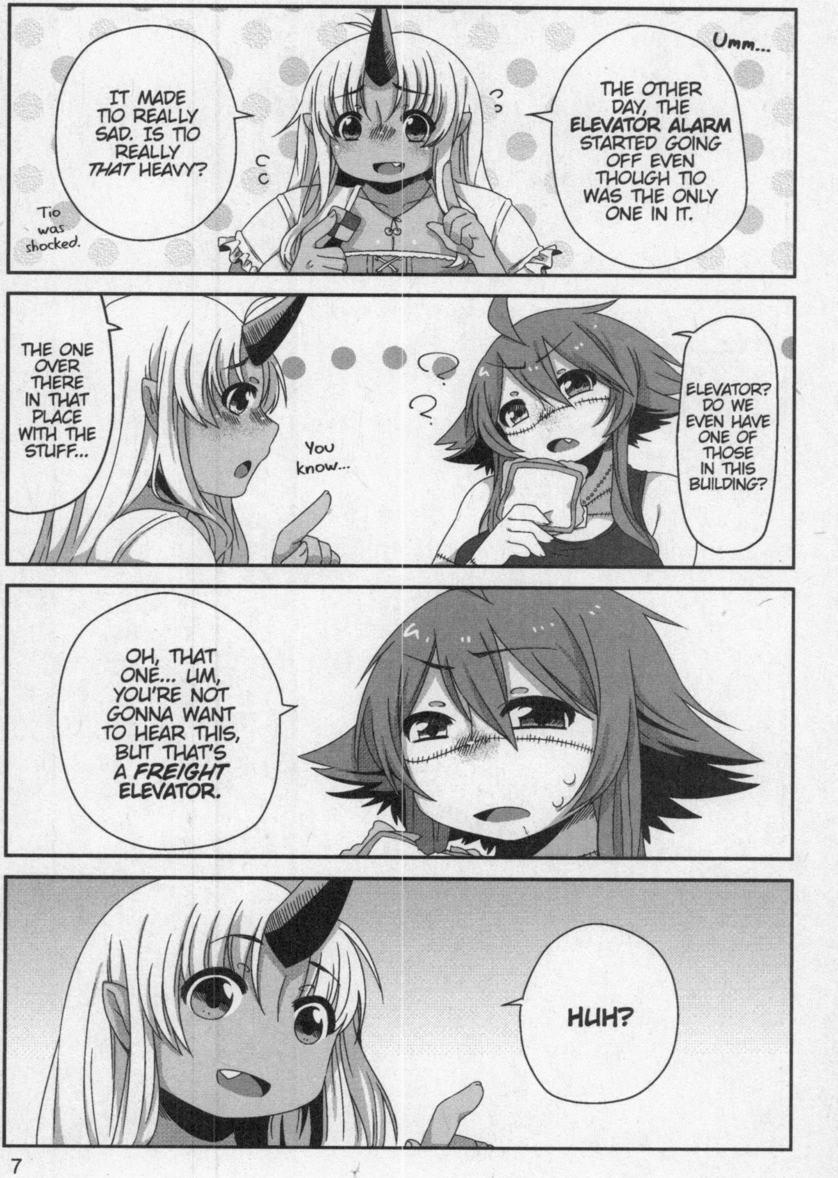

Umm...
THE OTHER DAY, THE ELEVATOR ALARM STARTED GOING OFF EVEN THOUGH TIO WAS THE ONLY ONE IN IT.
IT MADE TIO REALLY SAD. IS TIO REALLY *THAT* HEAVY?
Tio was shocked.
ELEVATOR? DO WE EVEN HAVE ONE OF THOSE IN THIS BUILDING?
THE ONE OVER THERE IN THAT PLACE WITH THE STUFF...
You know...
OH, THAT ONE... UM, YOU'RE NOT GONNA WANT TO HEAR THIS, BUT THAT'S A *FREIGHT* ELEVATOR.
HUH?

Manako's Problem

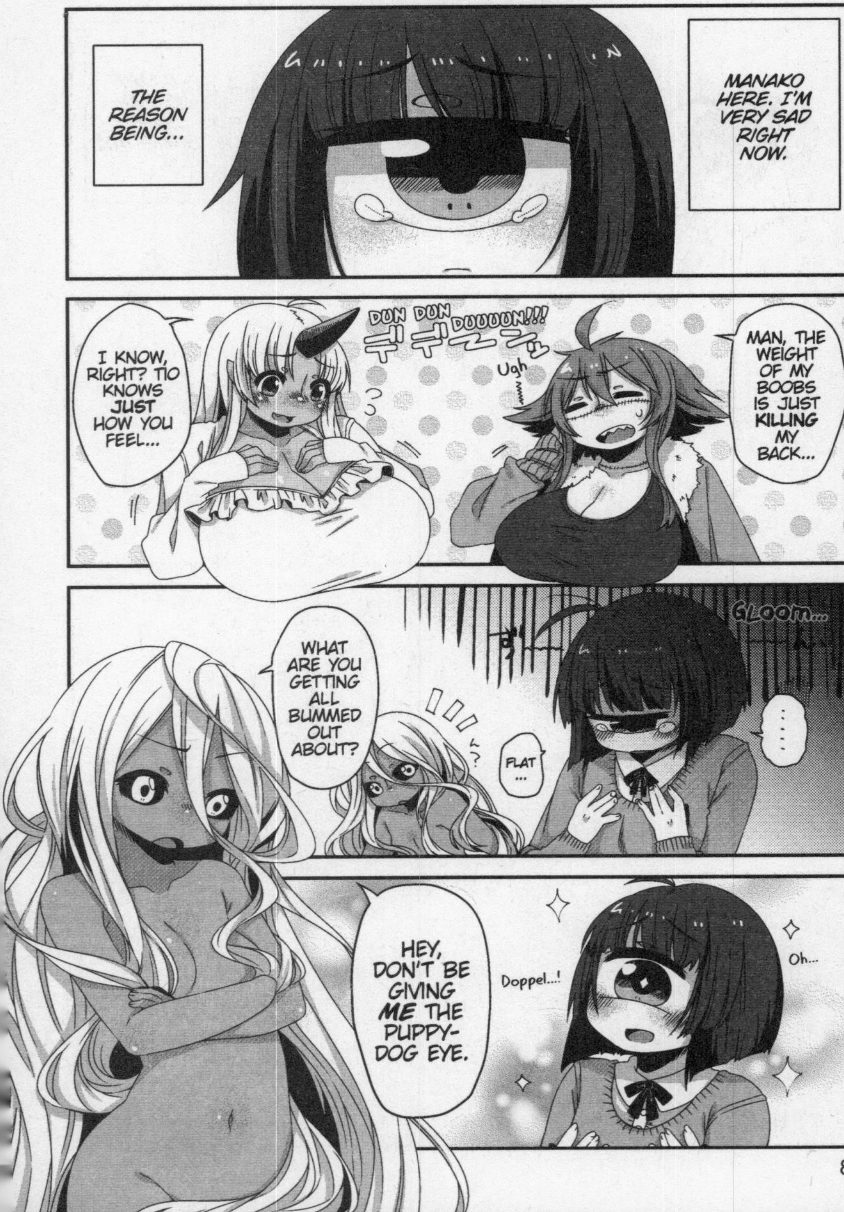
MANAKO HERE. I'M VERY SAD RIGHT NOW.
THE REASON BEING...
MAN, THE WEIGHT OF MY BOOBS IS JUST KILLING MY BACK...
Ugh
DUN DUN DUUUUN!!!
I KNOW, RIGHT? TIO KNOWS JUST HOW YOU FEEL...
GLOOM...
......
FLAT...
WHAT ARE YOU GETTING ALL BUMMED OUT ABOUT?
Oh...
Doppel...!
HEY, DON'T BE GIVING ME THE PUPPY-DOG EYE.

Tio's Birthday

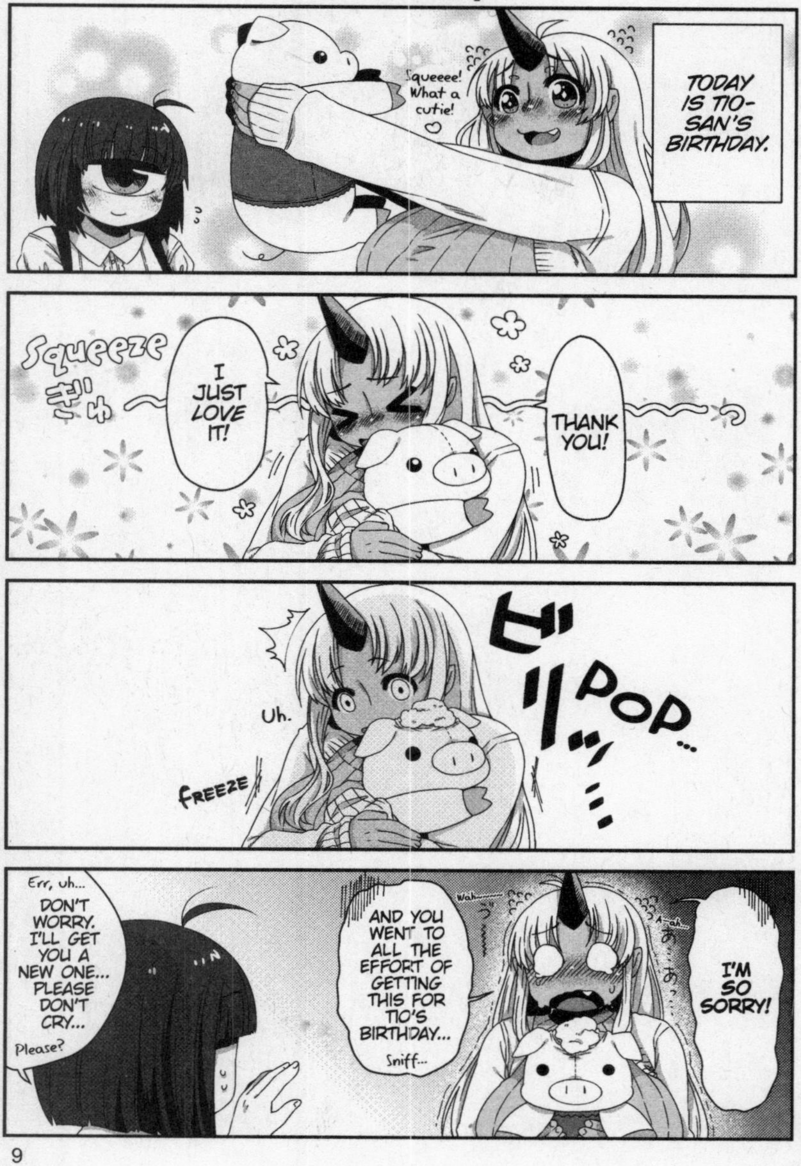

TODAY IS TIO-SAN'S BIRTHDAY.
Squeeee! What a cutie!
THANK YOU!
I JUST LOVE IT!
Squeeze
ぎゅ
ビリッ
POP...
Uh.
FREEZE
I'M SO SORRY!
A-ah...
Wah......
AND YOU WENT TO ALL THE EFFORT OF GETTING THIS FOR TIO'S BIRTHDAY...
Sniff...
Err, uh...
DON'T WORRY. I'LL GET YOU A NEW ONE... PLEASE DON'T CRY...
Please?

Tio & Manako

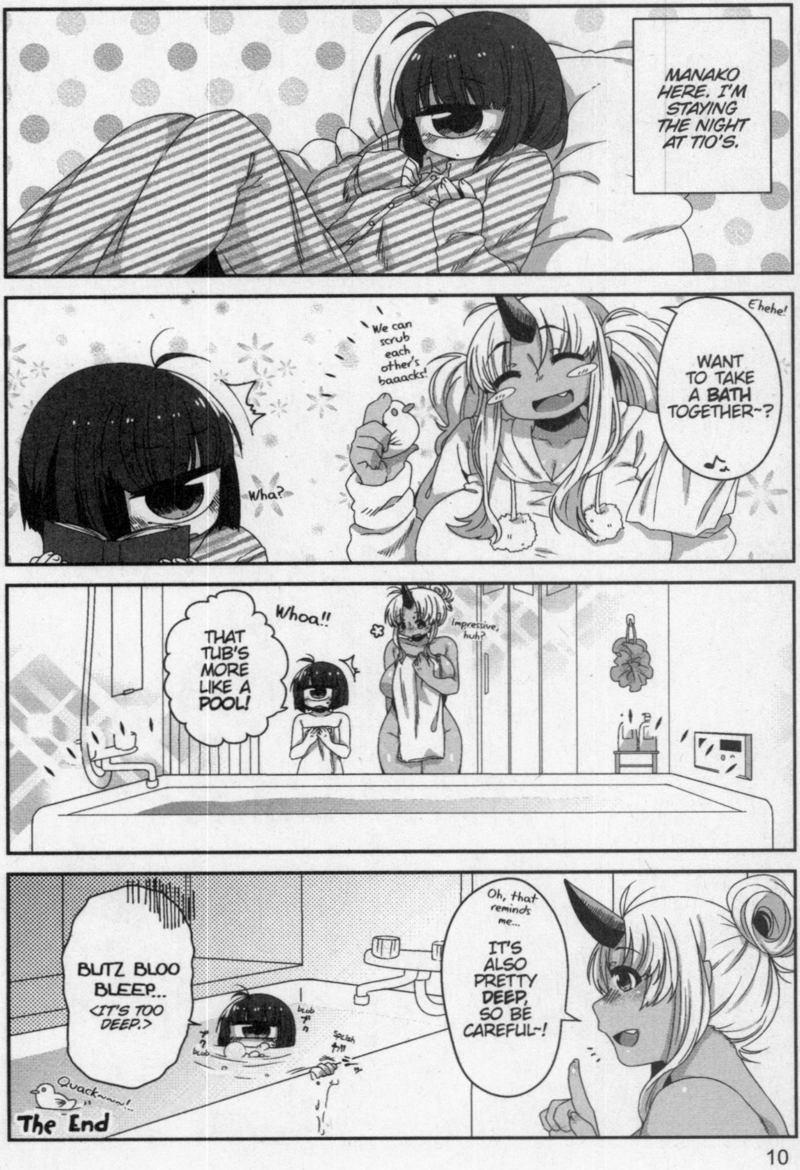
MANAKO HERE. I'M STAYING THE NIGHT AT TIO'S.
Ehehe!
WANT TO TAKE A BATH TOGETHER~?
We can scrub each other's baaacks!
Wha?
Impressive, huh?
Whoa!!
THAT TUB'S MORE LIKE A POOL!
Oh, that reminds me...
IT'S ALSO PRETTY DEEP, SO BE CAREFUL~!
Splish
blob
blob
BUTZ BLOO BLEEP...
<IT'S TOO DEEP.>
Quack~~!
The End

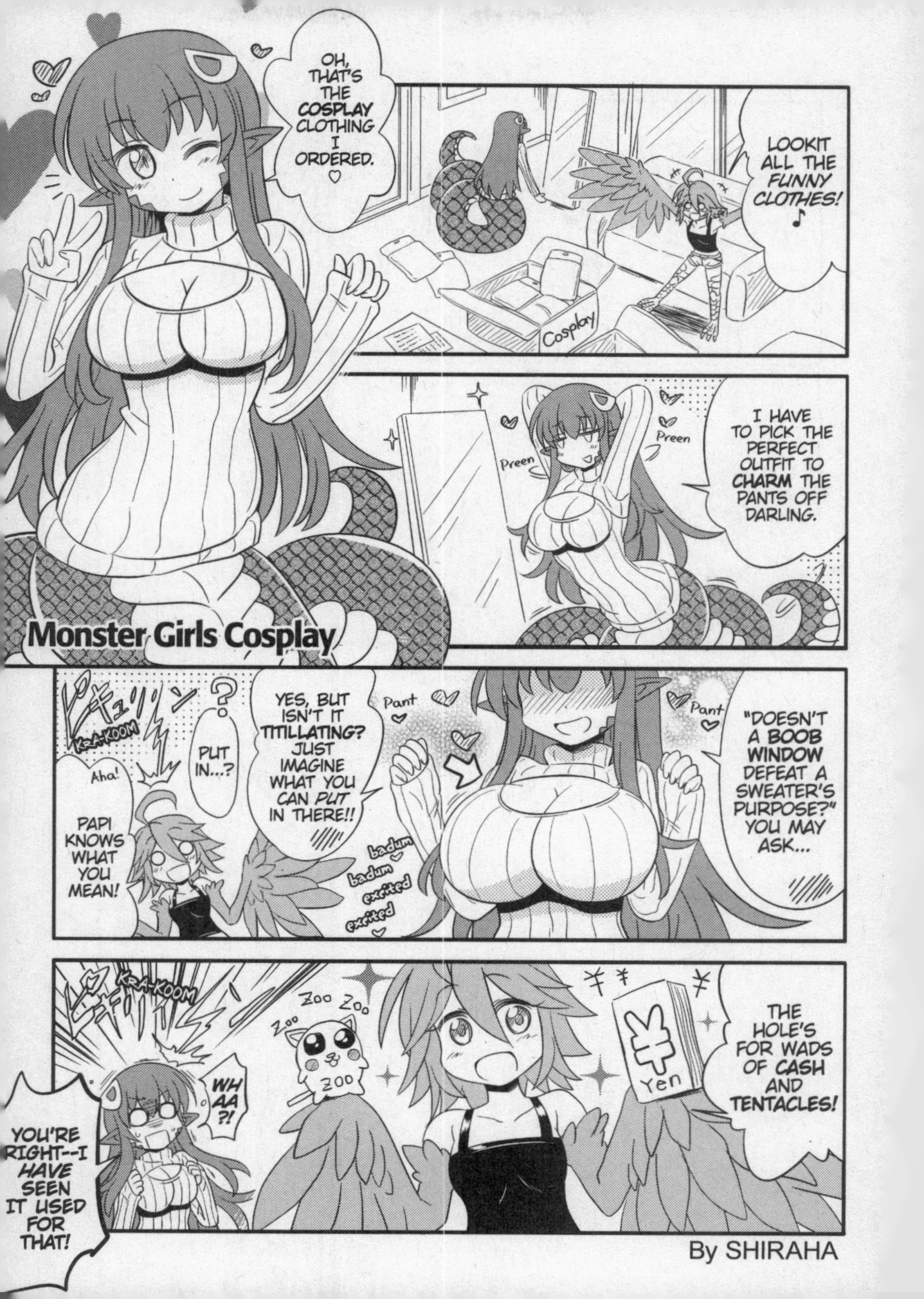

LOOKIT ALL THE FUNNY CLOTHES! ♪
OH, THAT'S THE COSPLAY CLOTHING I ORDERED. ♡
Cosplay
I HAVE TO PICK THE PERFECT OUTFIT TO CHARM THE PANTS OFF DARLING.
Preen
Preen
Monster Girls Cosplay
"DOESN'T A BOOB WINDOW DEFEAT A SWEATER'S PURPOSE?" YOU MAY ASK...
Pant
Pant
YES, BUT ISN'T IT TITILLATING? JUST IMAGINE WHAT YOU CAN PUT IN THERE!!
badum
badum
excited
excited
PUT IN...?
KRA-KOOM
Aha!
PAPI KNOWS WHAT YOU MEAN!
THE HOLE'S FOR WADS OF CASH AND TENTACLES!
Yen
Zoo Zoo
Zoo
ZOO
KRA-KOOM
WHAA?!
YOU'RE RIGHT--I HAVE SEEN IT USED FOR THAT!
By SHIRAHA

Papi Dresses Up

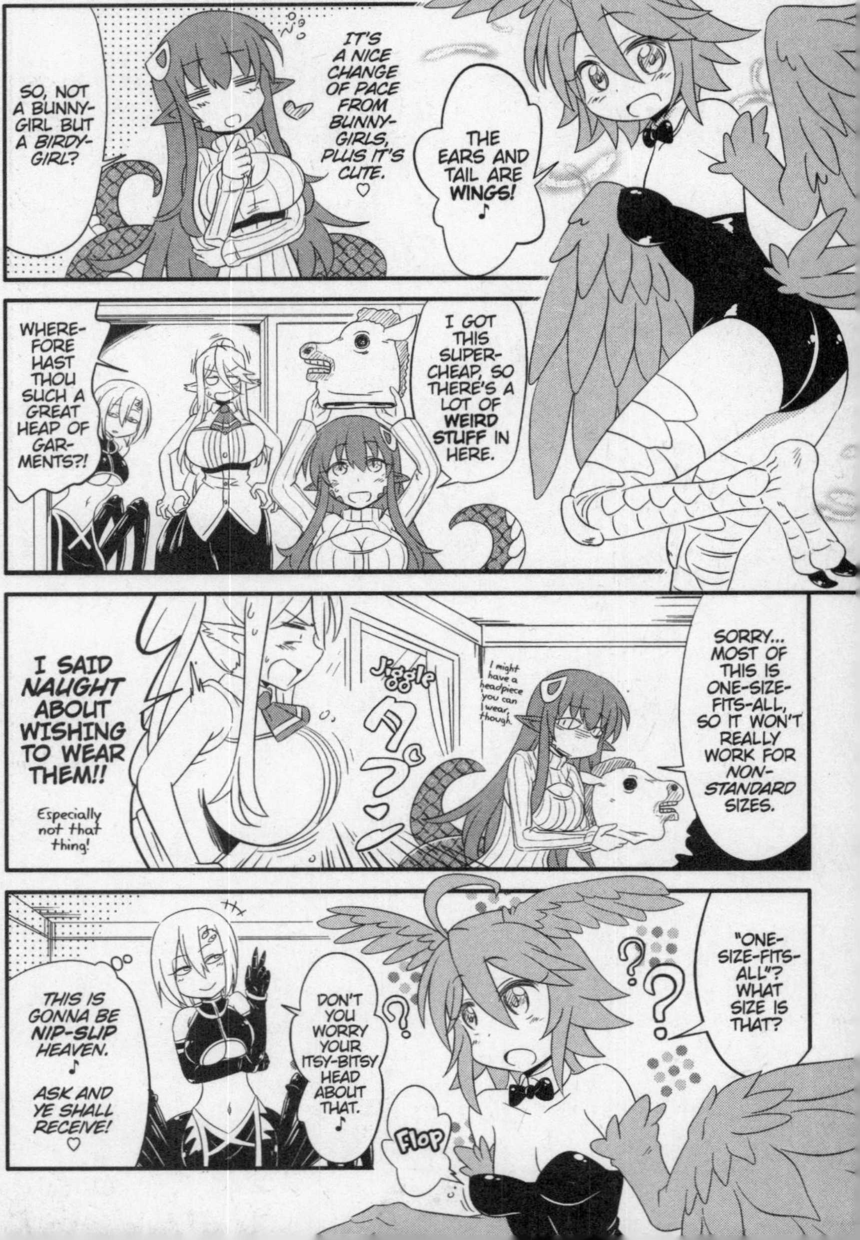
THE EARS AND TAIL ARE WINGS! ♪
IT'S A NICE CHANGE OF PACE FROM BUNNY-GIRLS, PLUS IT'S CUTE. ♡
SO, NOT A BUNNY-GIRL BUT A BIRDY-GIRL?
I GOT THIS SUPER-CHEAP, SO THERE'S A LOT OF WEIRD STUFF IN HERE.
WHEREFORE HAST THOU SUCH A GREAT HEAP OF GARMENTS?!
SORRY... MOST OF THIS IS ONE-SIZE-FITS-ALL, SO IT WON'T REALLY WORK FOR NON-STANDARD SIZES.
I might have a headpiece you can wear, though.
Jiggle
I SAID NAUGHT ABOUT WISHING TO WEAR THEM!!
Especially not that thing!
"ONE-SIZE-FITS-ALL"? WHAT SIZE IS THAT?
DON'T YOU WORRY YOUR ITSY-BITSY HEAD ABOUT THAT. ♪
Flop
THIS IS GONNA BE NIP-SLIP HEAVEN. ♪
ASK AND YE SHALL RECEIVE! ♡

Rachnera Dresses Up

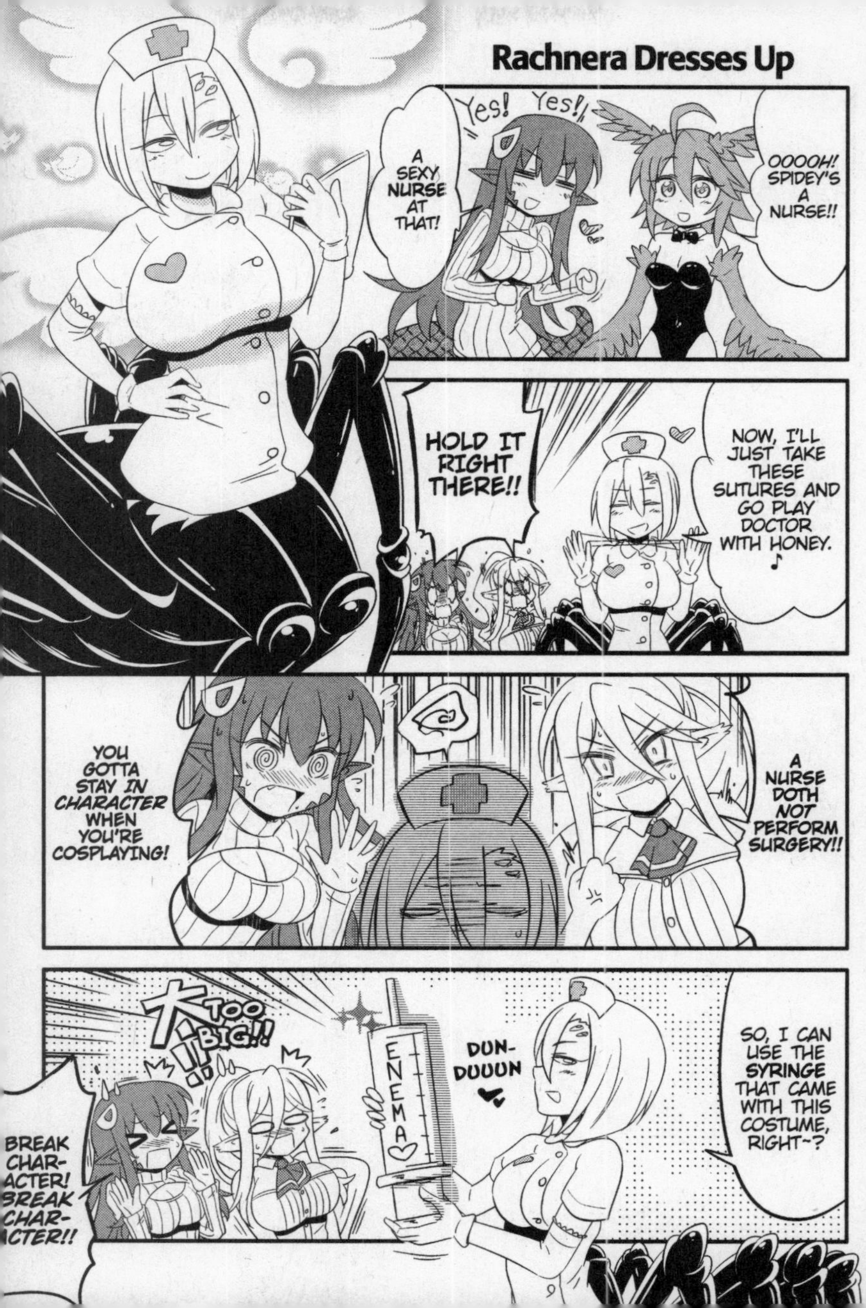

OOOOH! SPIDEY'S A NURSE!!
Yes!
Yes!
A SEXY NURSE AT THAT!
NOW, I'LL JUST TAKE THESE SUTURES AND GO PLAY DOCTOR WITH HONEY. ♪
HOLD IT RIGHT THERE!!
A NURSE DOTH NOT PERFORM SURGERY!!
YOU GOTTA STAY IN CHARACTER WHEN YOU'RE COSPLAYING!
SO, I CAN USE THE SYRINGE THAT CAME WITH THIS COSTUME, RIGHT~?
DUN-DUUUN
ENEMA
TOO BIG!!
BREAK CHARACTER! BREAK CHARACTER!!

Cerea Dresses Up

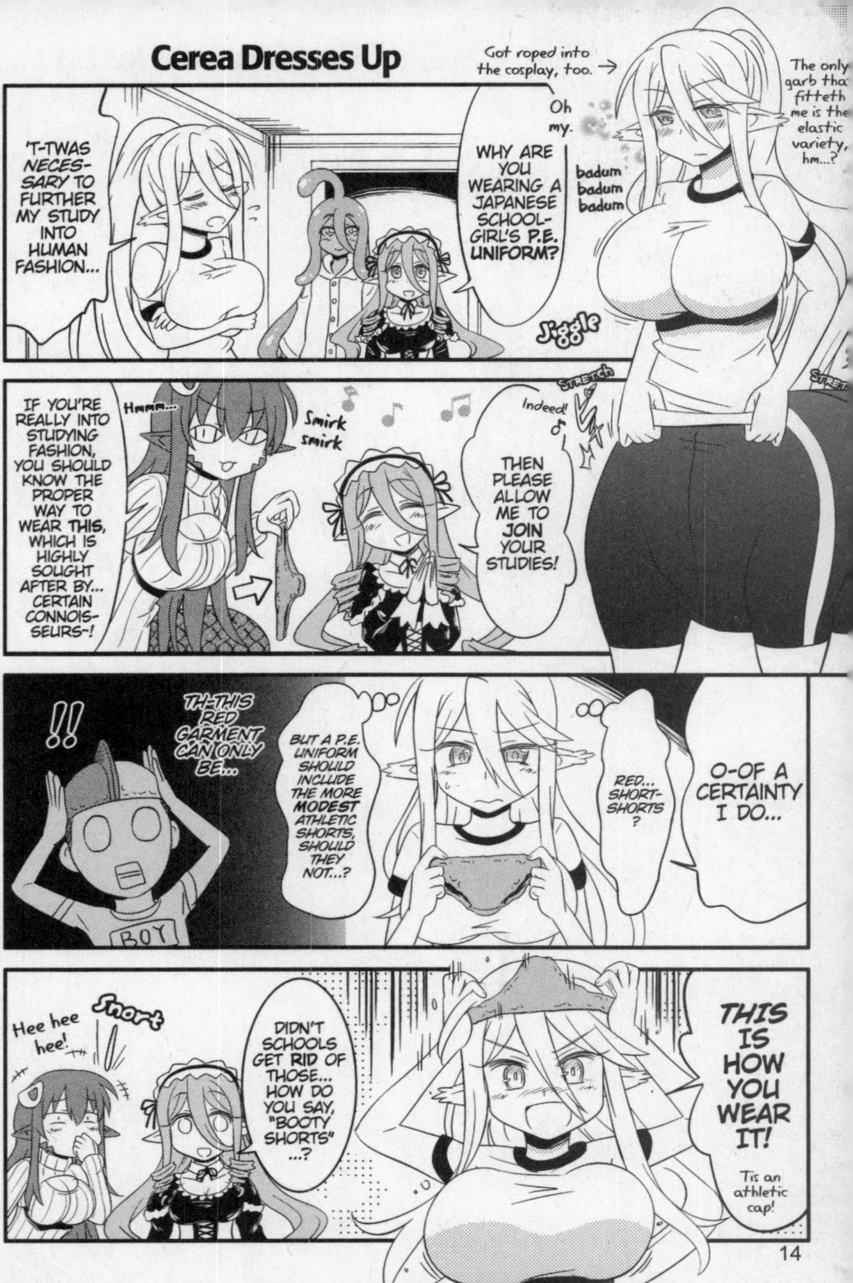

Got roped into the cosplay, too.
The only garb that fitteth me is the elastic variety, hm...?
badum badum badum
Jiggle
STRETCH
STRETCH
Oh my.
WHY ARE YOU WEARING A JAPANESE SCHOOL-GIRL'S P.E. UNIFORM?
'T-TWAS NECES-SARY TO FURTHER MY STUDY INTO HUMAN FASHION...
Indeed! ♪
THEN PLEASE ALLOW ME TO JOIN YOUR STUDIES!
Smirk smirk
Hmmm...
IF YOU'RE REALLY INTO STUDYING FASHION, YOU SHOULD KNOW THE PROPER WAY TO WEAR THIS, WHICH IS HIGHLY SOUGHT AFTER BY... CERTAIN CONNOISSEURS~!
O-OF A CERTAINTY I DO...
RED... SHORT-SHORTS?
BUT A P.E. UNIFORM SHOULD INCLUDE THE MORE MODEST ATHLETIC SHORTS, SHOULD THEY NOT...?
TH-THIS RED GARMENT CAN ONLY BE...
!!
BOY
Tis an athletic cap!
THIS IS HOW YOU WEAR IT!
DIDN'T SCHOOLS GET RID OF THOSE... HOW DO YOU SAY, "BOOTY SHORTS"...?
Snort
Hee hee hee!

Mero Dresses Up

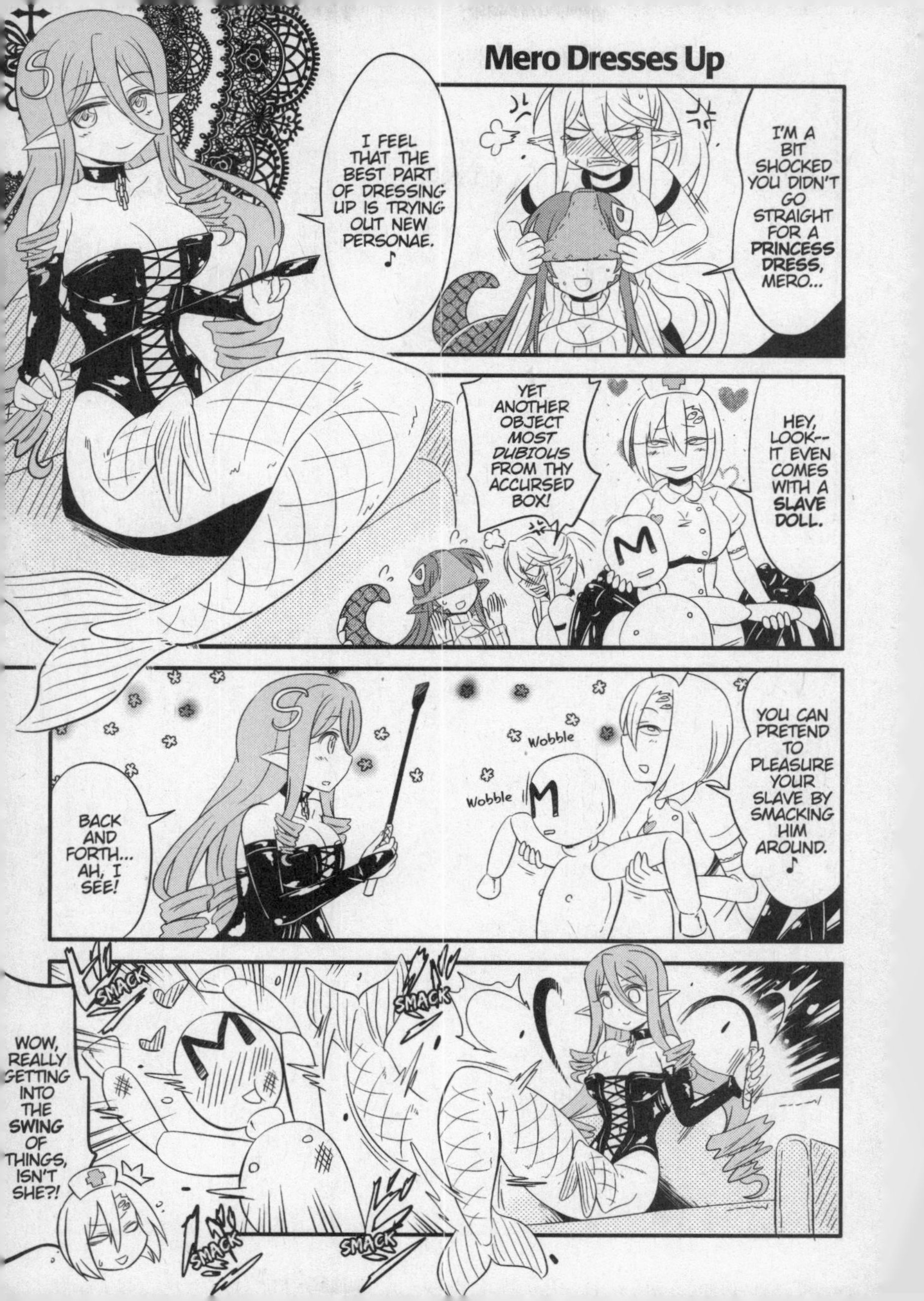
I'M A BIT SHOCKED YOU DIDN'T GO STRAIGHT FOR A PRINCESS DRESS, MERO...
HEY, LOOK-- IT EVEN COMES WITH A SLAVE DOLL.
YET ANOTHER OBJECT MOST DUBIOUS FROM THY ACCURSED BOX!
I FEEL THAT THE BEST PART OF DRESSING UP IS TRYING OUT NEW PERSONAE. ♪
YOU CAN PRETEND TO PLEASURE YOUR SLAVE BY SMACKING HIM AROUND. ♪
Wobble
Wobble
BACK AND FORTH... AH, I SEE!
SMACK
SMACK
SMACK
SMACK
WOW, REALLY GETTING INTO THE SWING OF THINGS, ISN'T SHE?!

Suu Dresses Up

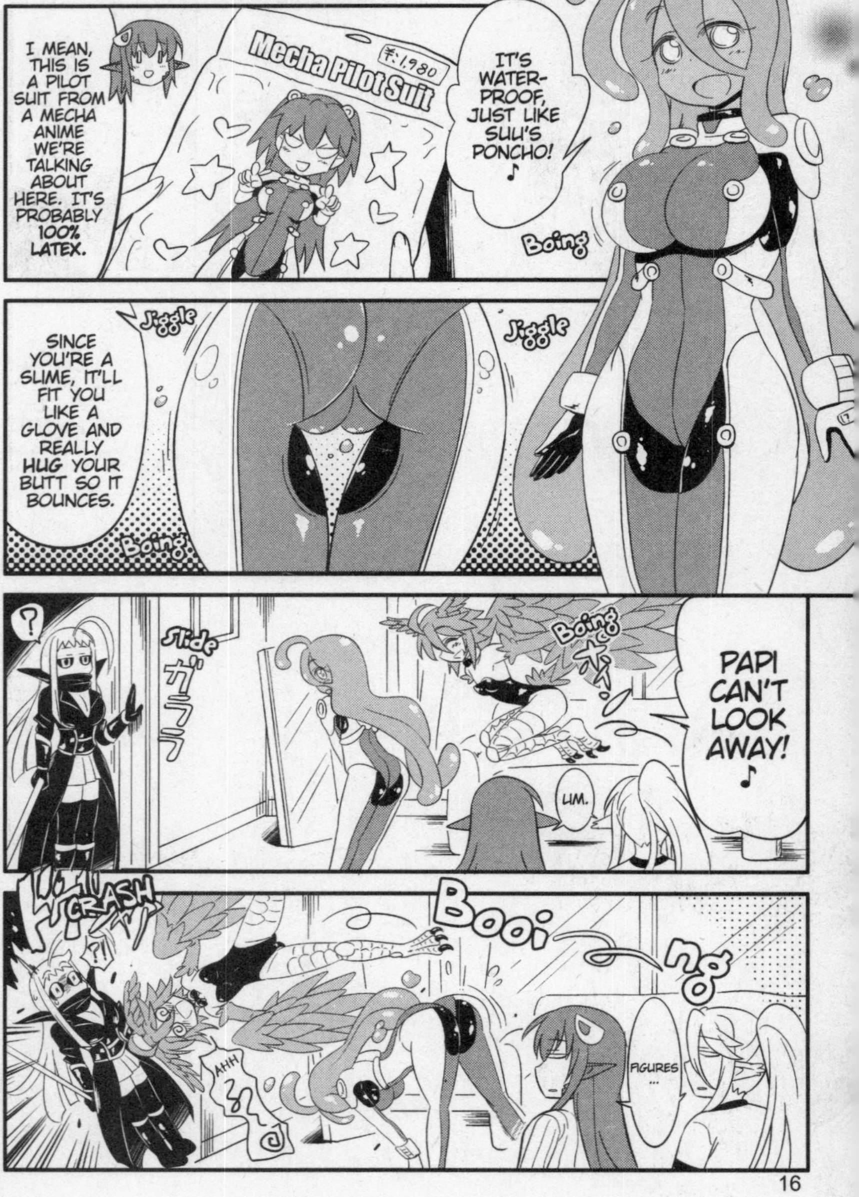

Boing
IT'S WATERPROOF, JUST LIKE SUU'S PONCHO! ♪
Mecha Pilot Suit
¥1,980
I MEAN, THIS IS A PILOT SUIT FROM A MECHA ANIME WE'RE TALKING ABOUT HERE. IT'S PROBABLY 100% LATEX.
Jiggle
Jiggle
SINCE YOU'RE A SLIME, IT'LL FIT YOU LIKE A GLOVE AND REALLY HUG YOUR BUTT SO IT BOUNCES.
Boing
PAPI CAN'T LOOK AWAY! ♪
Boing
UM.
Slide
?
Booi
ng
FIGURES...
AHH
?!
CRASH

Lala Dresses Up

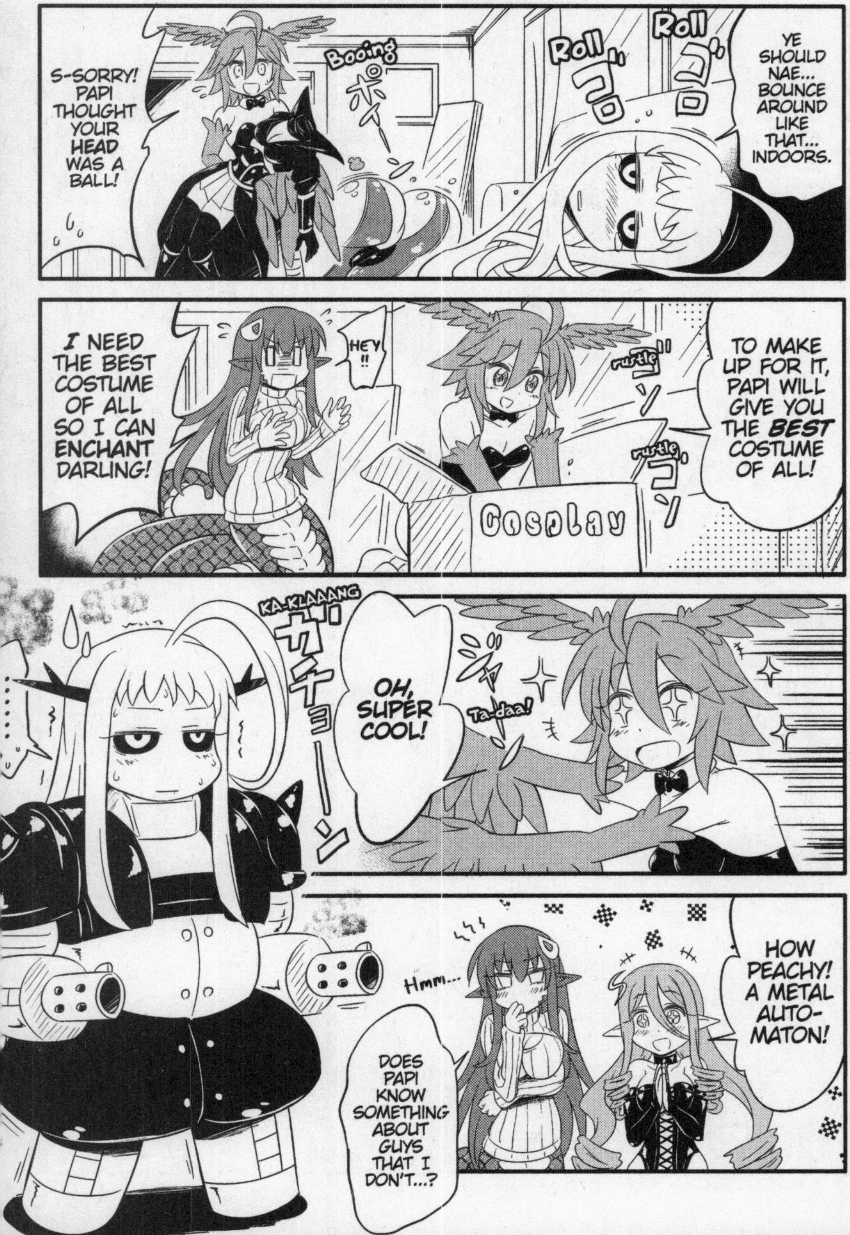
YE SHOULD NAE... BOUNCE AROUND LIKE THAT... INDOORS.
Roll
Roll
Booing
S-SORRY! PAPI THOUGHT YOUR HEAD WAS A BALL!
TO MAKE UP FOR IT, PAPI WILL GIVE YOU THE *BEST* COSTUME OF ALL!
rustle
rustle
Cosplay
HEY!!
I NEED THE BEST COSTUME OF ALL SO I CAN ENCHANT DARLING!
Ta-daa!
OH, SUPER COOL!
KA-KLAAANG
HOW PEACHY! A METAL AUTO-MATON!
Hmm...
DOES PAPI KNOW SOMETHING ABOUT GUYS THAT I DON'T...?

MON Dresses Up

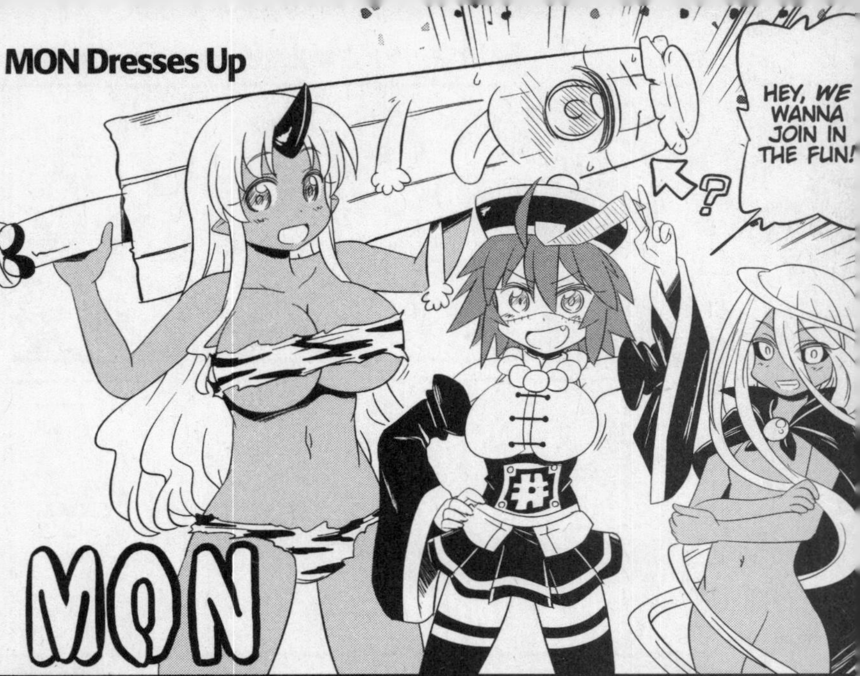
HEY, *WE* WANNA JOIN IN THE FUN!
?
MON

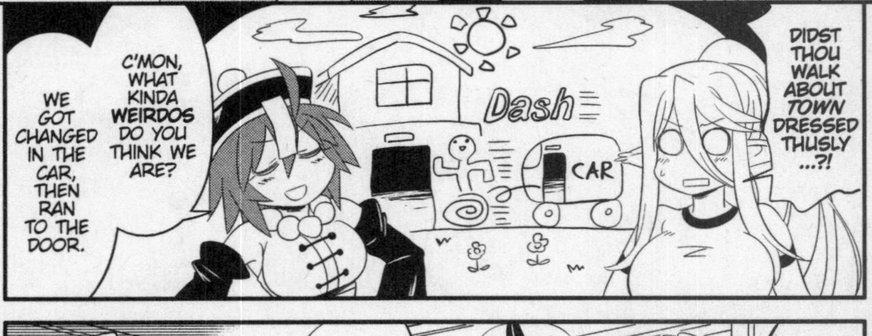
DIDST THOU WALK ABOUT *TOWN* DRESSED THUSLY ...?!
C'MON, WHAT KINDA **WEIRDOS** DO YOU THINK WE ARE?
WE GOT CHANGED IN THE CAR, THEN RAN TO THE DOOR.
Dash
CAR

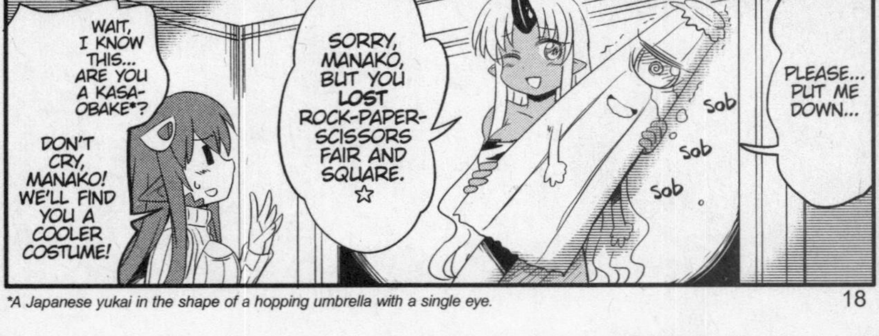
PLEASE... PUT ME DOWN...
Sob
Sob
Sob
SORRY, MANAKO, BUT YOU **LOST** ROCK-PAPER-SCISSORS FAIR AND SQUARE. ☆
WAIT, I KNOW THIS... ARE YOU A KASA-OBAKE*?
DON'T CRY, MANAKO! WE'LL FIND YOU A COOLER COSTUME!

*A Japanese yukai in the shape of a hopping umbrella with a single eye.

Zombina Dresses Up

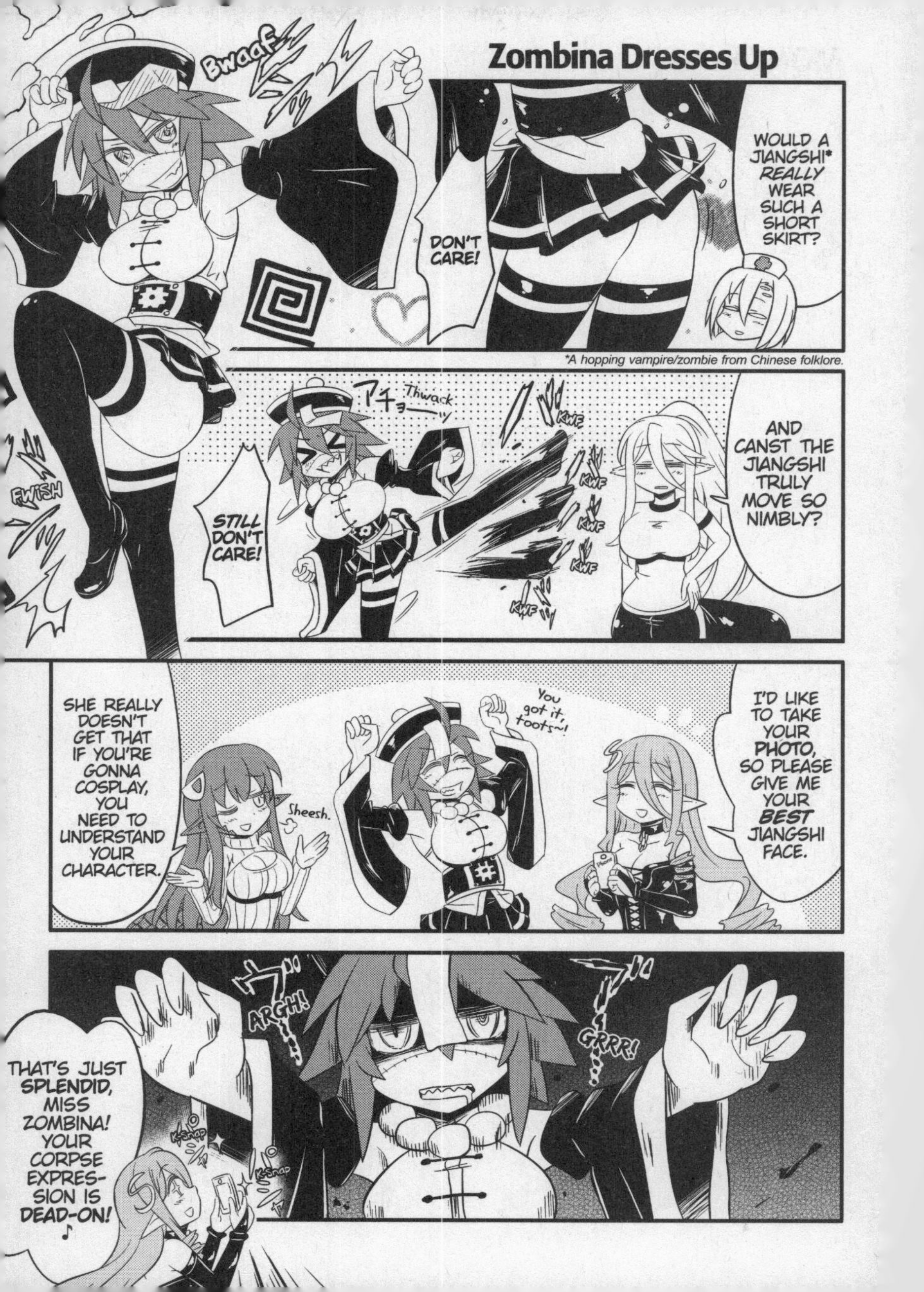
WOULD A JIANGSHI* *REALLY* WEAR SUCH A SHORT SKIRT?
DON'T CARE!
AND CANST THE JIANGSHI TRULY MOVE SO NIMBLY?
アチョーッ
Thwack
KWF
KWF
KWF
KWF
KWF
STILL DON'T CARE!
Bwaaf
FWISH
I'D LIKE TO TAKE YOUR PHOTO, SO PLEASE GIVE ME YOUR *BEST* JIANGSHI FACE.
You got it, toots~!
Sheesh.
SHE REALLY DOESN'T GET THAT IF YOU'RE GONNA COSPLAY, YOU NEED TO UNDERSTAND YOUR CHARACTER.
GRRR!
ARGH!
K-Snap
K-Snap
THAT'S JUST **SPLENDID**, MISS ZOMBINA! YOUR CORPSE EXPRESSION IS **DEAD-ON!** ♪

*A hopping vampire/zombie from Chinese folklore.

Tio Dresses Up

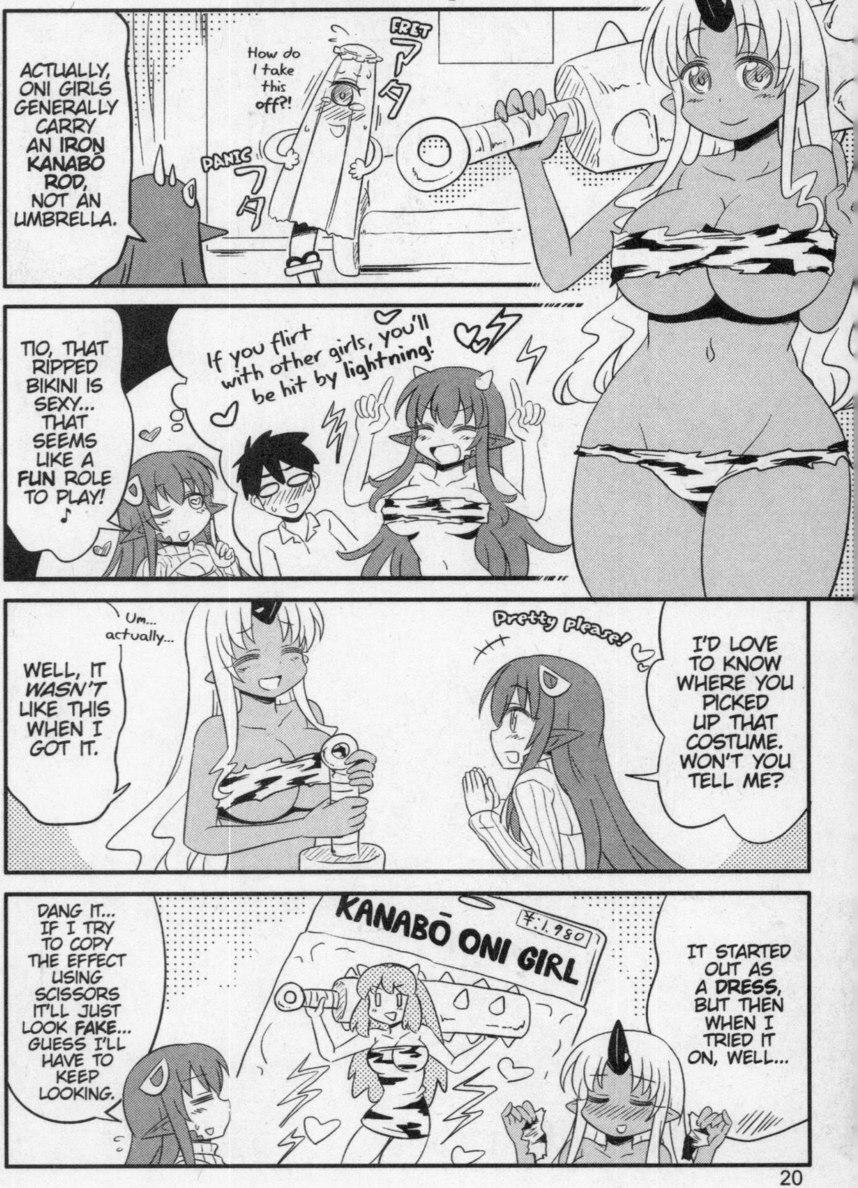
FRET
アタ
How do I take this off?!
PANIC
フタ
ACTUALLY, ONI GIRLS GENERALLY CARRY AN IRON KANABŌ ROD, NOT AN UMBRELLA.
If you flirt with other girls, you'll be hit by lightning!
TIO, THAT RIPPED BIKINI IS SEXY... THAT SEEMS LIKE A FUN ROLE TO PLAY! ♪
Pretty please!
I'D LOVE TO KNOW WHERE YOU PICKED UP THAT COSTUME. WON'T YOU TELL ME?
Um... actually...
WELL, IT WASN'T LIKE THIS WHEN I GOT IT.
IT STARTED OUT AS A DRESS, BUT THEN WHEN I TRIED IT ON, WELL...
KANABŌ ONI GIRL
¥1.980
DANG IT... IF I TRY TO COPY THE EFFECT USING SCISSORS IT'LL JUST LOOK FAKE... GUESS I'LL HAVE TO KEEP LOOKING.

Manako Dresses Up

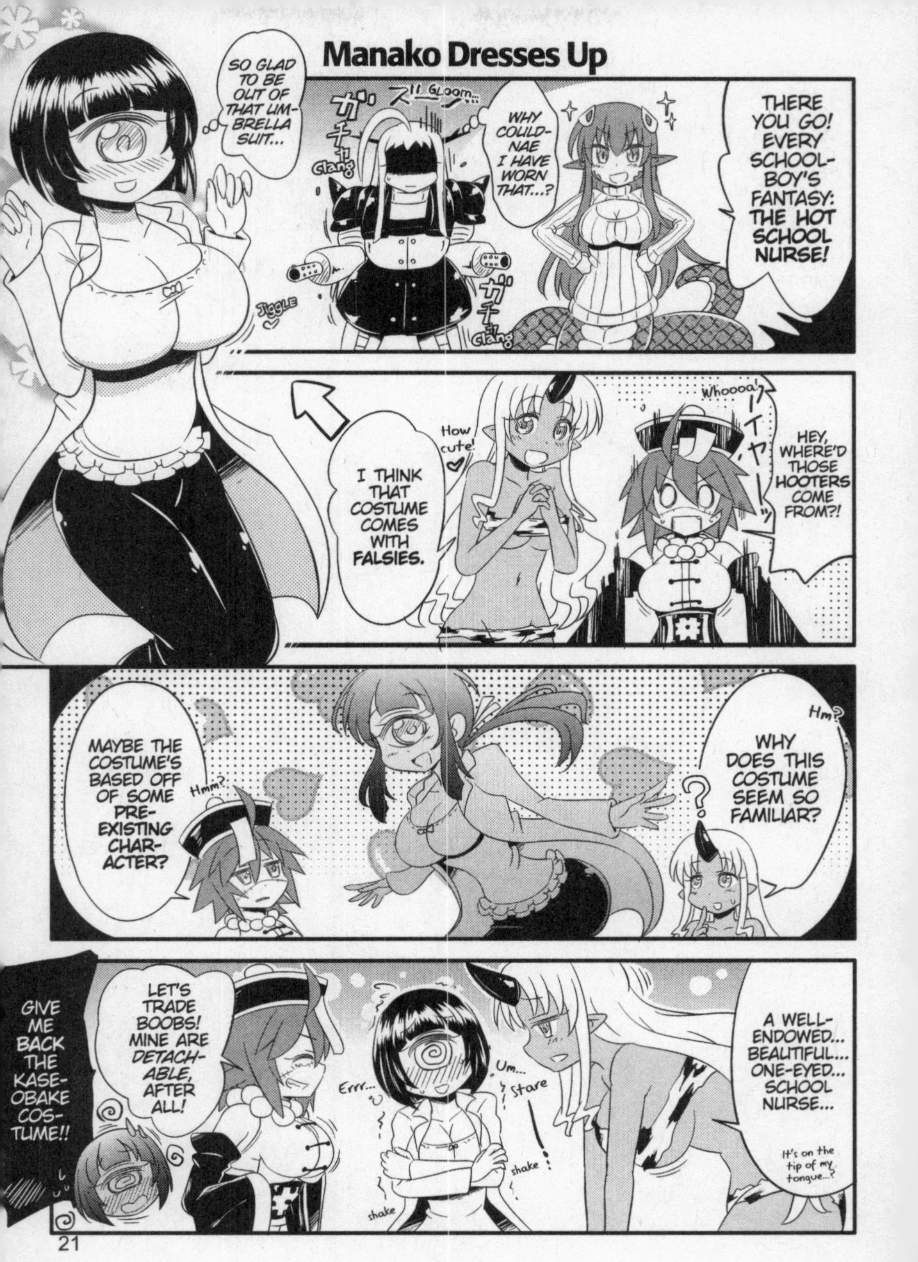
THERE YOU GO! EVERY SCHOOLBOY'S FANTASY: THE HOT SCHOOL NURSE!
WHY COULDNAE I HAVE WORN THAT...?
Gloom...
Clang
Clang
HEY, WHERE'D THOSE HOOTERS COME FROM?!
Whoooa!
How cute!
I THINK THAT COSTUME COMES WITH FALSIES.
SO GLAD TO BE OUT OF THAT UMBRELLA SUIT...
Jiggle
Hm?
WHY DOES THIS COSTUME SEEM SO FAMILIAR?
Hmm?
MAYBE THE COSTUME'S BASED OFF OF SOME PRE-EXISTING CHARACTER?
A WELL-ENDOWED... BEAUTIFUL... ONE-EYED... SCHOOL NURSE...
It's on the tip of my tongue...?
Stare
Um...
shake
shake
Err...
LET'S TRADE BOOBS! MINE ARE DETACHABLE, AFTER ALL!
GIVE ME BACK THE KASE-OBAKE COSTUME!!

Doppel Dresses Up

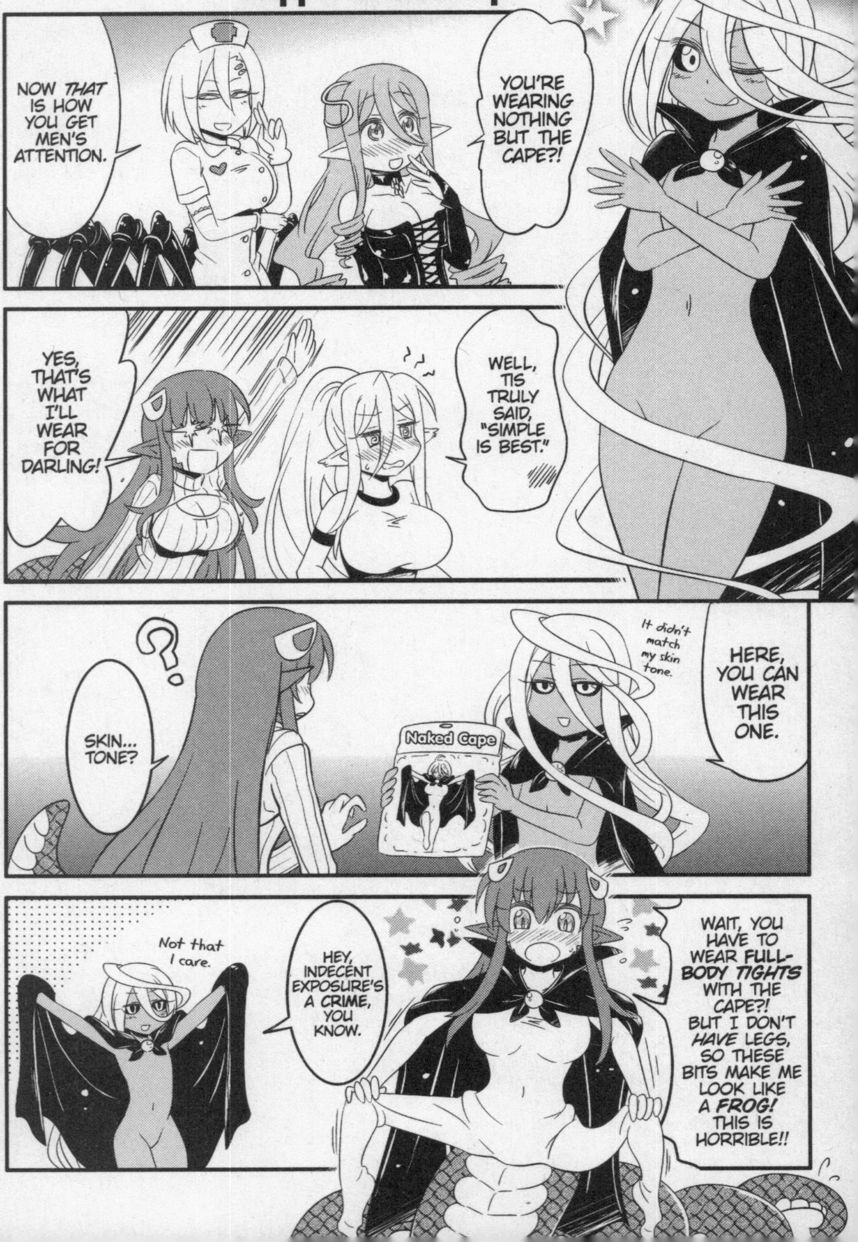
YOU'RE WEARING NOTHING BUT THE CAPE?!
NOW *THAT* IS HOW YOU GET MEN'S ATTENTION.
WELL, TIS TRULY SAID, "SIMPLE IS BEST."
YES, THAT'S WHAT I'LL WEAR FOR DARLING!
HERE, YOU CAN WEAR THIS ONE.
It didn't match my skin tone.
Naked Cape
SKIN... TONE?
WAIT, YOU HAVE TO WEAR **FULL-BODY *TIGHTS*** WITH THE CAPE?! BUT I DON'T *HAVE* LEGS, SO THESE BITS MAKE ME LOOK LIKE A ***FROG!*** THIS IS HORRIBLE!!
HEY, INDECENT EXPOSURE'S A **CRIME**, YOU KNOW.
Not that I care.

モンスター娘のいる日常
4コマアンソロジー

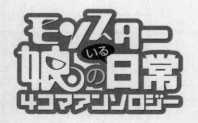

Hmm?

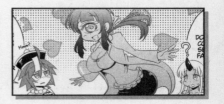

Drink Responsibly

By stealth kaigyou

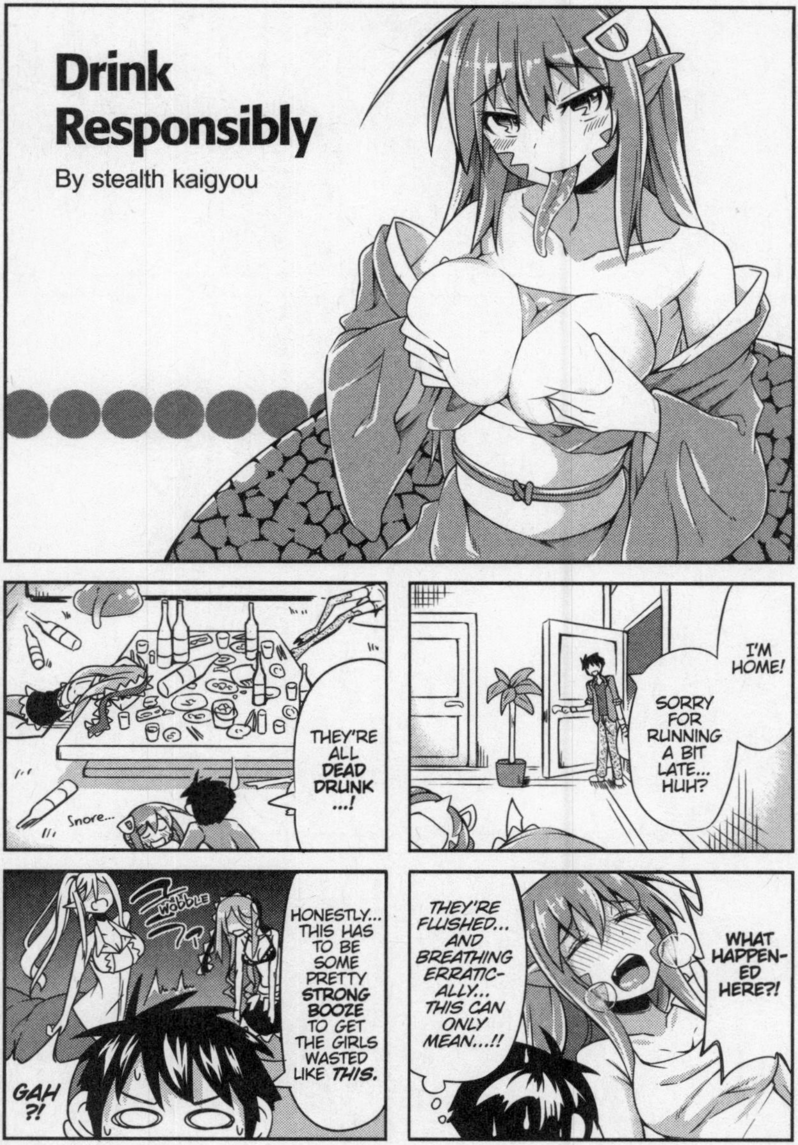

I'M HOME!
SORRY FOR RUNNING A BIT LATE... HUH?
THEY'RE ALL DEAD DRUNK ...!
Snore...
WHAT HAPPEN-ED HERE?!
THEY'RE FLUSHED... AND BREATHING ERRATIC-ALLY... THIS CAN ONLY MEAN...!!
HONESTLY... THIS HAS TO BE SOME PRETTY STRONG BOOZE TO GET THE GIRLS WASTED LIKE THIS.
WOBBLE
GAH ?!

Wound-up Drunks

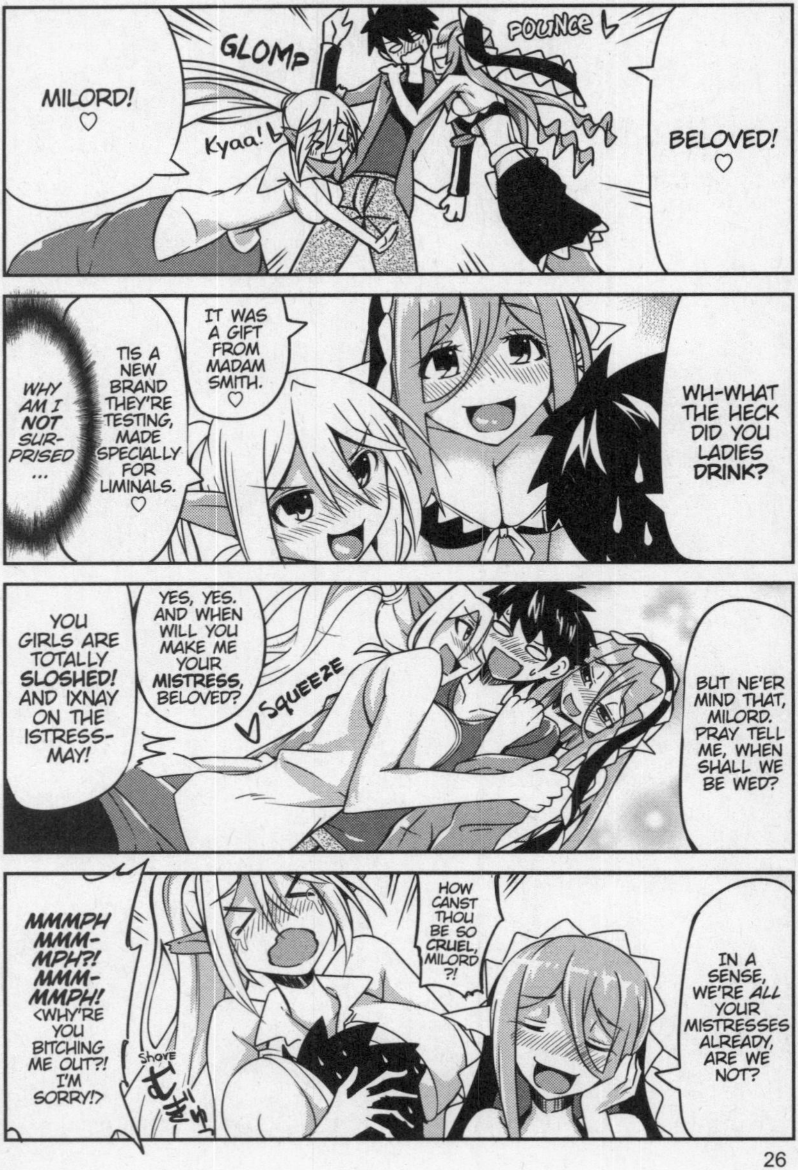
POUNCE
BELOVED! ♡
GLOMP
MILORD! ♡
Kyaa!
WH-WHAT THE HECK DID YOU LADIES DRINK?
IT WAS A GIFT FROM MADAM SMITH. ♡
TIS A NEW BRAND THEY'RE TESTING, MADE SPECIALLY FOR LIMINALS. ♡
WHY AM I NOT SURPRISED...
BUT NE'ER MIND THAT, MILORD. PRAY TELL ME, WHEN SHALL WE BE WED?
YES, YES. AND WHEN WILL YOU MAKE ME YOUR MISTRESS, BELOVED?
SQUEEZE
YOU GIRLS ARE TOTALLY SLOSHED! AND IXNAY ON THE ISTRESS-MAY!
IN A SENSE, WE'RE ALL YOUR MISTRESSES ALREADY, ARE WE NOT?
HOW CANST THOU BE SO CRUEL, MILORD?!
MMMPH MMM-MPH?! MMM-MMPH! <WHY'RE YOU BITCHING ME OUT?! I'M SORRY!>
Shove

Tied-up Drunks

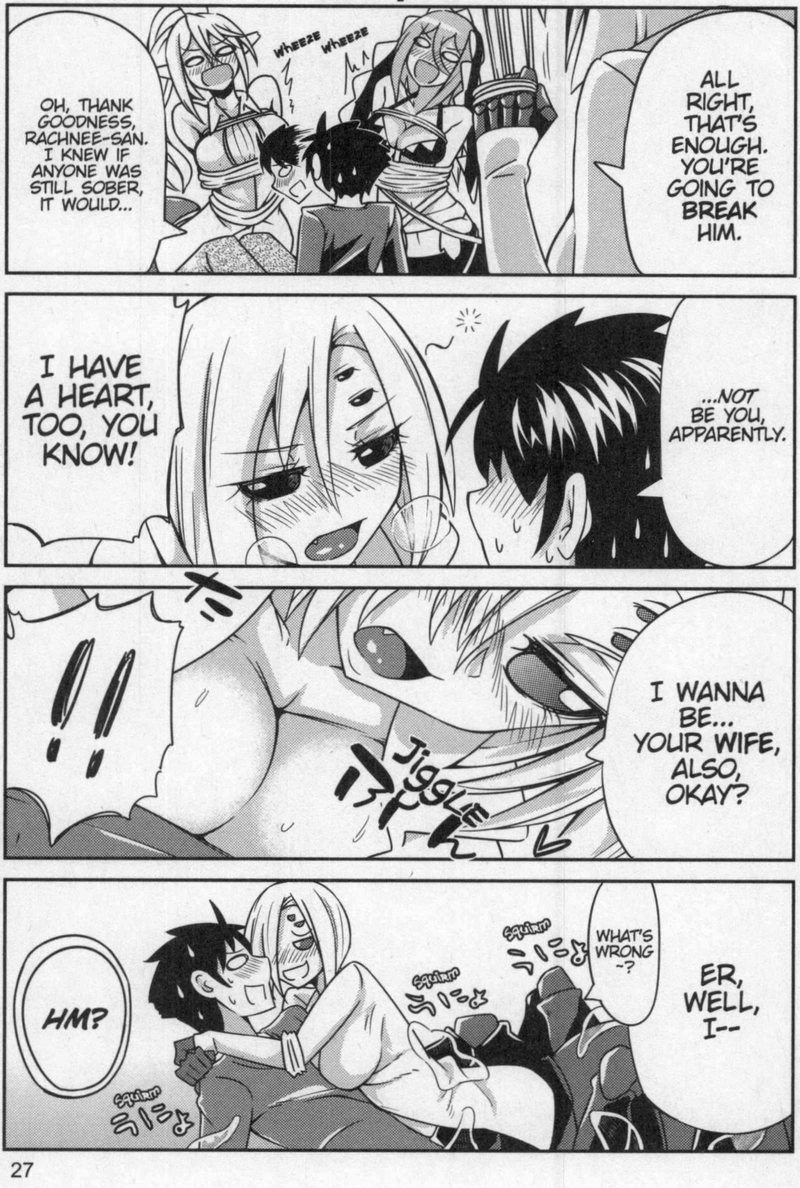

ALL RIGHT, THAT'S ENOUGH. YOU'RE GOING TO BREAK HIM.
WHEEZE WHEEZE
OH, THANK GOODNESS, RACHNEE-SAN. I KNEW IF ANYONE WAS STILL SOBER, IT WOULD...
...NOT BE YOU, APPARENTLY.
I HAVE A HEART, TOO, YOU KNOW!
I WANNA BE... YOUR WIFE, ALSO, OKAY?
JIGGLE
!!
ER, WELL, I--
WHAT'S WRONG ~?
SQUIRM
SQUIRM
HM?
SQUIRM

Levels of Tolerance

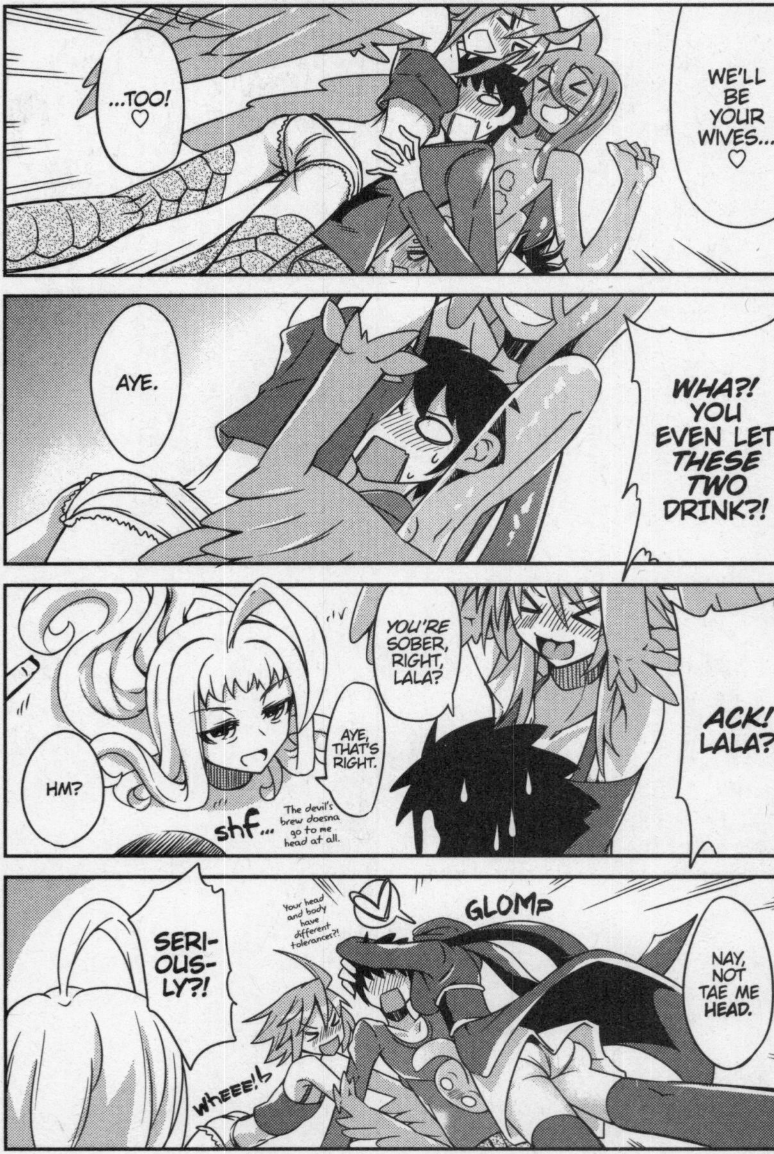
WE'LL BE YOUR WIVES... ♡
...TOO! ♡
WHA?! YOU EVEN LET THESE TWO DRINK?!
AYE.
ACK! LALA?!
YOU'RE SOBER, RIGHT, LALA?
AYE, THAT'S RIGHT.
The devil's brew doesna go to me head at all.
shf...
HM?
NAY, NOT TAE ME HEAD.
GLOMP
Your head and body have different tolerances?!
SERI-OUS-LY?!
wheee!

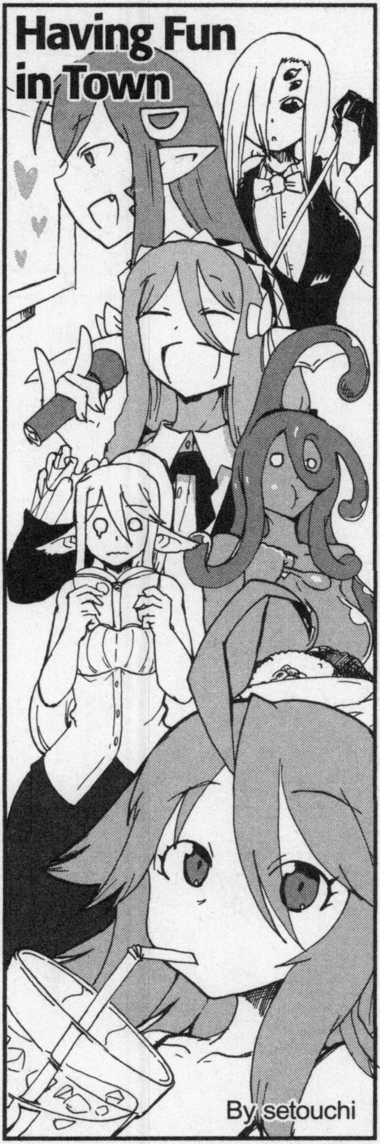
Having Fun in Town
By setouchi

Hodgepodges

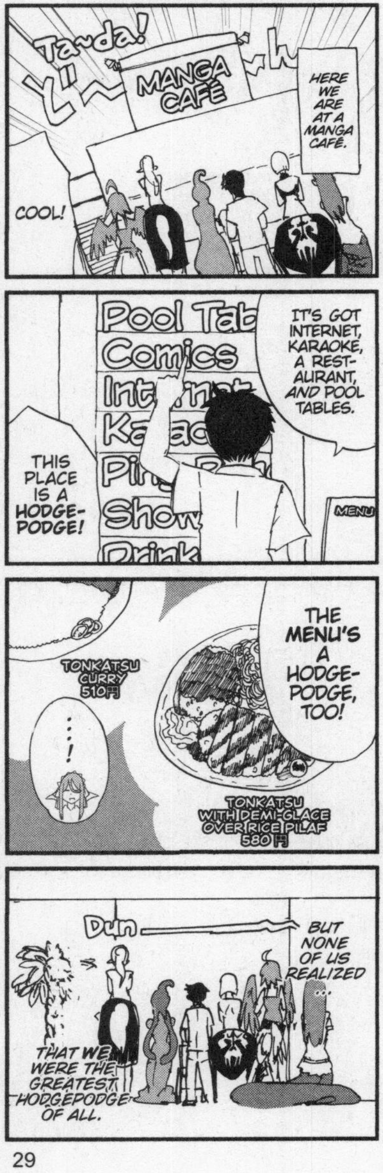
Ta~da!
MANGA CAFÉ
HERE WE ARE AT A MANGA CAFÉ.
COOL!
Pool Tab
Comics
IT'S GOT INTERNET, KARAOKE, A RESTAURANT, AND POOL TABLES.
THIS PLACE IS A HODGEPODGE!
MENU
THE MENU'S A HODGEPODGE, TOO!
TONKATSU CURRY 510円
...!
TONKATSU WITH DEMI-GLACE OVER RICE PILAF 580円
Dun
BUT NONE OF US REALIZED
THAT WE WERE THE GREATEST HODGEPODGE OF ALL.

Step And Repeat

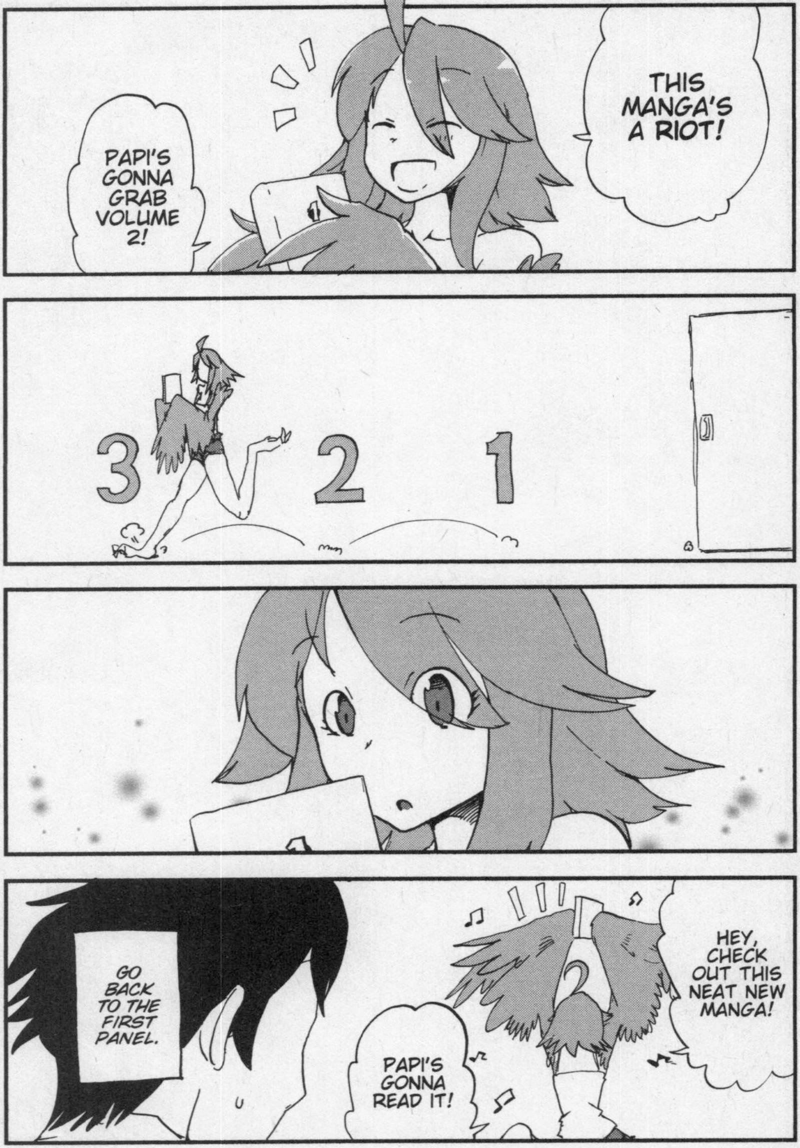

THIS MANGA'S A RIOT!
PAPI'S GONNA GRAB VOLUME 2!
3 2 1
HEY, CHECK OUT THIS NEAT NEW MANGA!
PAPI'S GONNA READ IT!
GO BACK TO THE FIRST PANEL.

The Trouble With Tall Girls

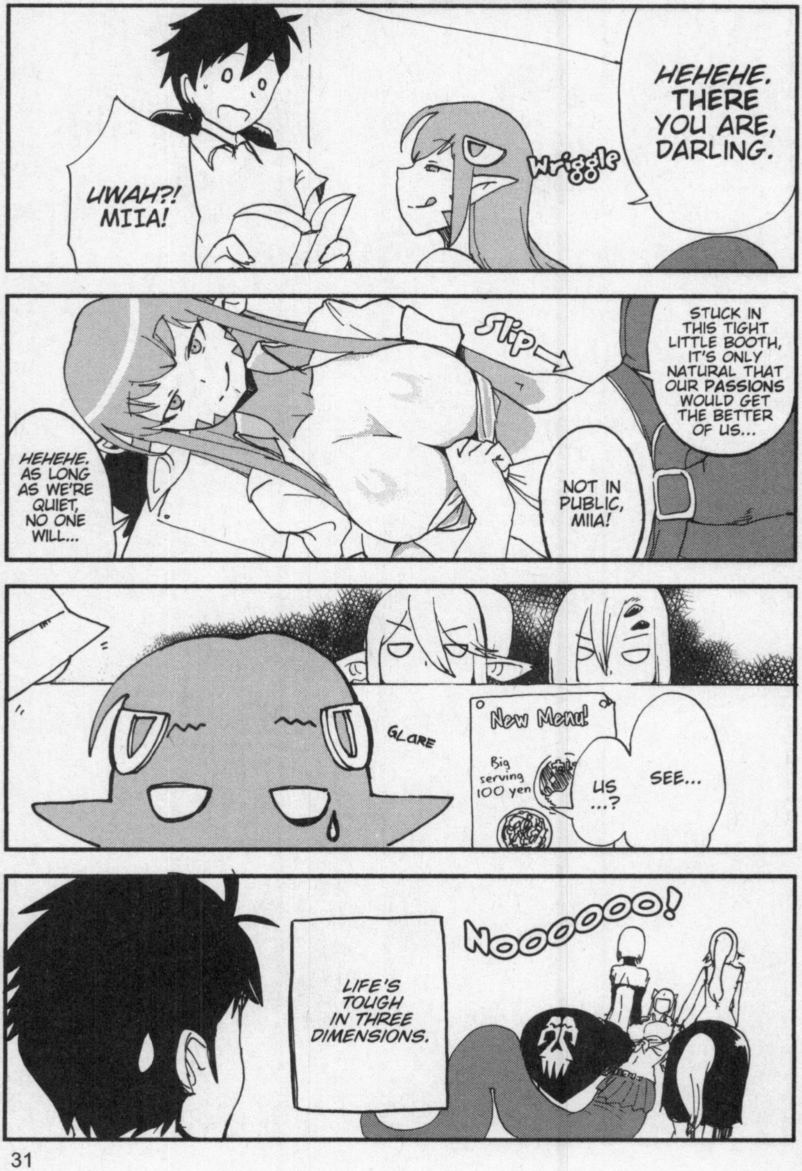
HEHEHE. THERE YOU ARE, DARLING.
Wriggle
UWAH?! MIIA!
STUCK IN THIS TIGHT LITTLE BOOTH, IT'S ONLY NATURAL THAT OUR PASSIONS WOULD GET THE BETTER OF US...
Slip
NOT IN PUBLIC, MIIA!
HEHEHE. AS LONG AS WE'RE QUIET, NO ONE WILL...
SEE...
US ...?
New Menu!
Big serving 100 yen
GLARE
Nooooooo!
LIFE'S TOUGH IN THREE DIMENSIONS.

Please Flip the Pages With Your Antenna

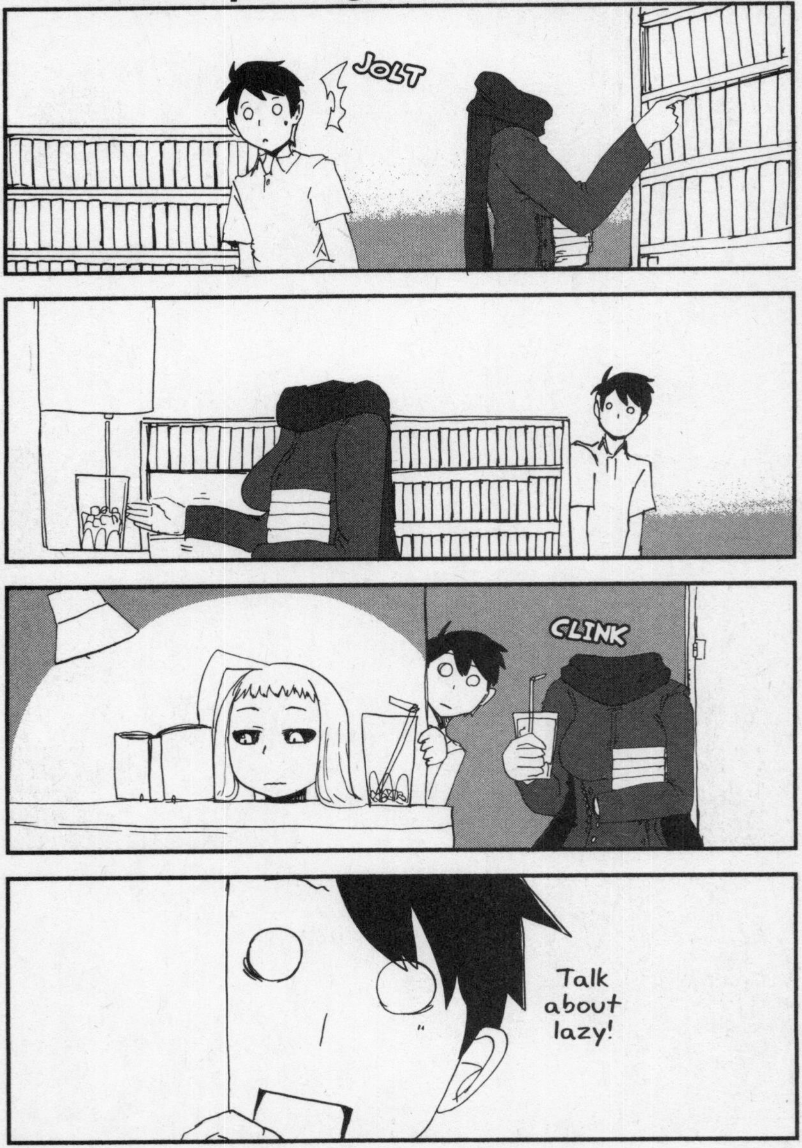
JOLT
CLINK
Talk about lazy!

A Certain Type of Romance

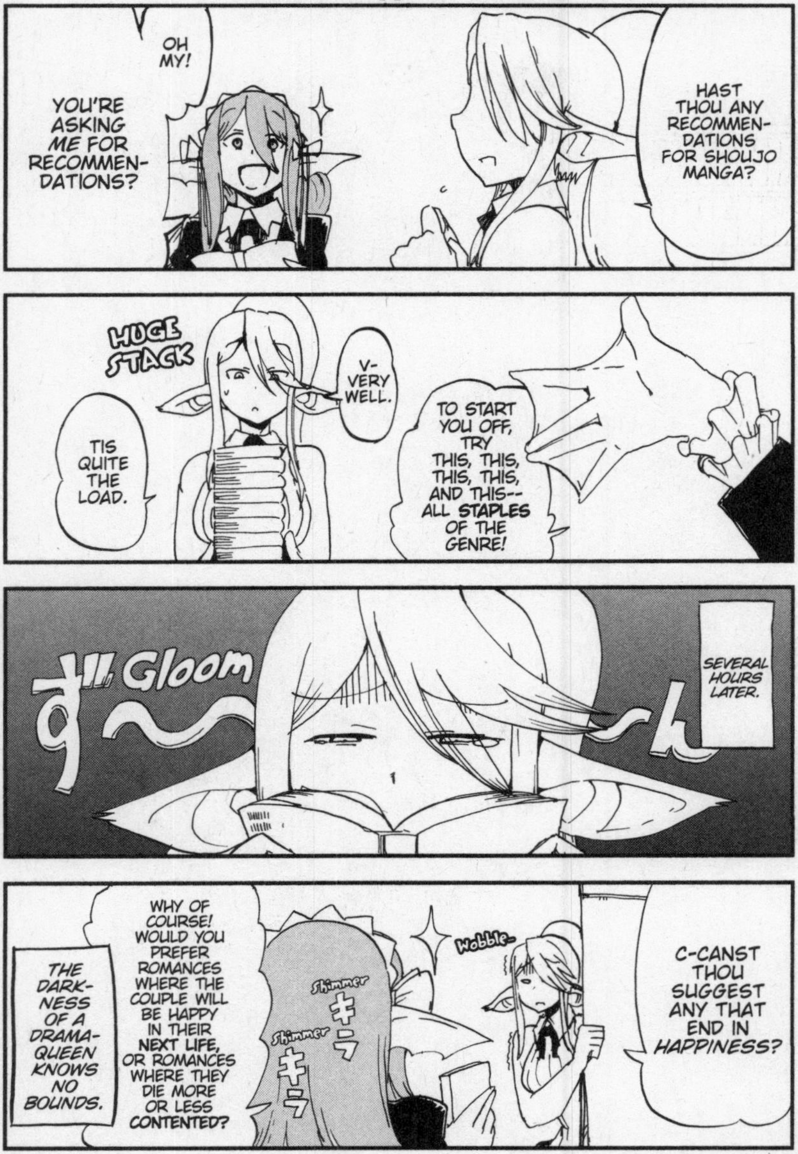
HAST THOU ANY RECOMMENDATIONS FOR SHOUJO MANGA?
OH MY!
YOU'RE ASKING ME FOR RECOMMENDATIONS?
TO START YOU OFF, TRY THIS, THIS, THIS, THIS, AND THIS--ALL STAPLES OF THE GENRE!
V-VERY WELL.
HUGE STACK
TIS QUITE THE LOAD.
SEVERAL HOURS LATER.
Gloom
C-CANST THOU SUGGEST ANY THAT END IN HAPPINESS?
Wobble-
Shimmer
Shimmer
WHY OF COURSE! WOULD YOU PREFER ROMANCES WHERE THE COUPLE WILL BE HAPPY IN THEIR NEXT LIFE, OR ROMANCES WHERE THEY DIE MORE OR LESS CONTENTED?
THE DARKNESS OF A DRAMA-QUEEN KNOWS NO BOUNDS.

Mixing Drinks

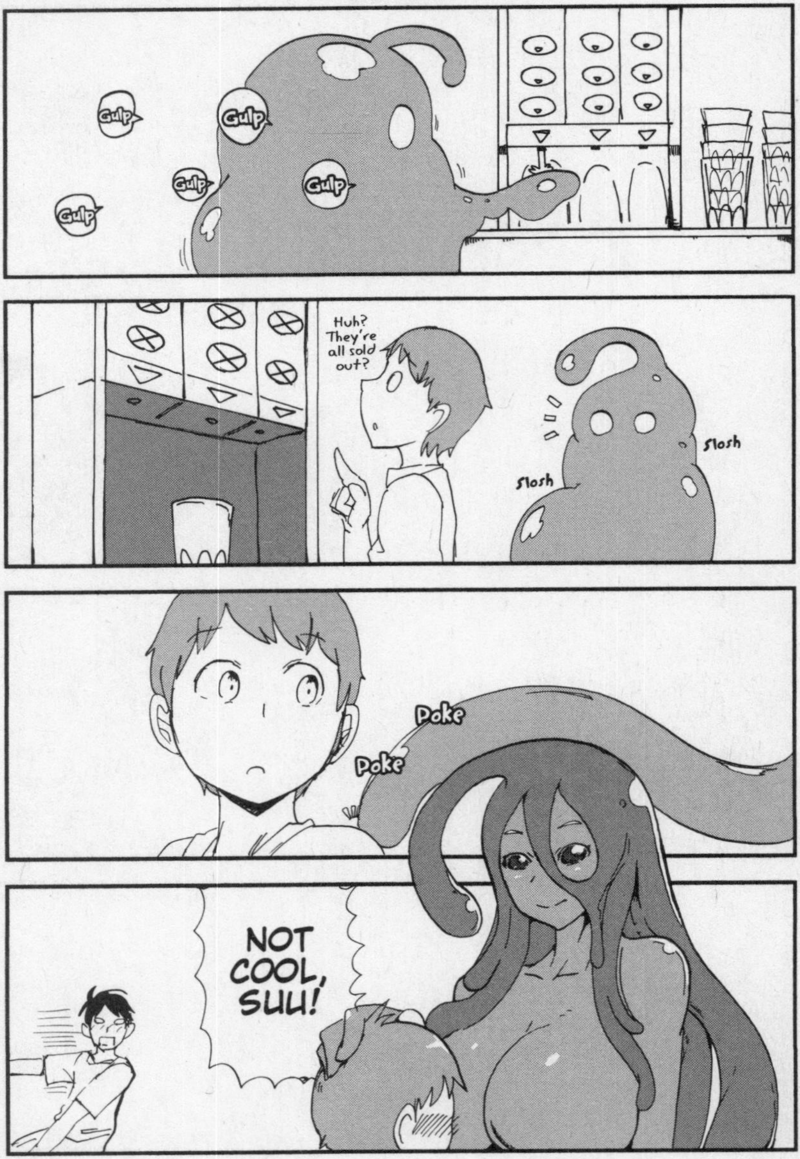

Gulp
Gulp
Gulp
Gulp
Gulp
Slosh
Huh? They're all sold out?
Slosh
Poke
Poke
NOT COOL, SUU!

Rachnee-san the Hustler

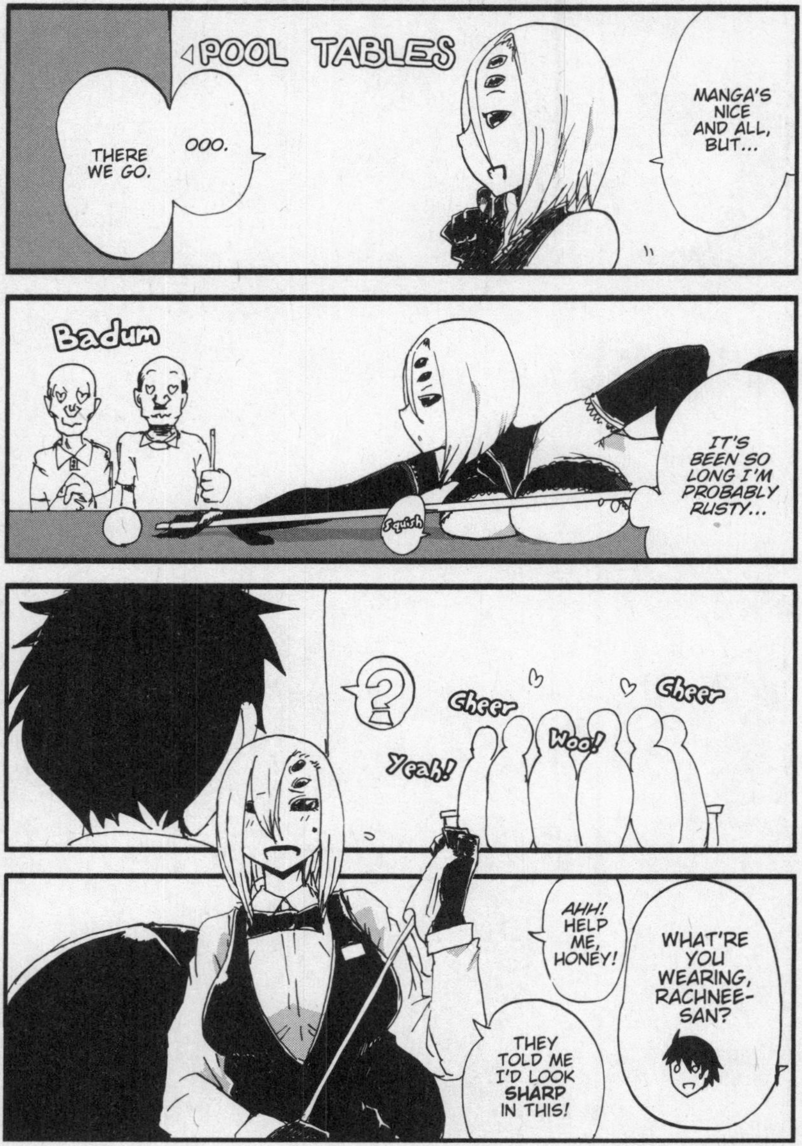

MANGA'S NICE AND ALL, BUT...
POOL TABLES
OOO.
THERE WE GO.
IT'S BEEN SO LONG I'M PROBABLY RUSTY...
Squish
Badum
Cheer
Woo!
Cheer
Yeah!
?
WHAT'RE YOU WEARING, RACHNEE-SAN?
AHH! HELP ME, HONEY!
THEY TOLD ME I'D LOOK SHARP IN THIS!

Monster-Sized Attraction

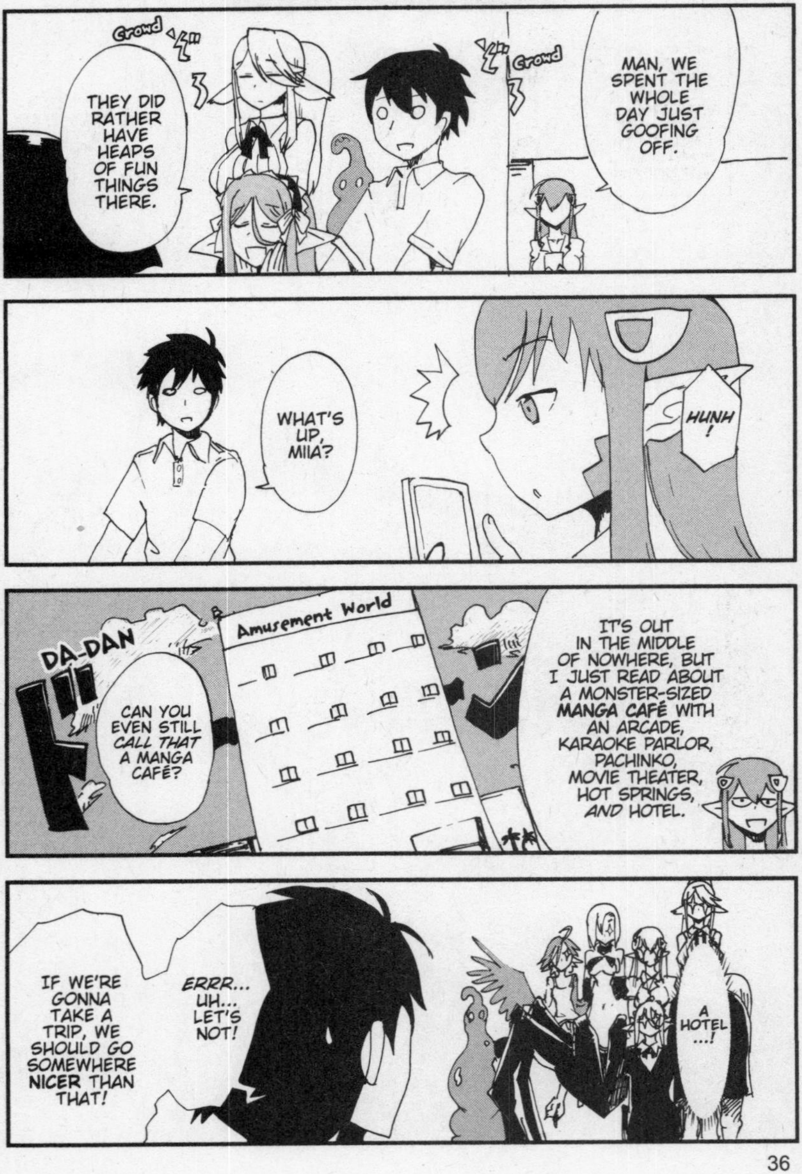
Crowd
MAN, WE SPENT THE WHOLE DAY JUST GOOFING OFF.
Crowd
THEY DID RATHER HAVE HEAPS OF FUN THINGS THERE.
HUNH!
WHAT'S UP, MIIA?
IT'S OUT IN THE MIDDLE OF NOWHERE, BUT I JUST READ ABOUT A MONSTER-SIZED MANGA CAFÉ WITH AN ARCADE, KARAOKE PARLOR, PACHINKO, MOVIE THEATER, HOT SPRINGS, AND HOTEL.
Amusement World
DA-DAN
CAN YOU EVEN STILL CALL THAT A MANGA CAFÉ?
A HOTEL...!
ERRR... UH... LET'S NOT!
IF WE'RE GONNA TAKE A TRIP, WE SHOULD GO SOMEWHERE NICER THAN THAT!

Cunning of the Lamia

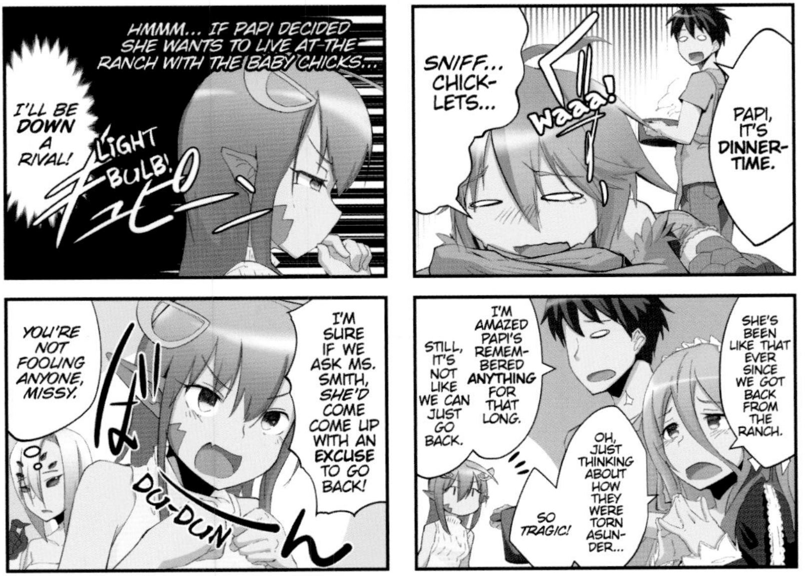
PAPI, IT'S DINNER-TIME.
SNIFF... CHICK-LETS...
WAAA!
HMMM... IF PAPI DECIDED SHE WANTS TO LIVE AT THE RANCH WITH THE BABY CHICKS...
LIGHT BULB!
I'LL BE DOWN A RIVAL!
SHE'S BEEN LIKE THAT EVER SINCE WE GOT BACK FROM THE RANCH.
I'M AMAZED PAPI'S REMEMBERED ANYTHING FOR THAT LONG.
STILL, IT'S NOT LIKE WE CAN JUST GO BACK.
OH, JUST THINKING ABOUT HOW THEY WERE TORN ASUNDER...
SO TRAGIC!
I'M SURE IF WE ASK MS. SMITH, SHE'D COME UP WITH AN EXCUSE TO GO BACK!
DU-DUN
YOU'RE NOT FOOLING ANYONE, MISSY.

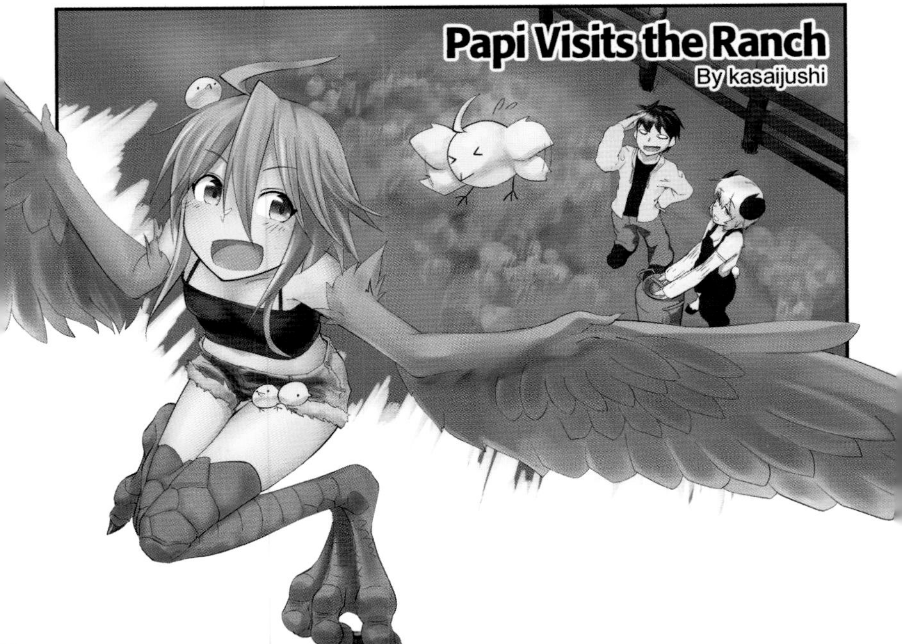
Papi Visits the Ranch
By kasaijushi

Smith-san Doesn't Want to Work

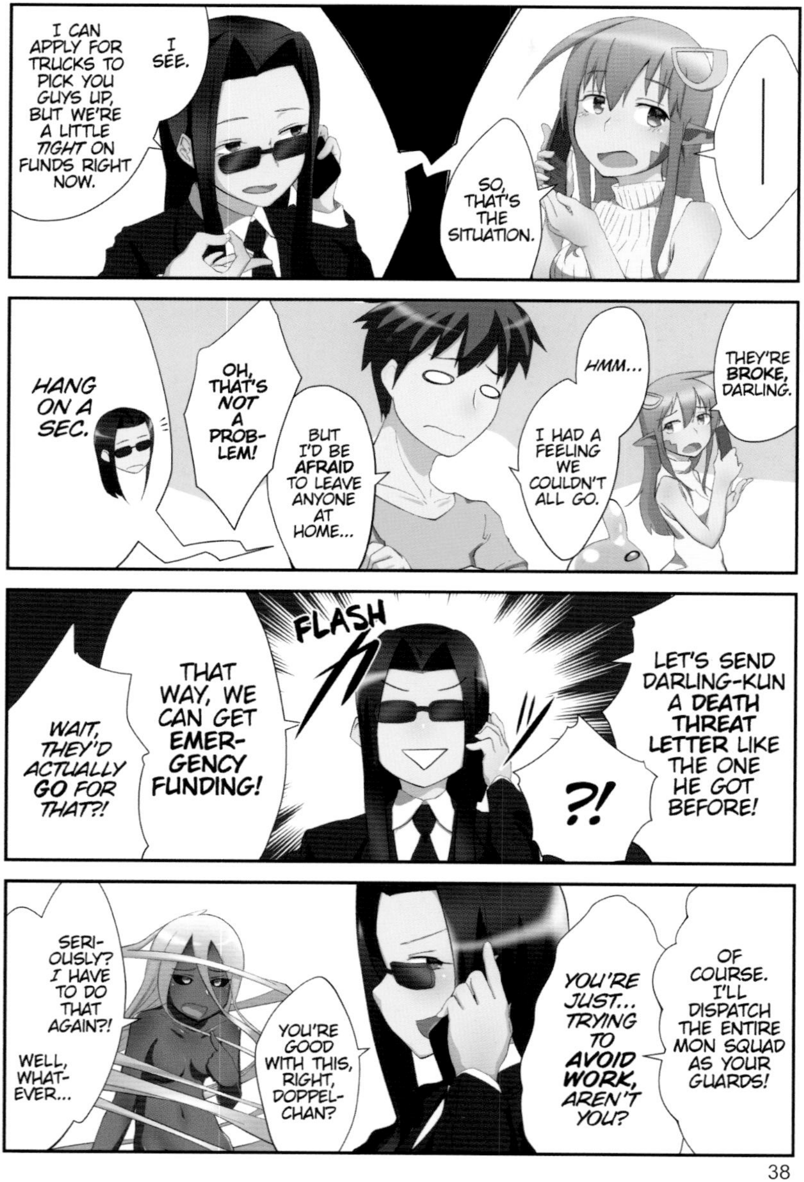
SO, THAT'S THE SITUATION.
I SEE.
I CAN APPLY FOR TRUCKS TO PICK YOU GUYS UP, BUT WE'RE A LITTLE *TIGHT* ON FUNDS RIGHT NOW.
THEY'RE **BROKE**, DARLING.
HMM...
I HAD A FEELING WE COULDN'T ALL GO.
BUT I'D BE **AFRAID** TO LEAVE ANYONE AT HOME...
OH, THAT'S ***NOT*** A PROBLEM!
HANG ON A SEC.
LET'S SEND DARLING-KUN A **DEATH THREAT LETTER** LIKE THE ONE HE GOT BEFORE!
?!
FLASH
THAT WAY, WE CAN GET **EMERGENCY FUNDING!**
WAIT, THEY'D ACTUALLY ***GO*** *FOR THAT?!*
OF COURSE. I'LL DISPATCH THE ENTIRE MON SQUAD AS YOUR GUARDS!
YOU'RE JUST... TRYING TO ***AVOID WORK,*** *AREN'T YOU?*
YOU'RE GOOD WITH THIS, RIGHT, DOPPEL-CHAN?
SERIOUSLY? I HAVE TO DO THAT AGAIN?!
WELL, WHATEVER...

We're Back

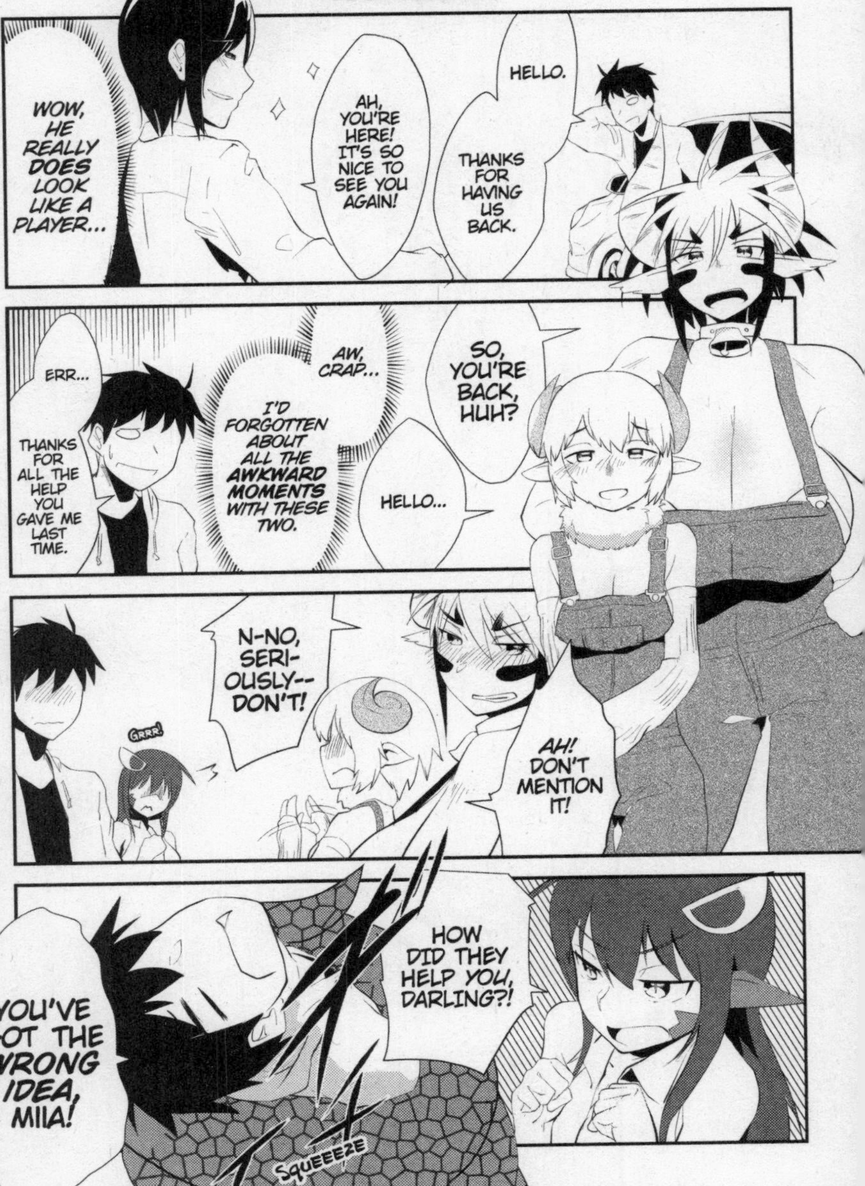
HELLO.
THANKS FOR HAVING US BACK.
AH, YOU'RE HERE! IT'S SO NICE TO SEE YOU AGAIN!
WOW, HE REALLY DOES LOOK LIKE A PLAYER...
SO, YOU'RE BACK, HUH?
HELLO...
AW, CRAP...
I'D FORGOTTEN ABOUT ALL THE AWKWARD MOMENTS WITH THESE TWO.
ERR...
THANKS FOR ALL THE HELP YOU GAVE ME LAST TIME.
AH! DON'T MENTION IT!
N-NO, SERI-OUSLY--DON'T!
GRRR!
HOW DID THEY HELP YOU, DARLING?!
YOU'VE GOT THE WRONG IDEA, MIIA!
SQUEEEZE

Suspicion

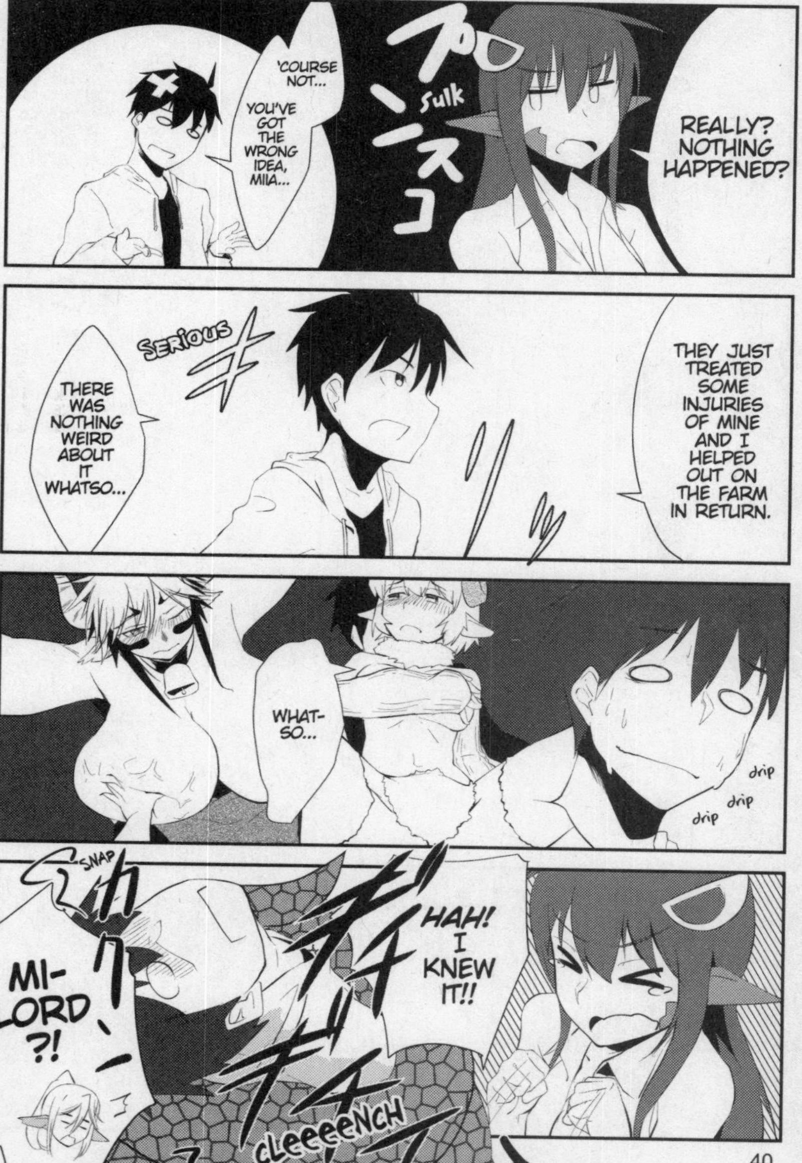
REALLY? NOTHING HAPPENED?
Sulk
'COURSE NOT... YOU'VE GOT THE WRONG IDEA, MIIA...
THEY JUST TREATED SOME INJURIES OF MINE AND I HELPED OUT ON THE FARM IN RETURN.
SERIOUS
THERE WAS NOTHING WEIRD ABOUT IT WHATSO...
drip drip drip
WHAT-SO...
HAH! I KNEW IT!!
CLEEEEENCH
SNAP
MI-LORD?!

Rival?

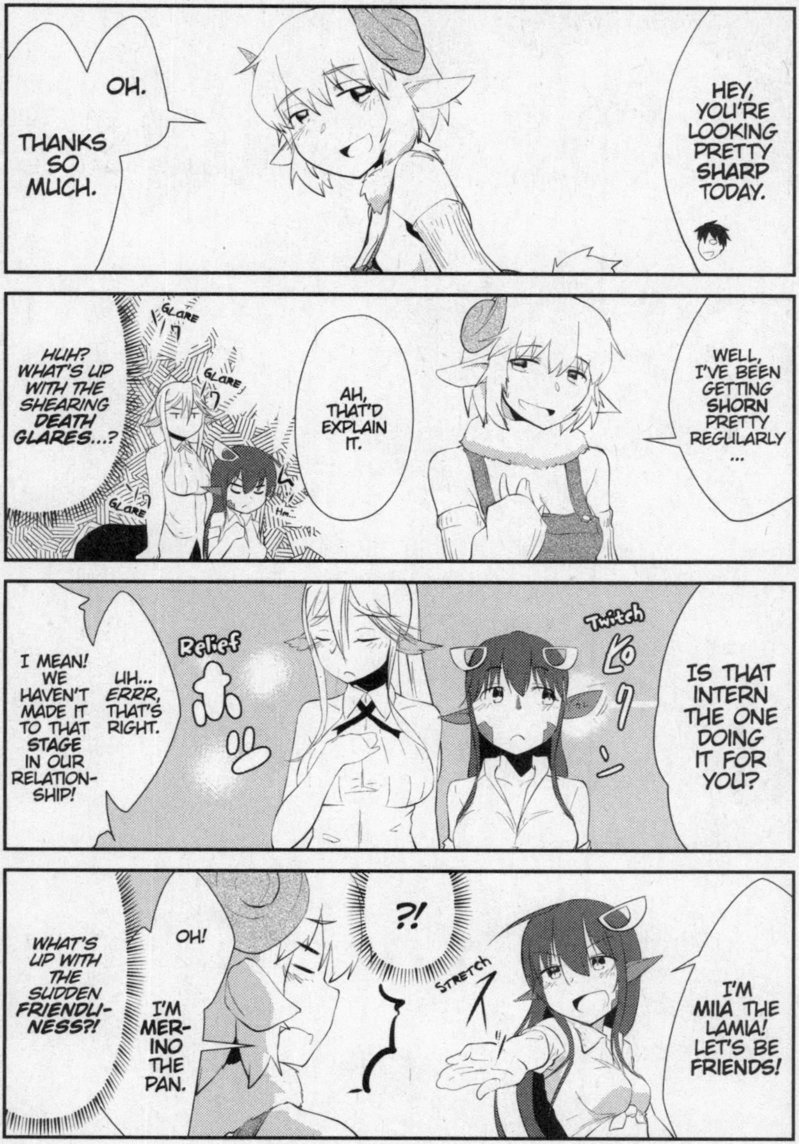
HEY, YOU'RE LOOKING PRETTY SHARP TODAY.
OH.
THANKS SO MUCH.
WELL, I'VE BEEN GETTING SHORN PRETTY REGULARLY ...
AH, THAT'D EXPLAIN IT.
GLARE
GLARE
Hm...
GLARE
HUH? WHAT'S UP WITH THE SHEARING DEATH GLARES...?
IS THAT INTERN THE ONE DOING IT FOR YOU?
Twitch
Relief
UH... ERRR, THAT'S RIGHT.
I MEAN! WE HAVEN'T MADE IT TO THAT STAGE IN OUR RELATION-SHIP!
I'M MIIA THE LAMIA! LET'S BE FRIENDS!
STRETCH
?!
OH!
I'M MER-INO THE PAN.
WHAT'S UP WITH THE SUDDEN FRIENDLI-NESS?!

Centaur-Based Memory

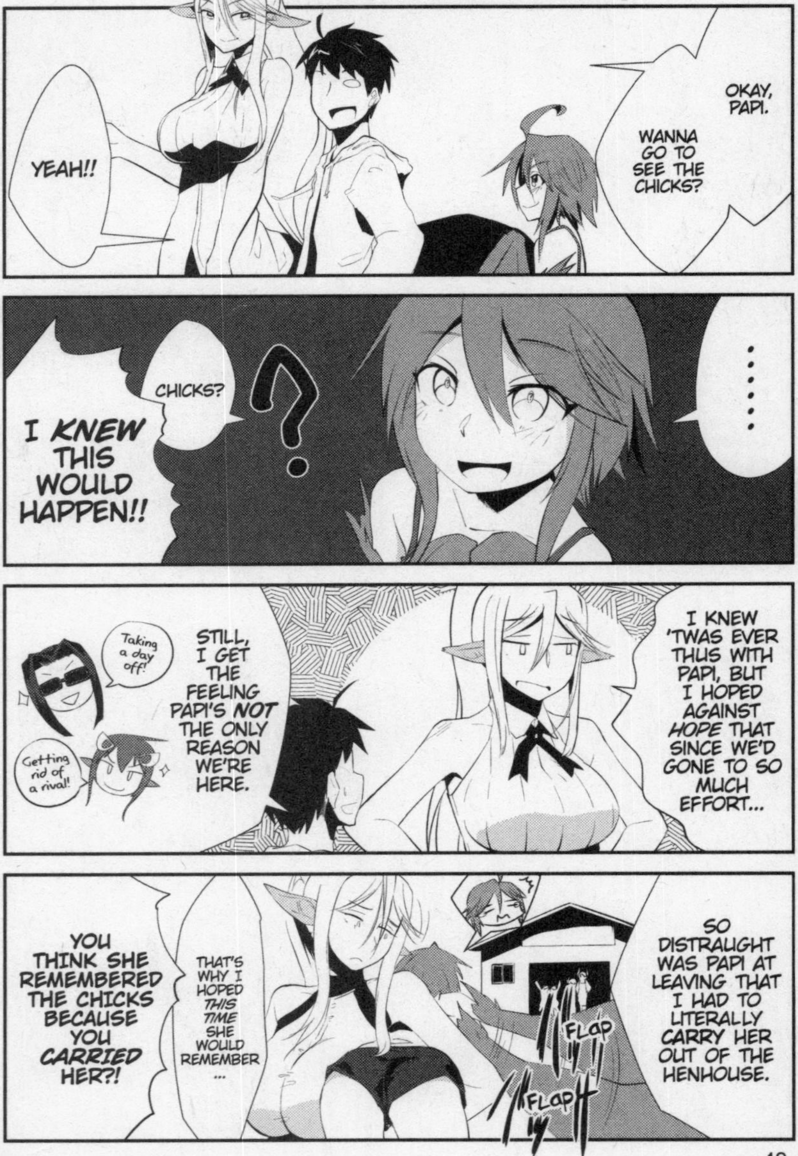
OKAY, PAPI.
WANNA GO TO SEE THE CHICKS?
YEAH!!
......
CHICKS?
I KNEW THIS WOULD HAPPEN!!
I KNEW 'TWAS EVER THUS WITH PAPI, BUT I HOPED AGAINST HOPE THAT SINCE WE'D GONE TO SO MUCH EFFORT...
STILL, I GET THE FEELING PAPI'S NOT THE ONLY REASON WE'RE HERE.
Taking a day off!
Getting rid of a rival!
SO DISTRAUGHT WAS PAPI AT LEAVING THAT I HAD TO LITERALLY CARRY HER OUT OF THE HENHOUSE.
FLAP
FLAP
THAT'S WHY I HOPED THIS TIME SHE WOULD REMEMBER...
YOU THINK SHE REMEMBERED THE CHICKS BECAUSE YOU CARRIED HER?!

Species-Specific Methods

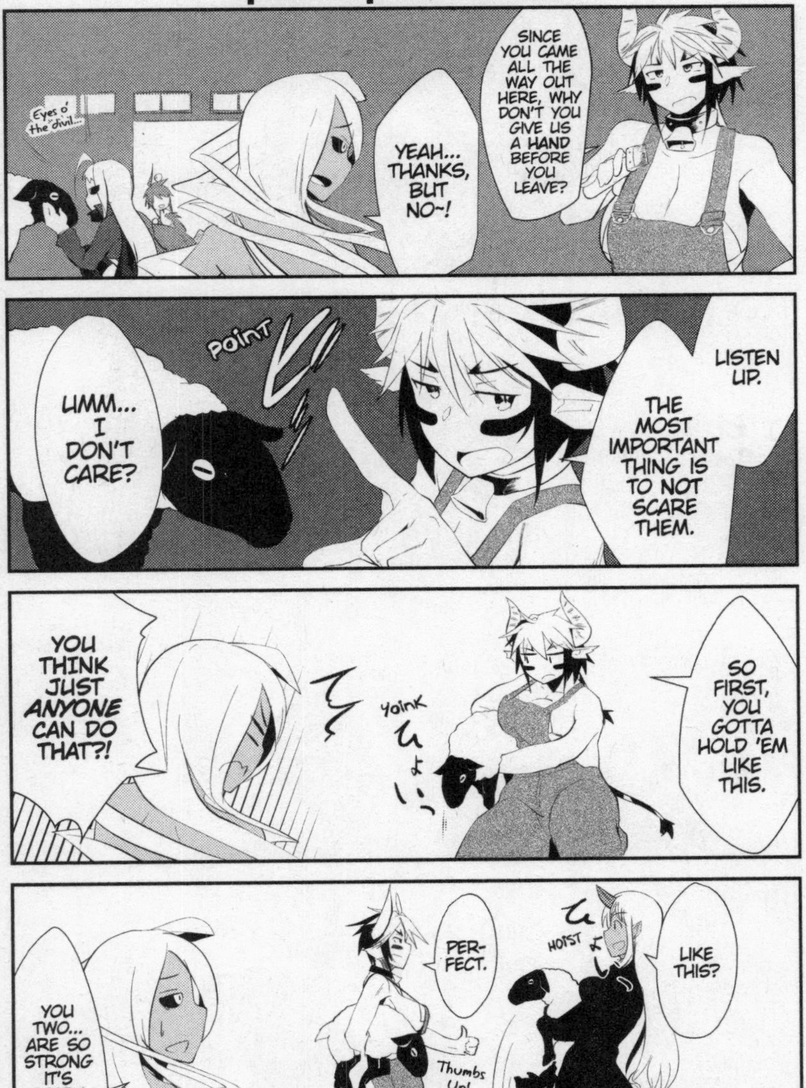
SINCE YOU CAME ALL THE WAY OUT HERE, WHY DON'T YOU GIVE US A HAND BEFORE YOU LEAVE?
YEAH... THANKS, BUT NO~!
Eyes o' the divil...
LISTEN UP.
THE MOST IMPORTANT THING IS TO NOT SCARE THEM.
POINT
UMM... I DON'T CARE?
SO FIRST, YOU GOTTA HOLD 'EM LIKE THIS.
Yoink
ひょいっ
YOU THINK JUST *ANYONE* CAN DO THAT?!
LIKE THIS?
HOIST
PERFECT.
Thumbs Up!
YOU TWO... ARE SO STRONG IT'S SCARY.

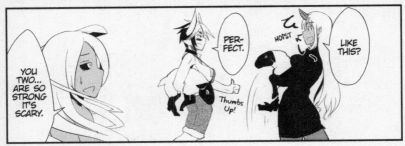

Not My Style

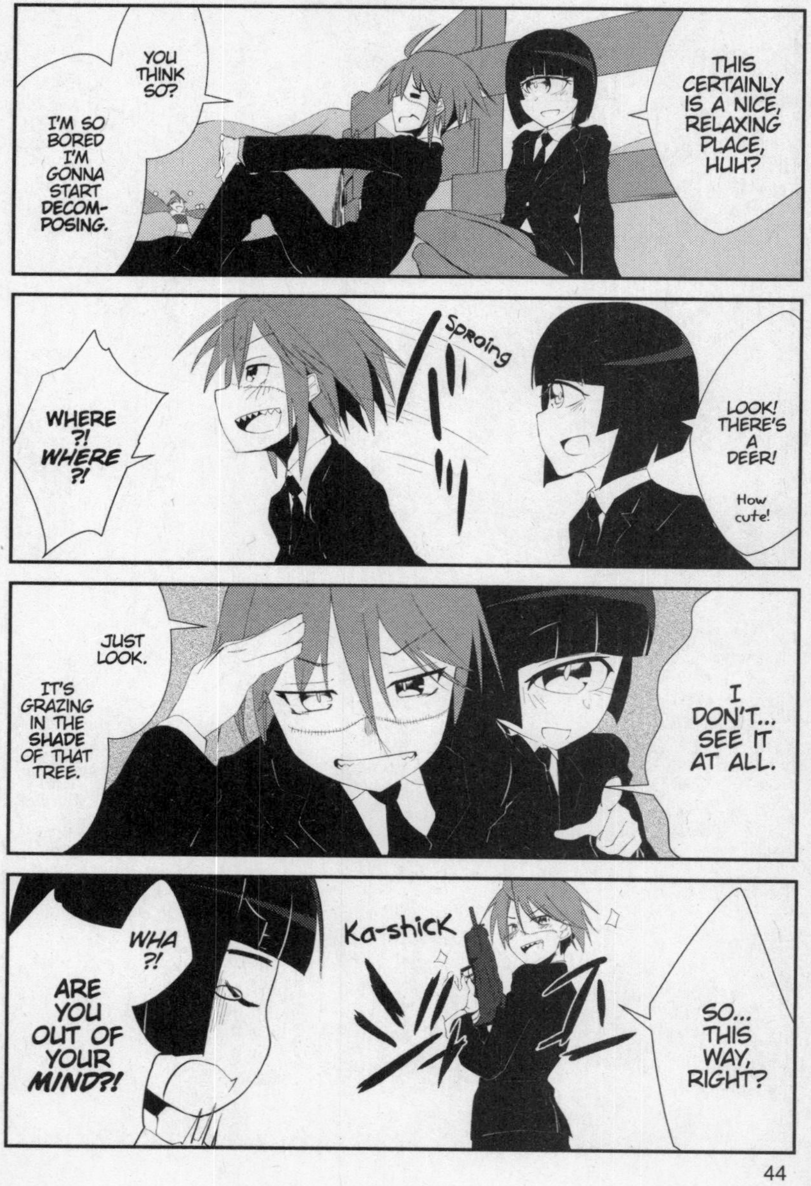
THIS CERTAINLY IS A NICE, RELAXING PLACE, HUH?
YOU THINK SO?
I'M SO BORED I'M GONNA START DECOMPOSING.
LOOK! THERE'S A DEER!
How cute!
Sproing
WHERE?! WHERE?!
I DON'T... SEE IT AT ALL.
JUST LOOK.
IT'S GRAZING IN THE SHADE OF THAT TREE.
SO... THIS WAY, RIGHT?
Ka-shick
WHA?!
ARE YOU OUT OF YOUR MIND?!

Wear and Tear

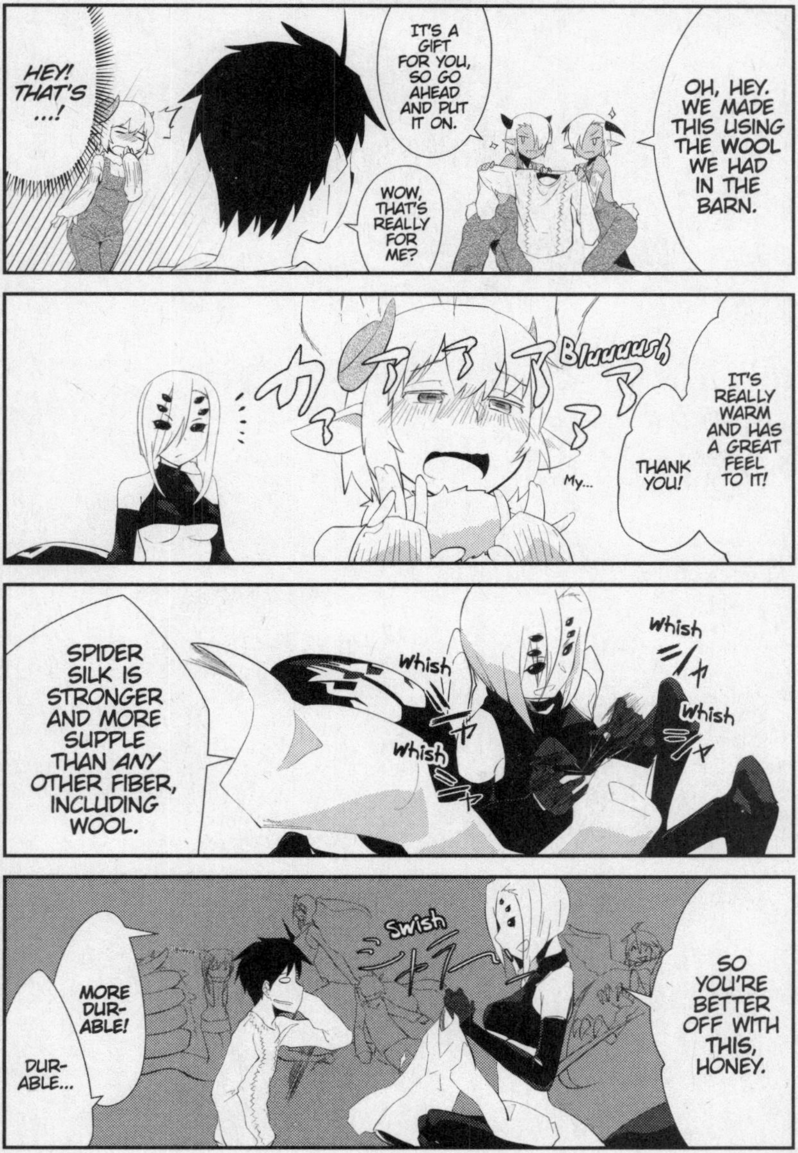
OH, HEY. WE MADE THIS USING THE WOOL WE HAD IN THE BARN.
IT'S A GIFT FOR YOU, SO GO AHEAD AND PUT IT ON.
WOW, THAT'S REALLY FOR ME?
HEY! THAT'S ...!
Bluuuush
IT'S REALLY WARM AND HAS A GREAT FEEL TO IT!
THANK YOU!
My...
Whish
Whish
Whish
Whish
SPIDER SILK IS STRONGER AND MORE SUPPLE THAN ANY OTHER FIBER, INCLUDING WOOL.
SO YOU'RE BETTER OFF WITH THIS, HONEY.
Swish
MORE DUR-ABLE!
DUR-ABLE...

We'll Be Back

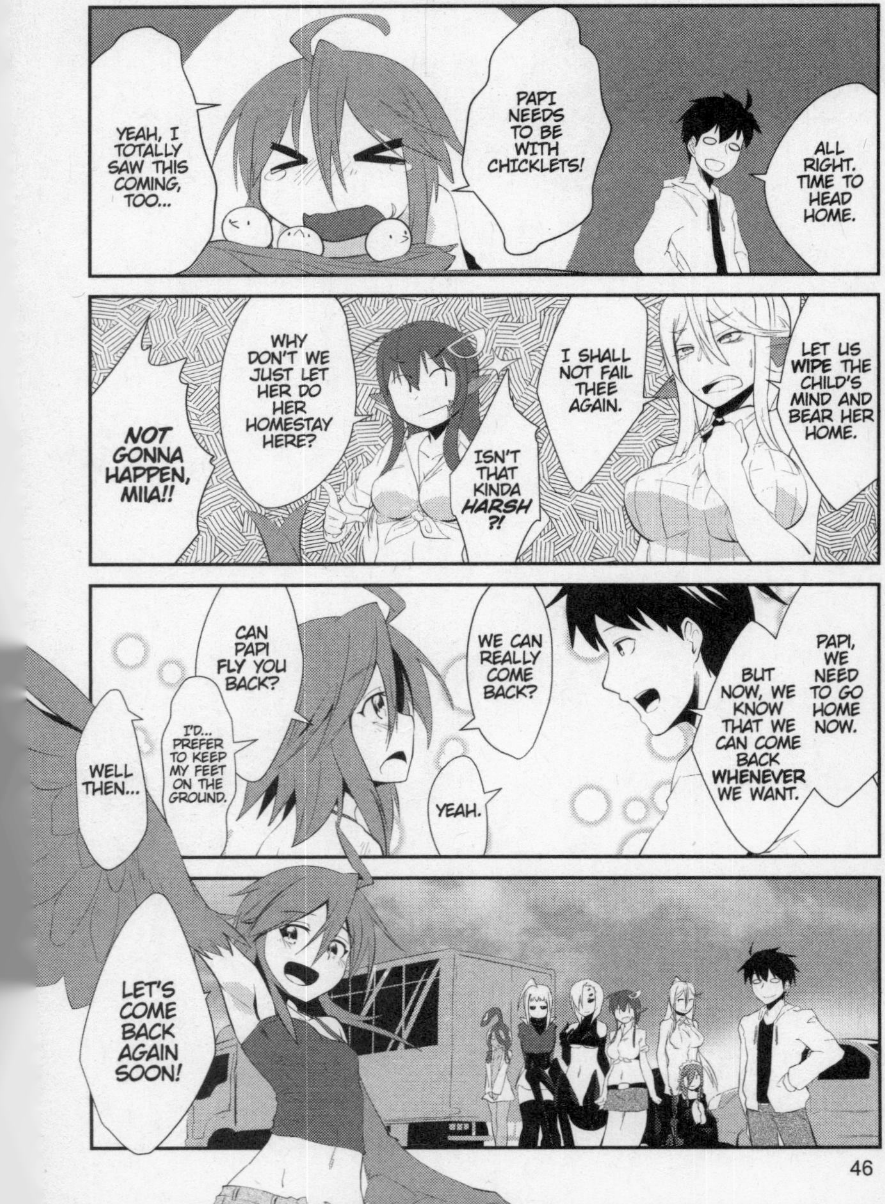
ALL RIGHT. TIME TO HEAD HOME.
PAPI NEEDS TO BE WITH CHICKLETS!
YEAH, I TOTALLY SAW THIS COMING, TOO...
LET US WIPE THE CHILD'S MIND AND BEAR HER HOME.
I SHALL NOT FAIL THEE AGAIN.
WHY DON'T WE JUST LET HER DO HER HOMESTAY HERE?
ISN'T THAT KINDA *HARSH* ?!
NOT GONNA HAPPEN, MIIA!!
PAPI, WE NEED TO GO HOME NOW.
BUT NOW, WE KNOW THAT WE CAN COME BACK WHENEVER WE WANT.
WE CAN REALLY COME BACK?
YEAH.
CAN PAPI FLY YOU BACK?
I'D... PREFER TO KEEP MY FEET ON THE GROUND.
WELL THEN...
LET'S COME BACK AGAIN SOON!

モンスター娘のいる日常
4コマアンソロジー

PAPI NEEDS TO BE WITH CHICKLETS!

Biological Instinct?

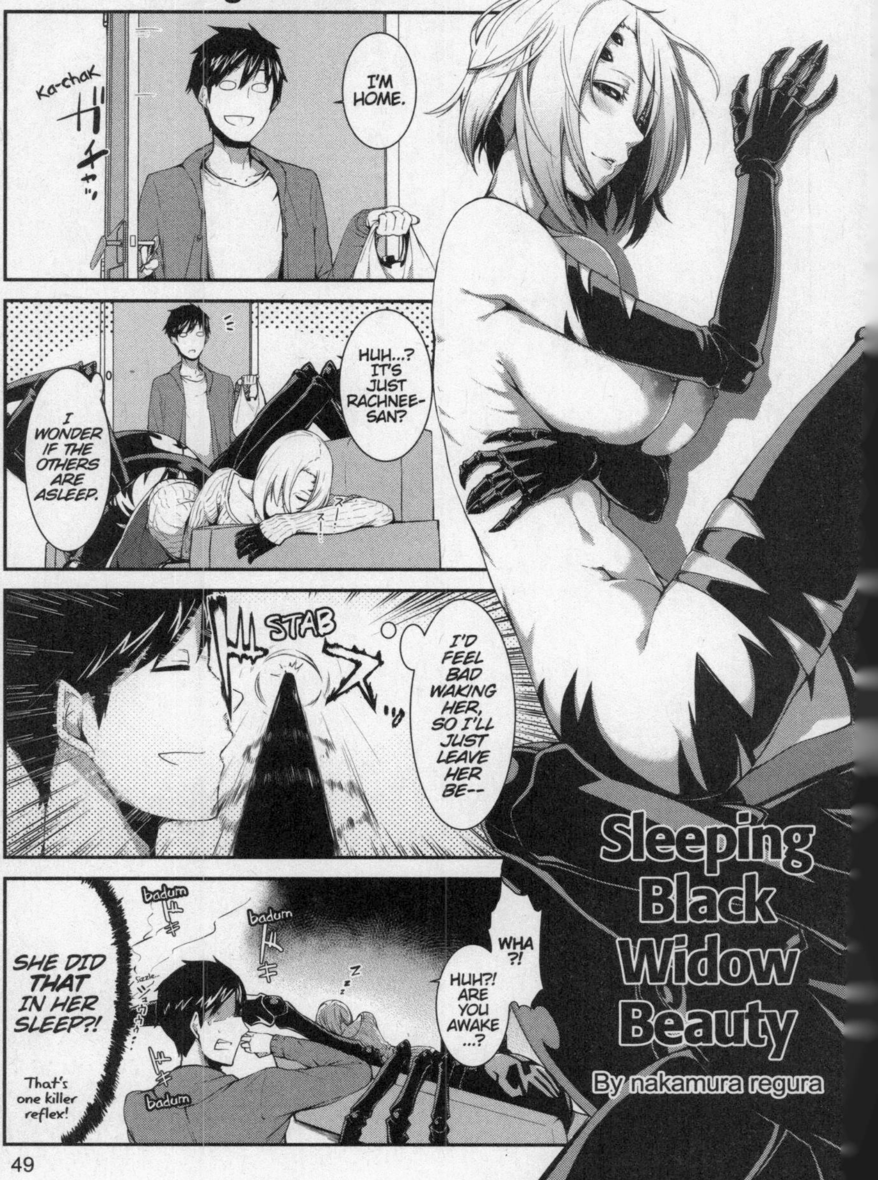
Sleeping Black Widow Beauty
By nakamura regura
I'M HOME.
Ka-chak
ガチャッ
HUH...? IT'S JUST RACHNEE-SAN?
I WONDER IF THE OTHERS ARE ASLEEP.
I'D FEEL BAD WAKING HER, SO I'LL JUST LEAVE HER BE--
STAB
ドス
WHA?!
HUH?! ARE YOU AWAKE ...?
badum
badum
Sizzle...
SHE DID THAT IN HER SLEEP?!
badum
That's one killer reflex!

Getting (Yellow)Tail

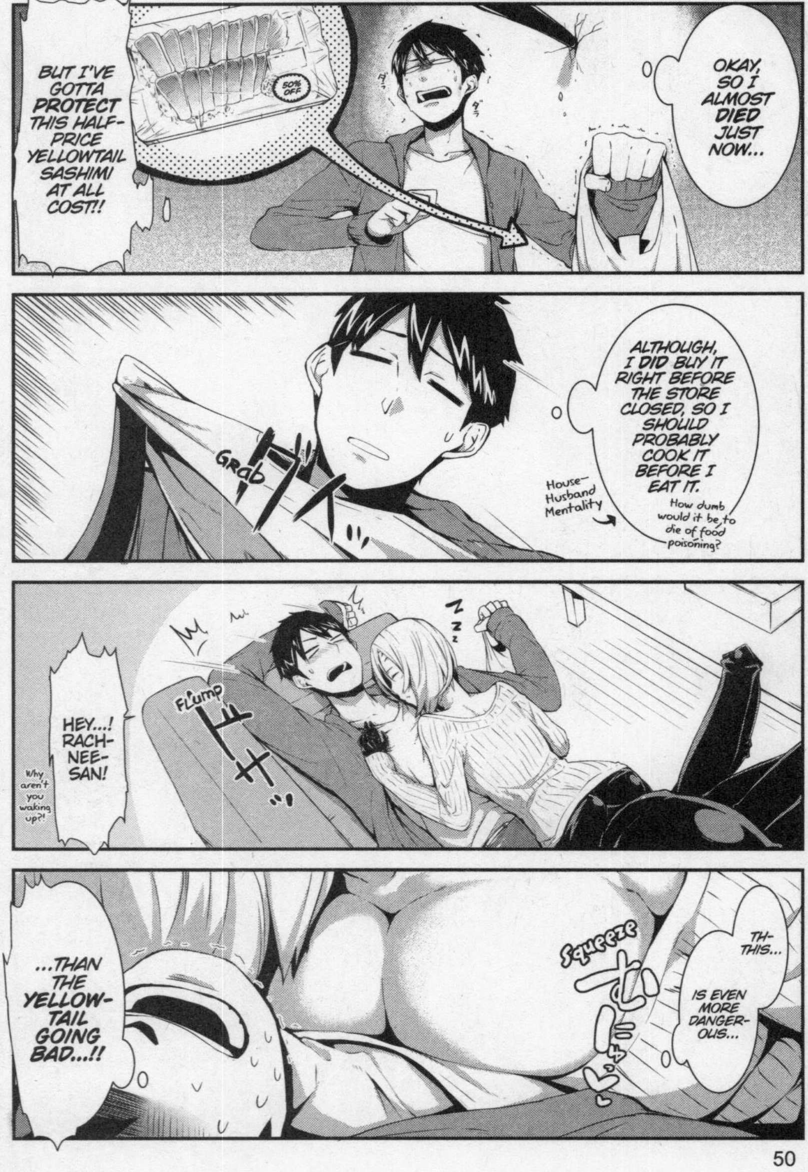
OKAY, SO I ALMOST DIED JUST NOW...
50% OFF
BUT I'VE GOTTA PROTECT THIS HALF-PRICE YELLOWTAIL SASHIMI AT ALL COST!!
ALTHOUGH, I DID BUY IT RIGHT BEFORE THE STORE CLOSED, SO I SHOULD PROBABLY COOK IT BEFORE I EAT IT.
How dumb would it be, to die of food poisoning?
House-Husband Mentality
Grab
Flump
HEY...! RACHNEE-SAN!
Why aren't you waking up?!
Squeeze
TH-THIS... IS EVEN MORE DANGER-OUS...
...THAN THE YELLOW-TAIL GOING BAD...!!

Dirty Sleep Talking

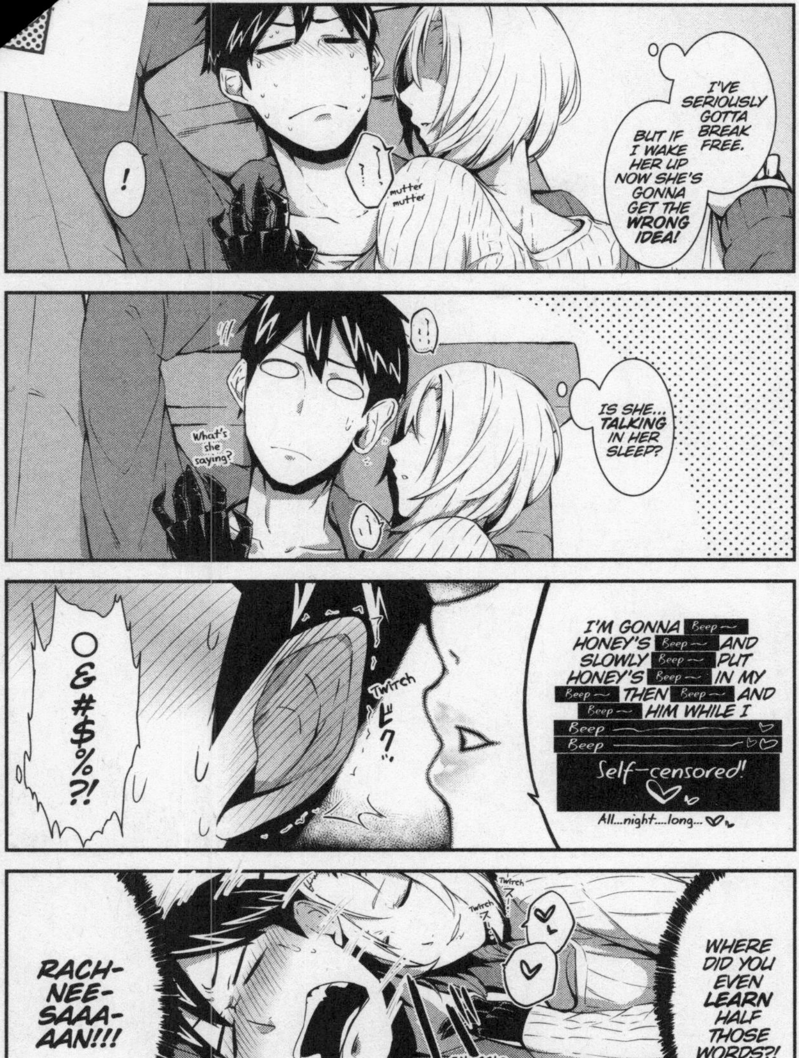

I'VE SERIOUSLY GOTTA BREAK FREE.
BUT IF I WAKE HER UP NOW SHE'S GONNA GET THE WRONG IDEA!
mutter mutter
!
IS SHE... TALKING IN HER SLEEP?
What's she saying?
I'M GONNA Beep~ HONEY'S Beep~ AND SLOWLY Beep~ PUT HONEY'S Beep~ IN MY Beep~ THEN Beep~ AND Beep~ HIM WHILE I Beep Beep Self-censored!
All...night....long...
Twitch
○&#$%?!
WHERE DID YOU EVEN LEARN HALF THOSE WORDS?!
Twitch
Twitch
SNUGGLE
RACH-NEE-SAAAA-AAN!!!

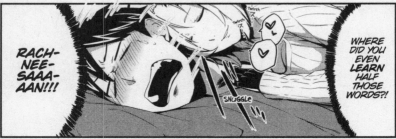

The Final Straw

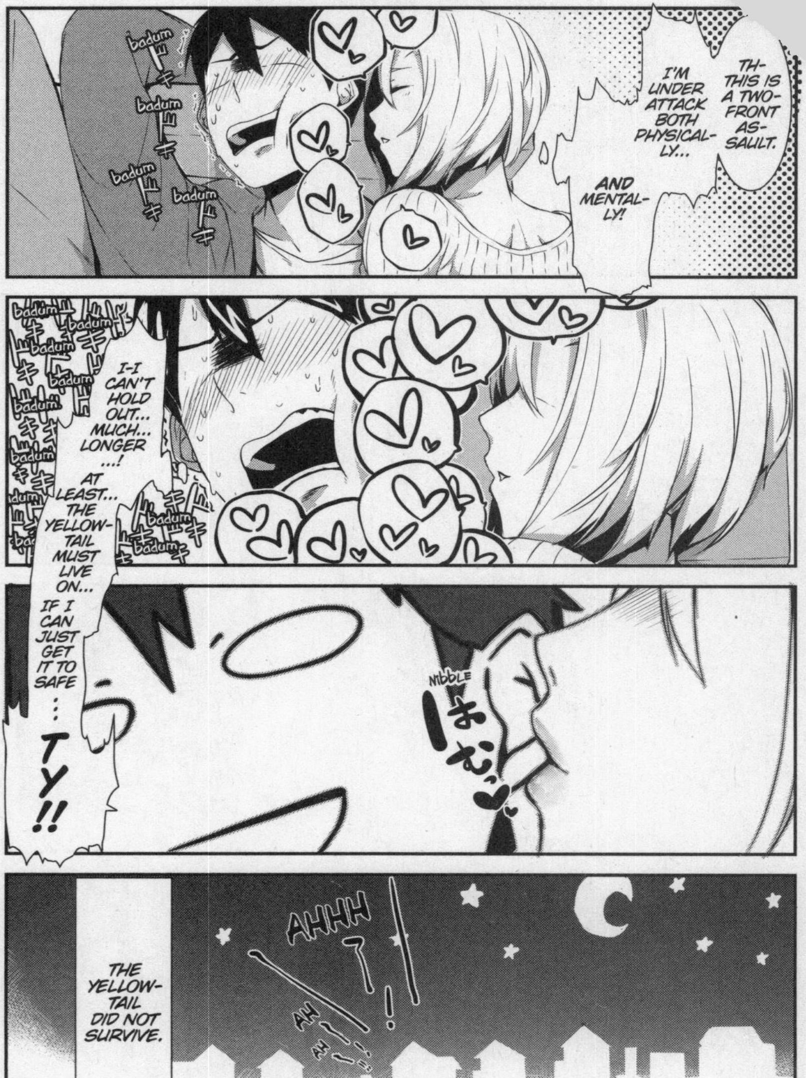

TH- THIS IS A TWO-FRONT AS-SAULT.
I'M UNDER ATTACK BOTH PHYSICAL-LY...
AND MENTAL-LY!
badum
badum
badum
badum
badum
I-I CAN'T HOLD OUT... MUCH... LONGER ...!
AT LEAST... THE YELLOW-TAIL MUST LIVE ON...
Nibble
IF I CAN JUST GET IT TO SAFE ... TY!!
AHHH
THE YELLOW-TAIL DID NOT SURVIVE.

Honey Trap

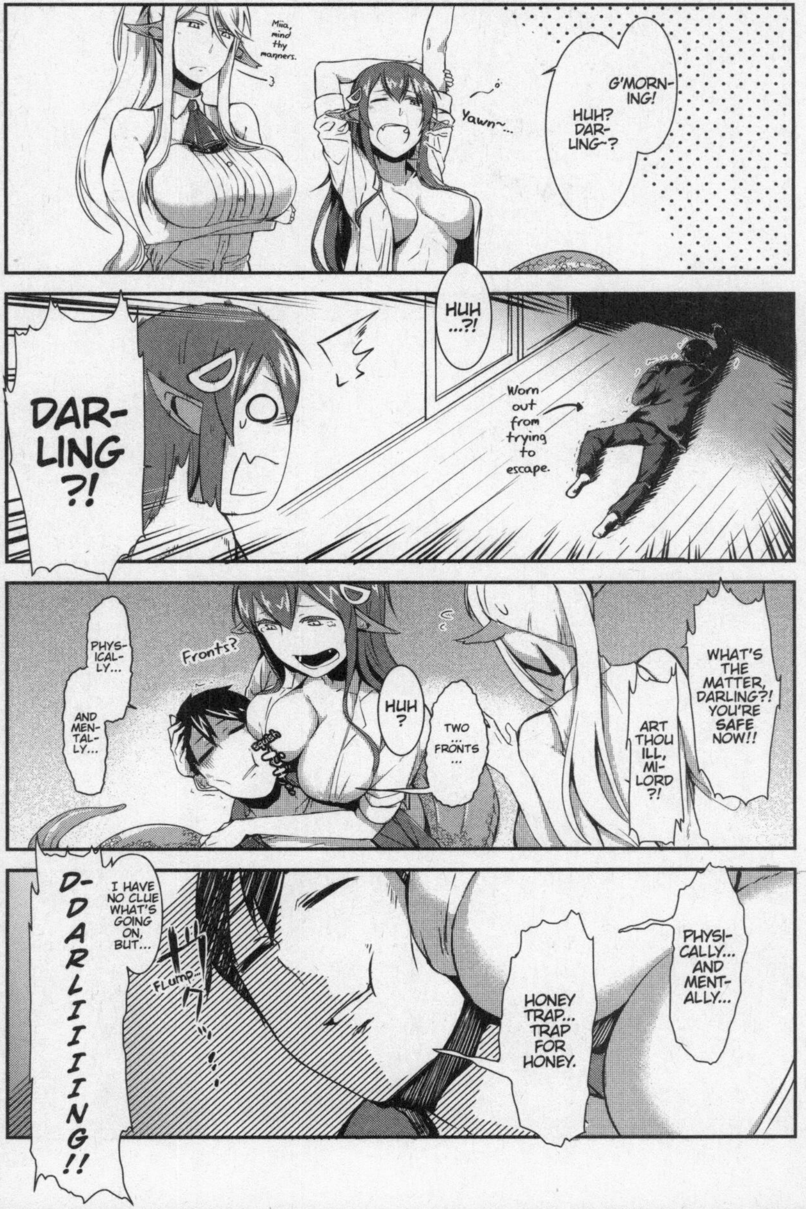
G'MORNING! HUH? DARLING~?
Yawn~...
Miia, mind thy manners.
HUH...?!
Worn out from trying to escape.
DARLING?!
WHAT'S THE MATTER, DARLING?! YOU'RE SAFE NOW!!
ART THOU ILL, MILORD?!
TWO... FRONTS...
HUH?
Fronts?
PHYSICALLY...
AND MENTALLY...
PHYSICALLY... AND MENTALLY...
HONEY TRAP... TRAP FOR HONEY.
I HAVE NO CLUE WHAT'S GOING ON, BUT...
Flump...
D-DARLIIIING!!

Trauma

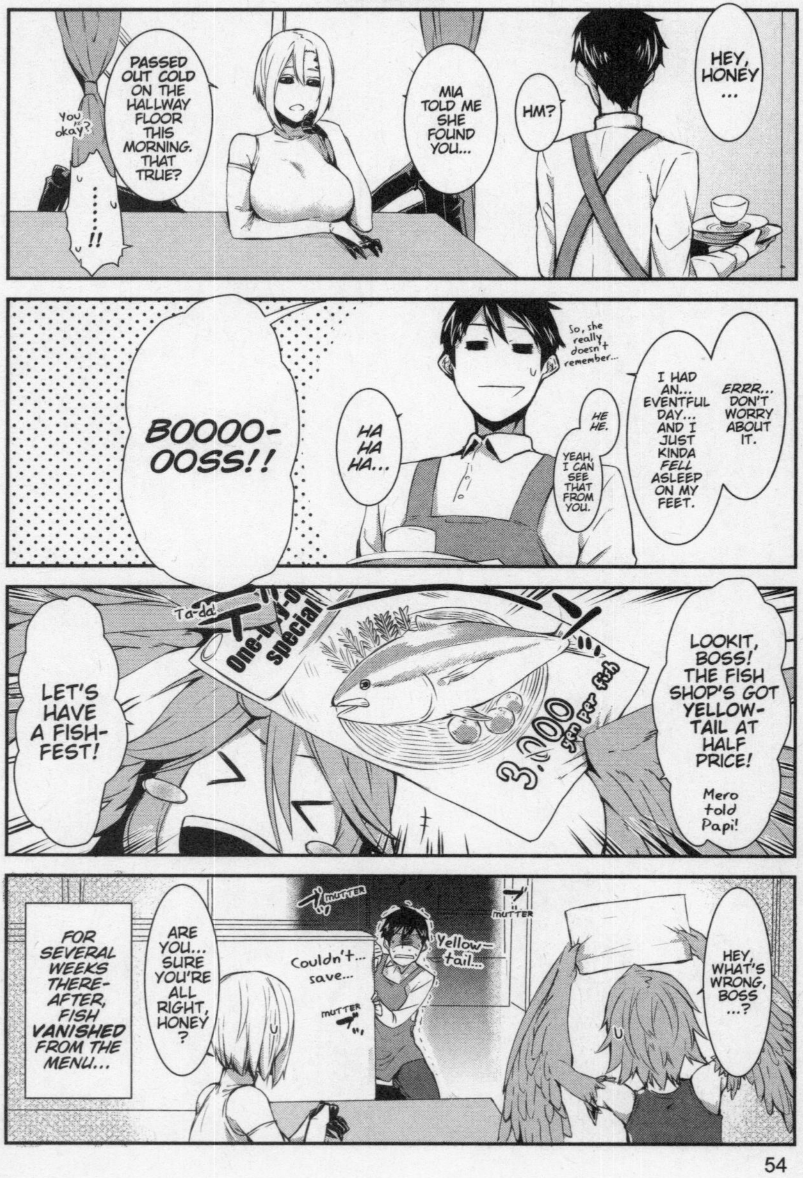
HEY, HONEY ...
HM?
MIA TOLD ME SHE FOUND YOU...
PASSED OUT COLD ON THE HALLWAY FLOOR THIS MORNING. THAT TRUE?
You okay?
......!!
ERRR... DON'T WORRY ABOUT IT.
I HAD AN... EVENTFUL DAY... AND I JUST KINDA FELL ASLEEP ON MY FEET.
So, she really doesn't remember...
HE HE.
YEAH, I CAN SEE THAT FROM YOU.
HA HA HA...
BOOOO-OOSS!!
LOOKIT, BOSS! THE FISH SHOP'S GOT YELLOW-TAIL AT HALF PRICE!
Mero told Papi!
Ta-da!
LET'S HAVE A FISH-FEST!
HEY, WHAT'S WRONG, BOSS ...?
mutter
Yellow-tail...
mutter
Couldn't... save...
mutter
ARE YOU... SURE YOU'RE ALL RIGHT, HONEY?
FOR SEVERAL WEEKS THEREAFTER, FISH VANISHED FROM THE MENU...

モンスター娘のいる日常
4コマアンソロジー

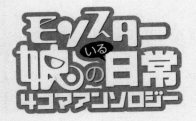

NIBBLE
はむっ♥

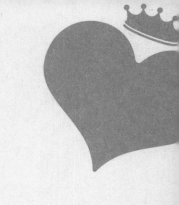

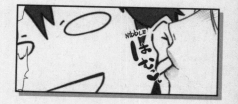

No Room

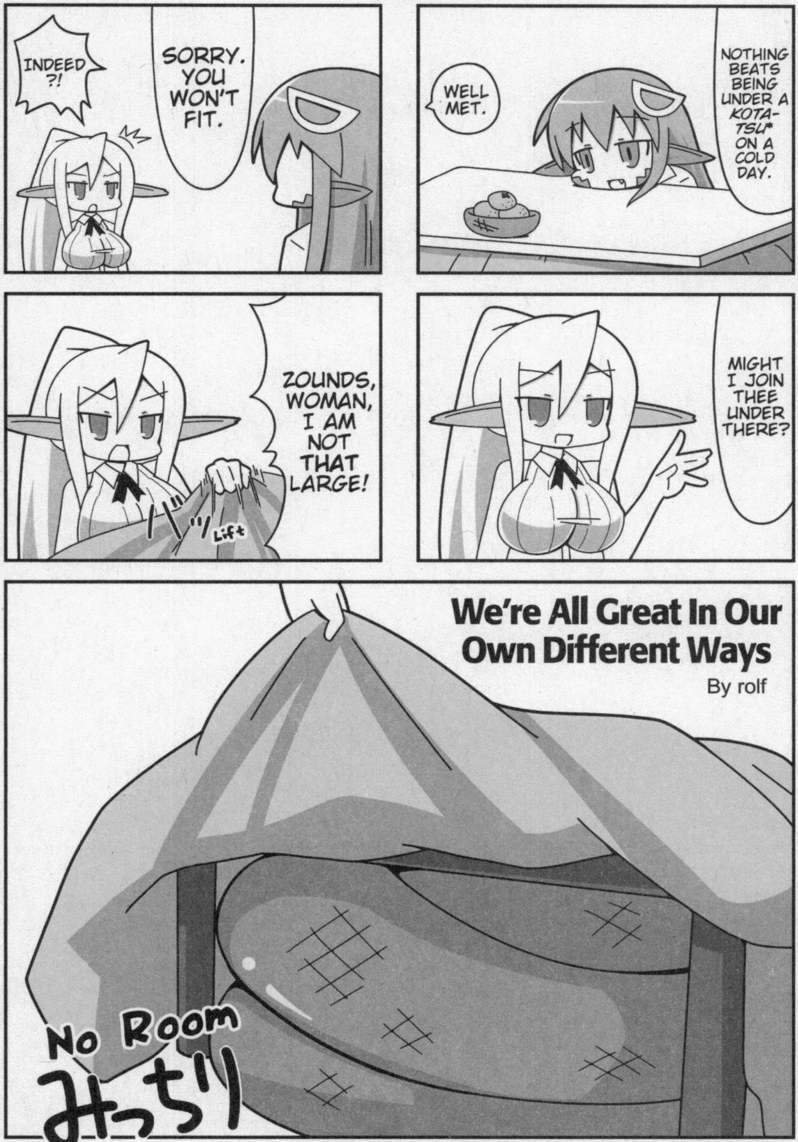
NOTHING BEATS BEING UNDER A KOTATSU* ON A COLD DAY.
WELL MET.
SORRY. YOU WON'T FIT.
INDEED ?!
MIGHT I JOIN THEE UNDER THERE?
ZOUNDS, WOMAN, I AM NOT THAT LARGE!
Lift
We're All Great In Our Own Different Ways
By rolf
No Room
みっちり

*A kotatsu is a table with a heat source underneath it, covered by a blanket.

Disarmed

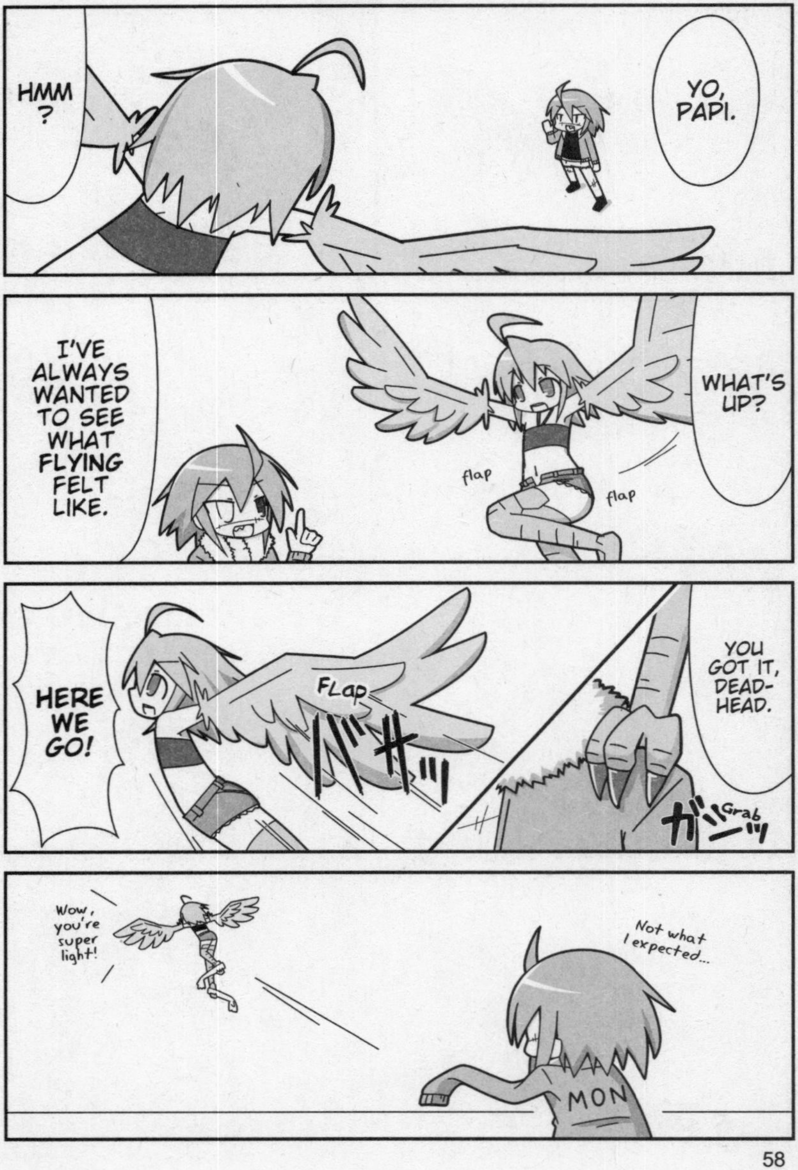
YO, PAPI.
HMM?
WHAT'S UP?
flap
flap
I'VE ALWAYS WANTED TO SEE WHAT FLYING FELT LIKE.
YOU GOT IT, DEAD-HEAD.
Grab
FLap
HERE WE GO!
Not what I expected...
MON
Wow, you're super light!

All Ears

BLAH BLAH BLAH...
BLAH-DE-BLAH BLAH...
CARROT.
Whisper
ビクッ
WHIP
BLAH-DE-BLAH.
Poke Poke

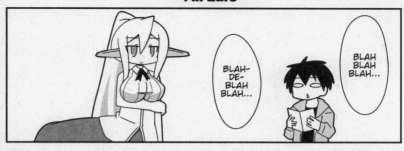

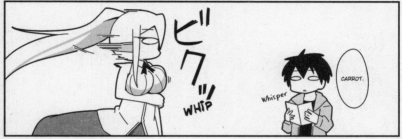

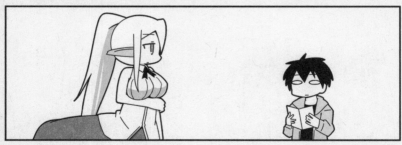

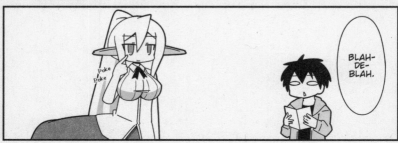

Snackrifice

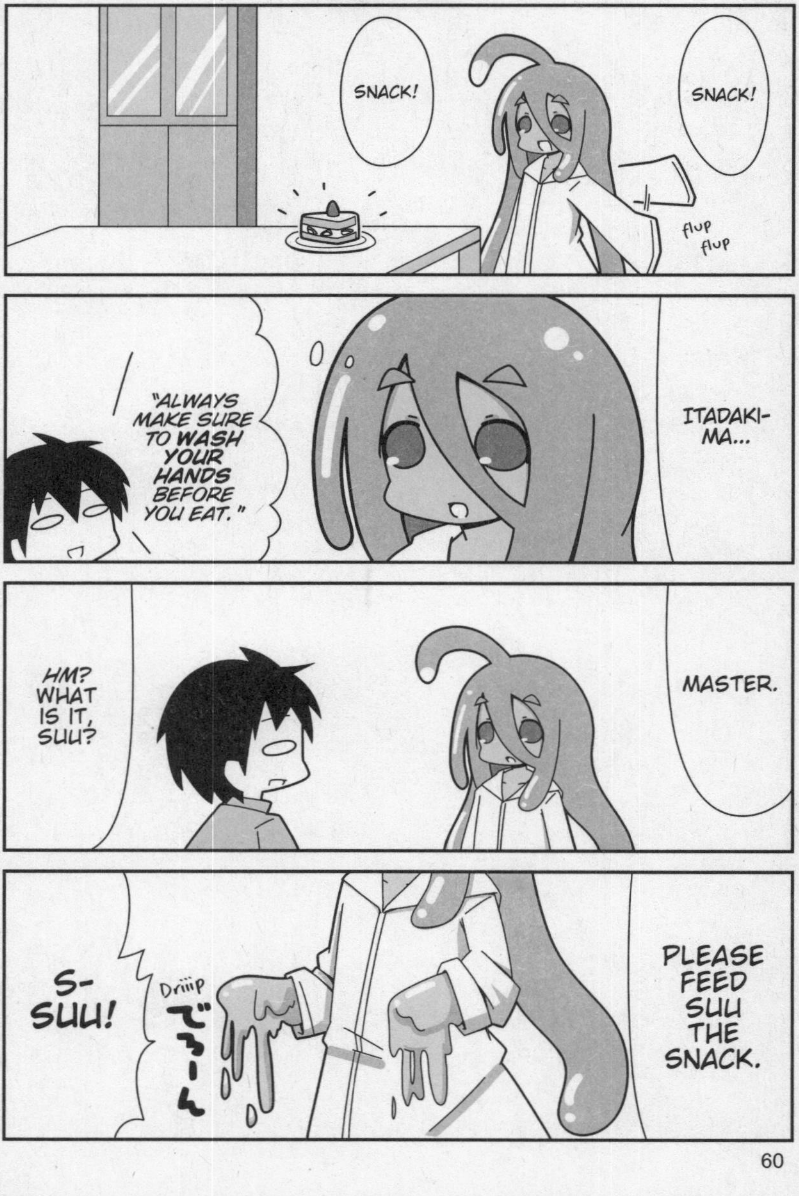
SNACK!
SNACK!
flup flup
ITADAKI-MA...
"ALWAYS MAKE SURE TO WASH YOUR HANDS BEFORE YOU EAT."
MASTER.
HM? WHAT IS IT, SUU?
PLEASE FEED SUU THE SNACK.
Driiip
でろーん
S-SUU!

If the Shoe Fits...

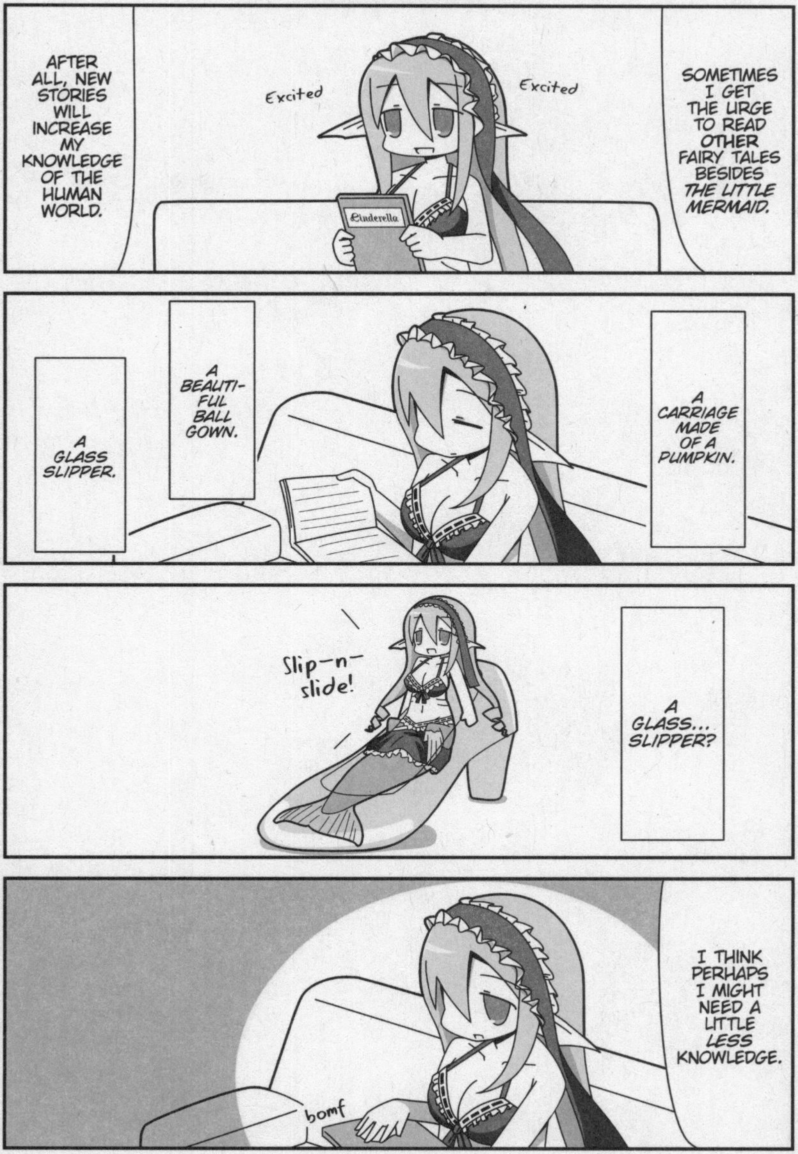
SOMETIMES I GET THE URGE TO READ OTHER FAIRY TALES BESIDES *THE LITTLE MERMAID.*
Excited
Excited
Cinderella
AFTER ALL, NEW STORIES WILL INCREASE MY KNOWLEDGE OF THE HUMAN WORLD.
A CARRIAGE MADE OF A PUMPKIN.
A BEAUTIFUL BALL GOWN.
A GLASS SLIPPER.
A GLASS... SLIPPER?
Slip-n-slide!
I THINK PERHAPS I MIGHT NEED A LITTLE *LESS* KNOWLEDGE.
bomf

Itsy Bitsy Effort

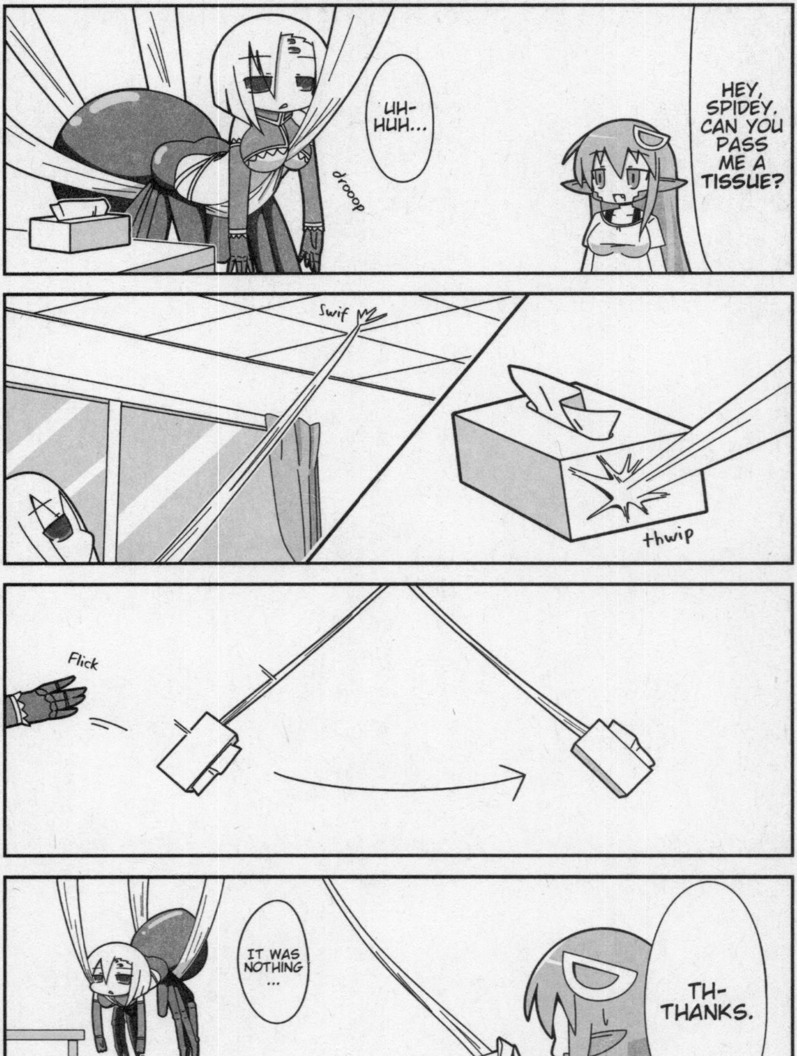
HEY, SPIDEY. CAN YOU PASS ME A TISSUE?
UH-HUH...
droooop
thwip
Swif
Flick
TH-THANKS.
IT WAS NOTHING ...

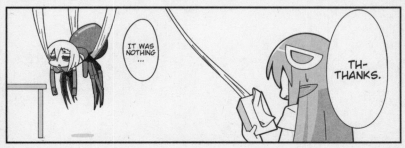

Trial By Fire

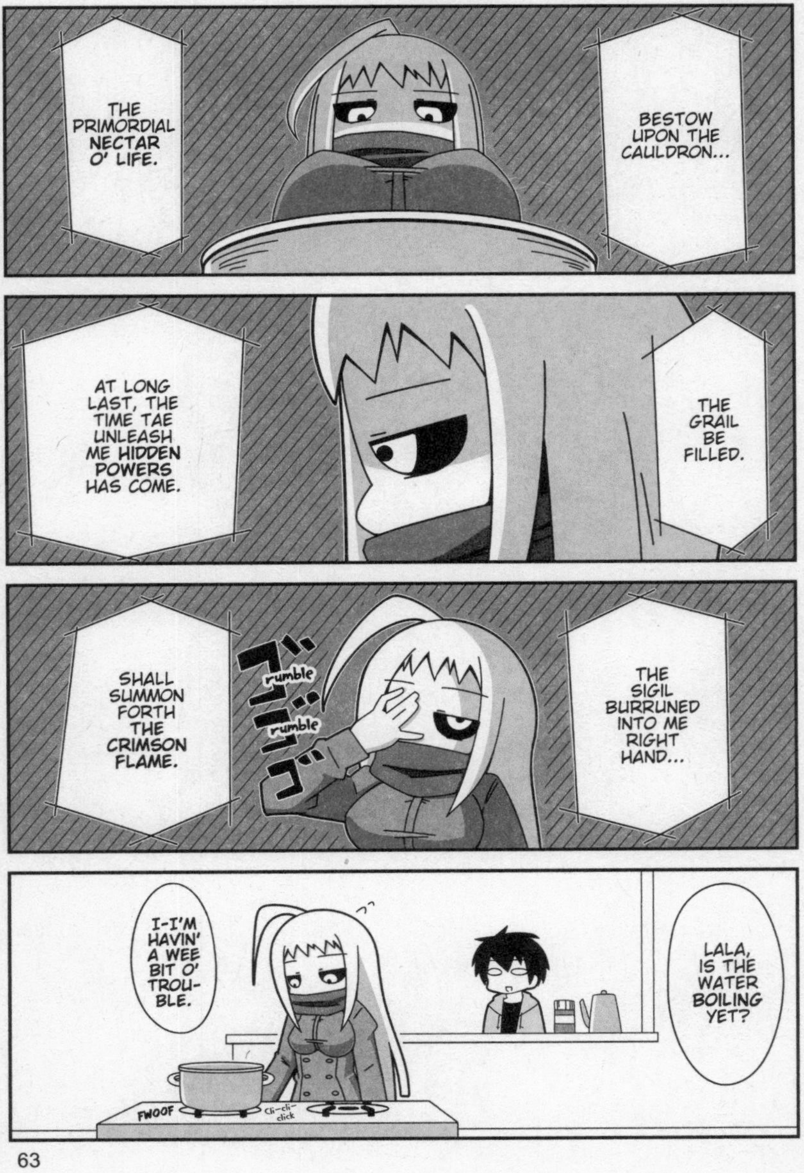
BESTOW UPON THE CAULDRON...
THE PRIMORDIAL NECTAR O' LIFE.
THE GRAIL BE FILLED.
AT LONG LAST, THE TIME TAE UNLEASH ME HIDDEN POWERS HAS COME.
THE SIGIL BURRUNED INTO ME RIGHT HAND...
rumble
rumble
SHALL SUMMON FORTH THE CRIMSON FLAME.
LALA, IS THE WATER BOILING YET?
I-I'M HAVIN' A WEE BIT O' TROU-BLE.
Cli-cli-click
FWOOF

Fee Fi Fo Fum

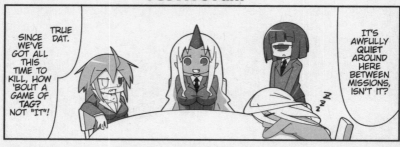

IT'S AWFULLY QUIET AROUND HERE BETWEEN MISSIONS, ISN'T IT?
TRUE DAT.
SINCE WE'VE GOT ALL THIS TIME TO KILL, HOW 'BOUT A GAME OF TAG? NOT "IT"!
Stare —
Stare —
WE'LL DO ROCK-PAPER-SCISSORS FOR "IT," OKAY?
GOOD CALL. AHA HA HA!
WHY DON'T WE JUST HAVE TIO BE "IT"?
"It" is written the same as "oni", after all.
Seems only fitting.
HEY, WE'RE TRYING NOT TO DISCRIMINATE, Y'KNOW?!
Just go back to sleep!

※ *The Japanese word for "it," as in "you're it," is written the same as "oni" (鬼).*

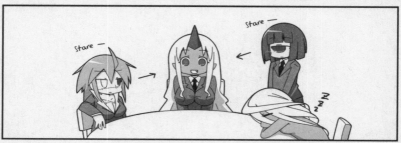

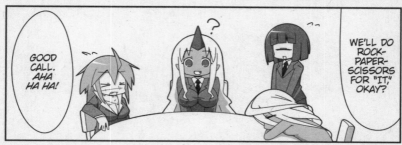

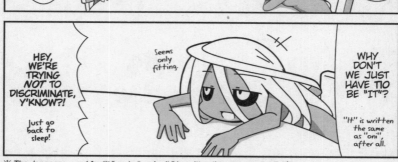

モンスター娘のいる日常
4コマアンソロジー

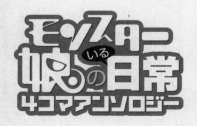

slip-n-
slide!

Early Bird

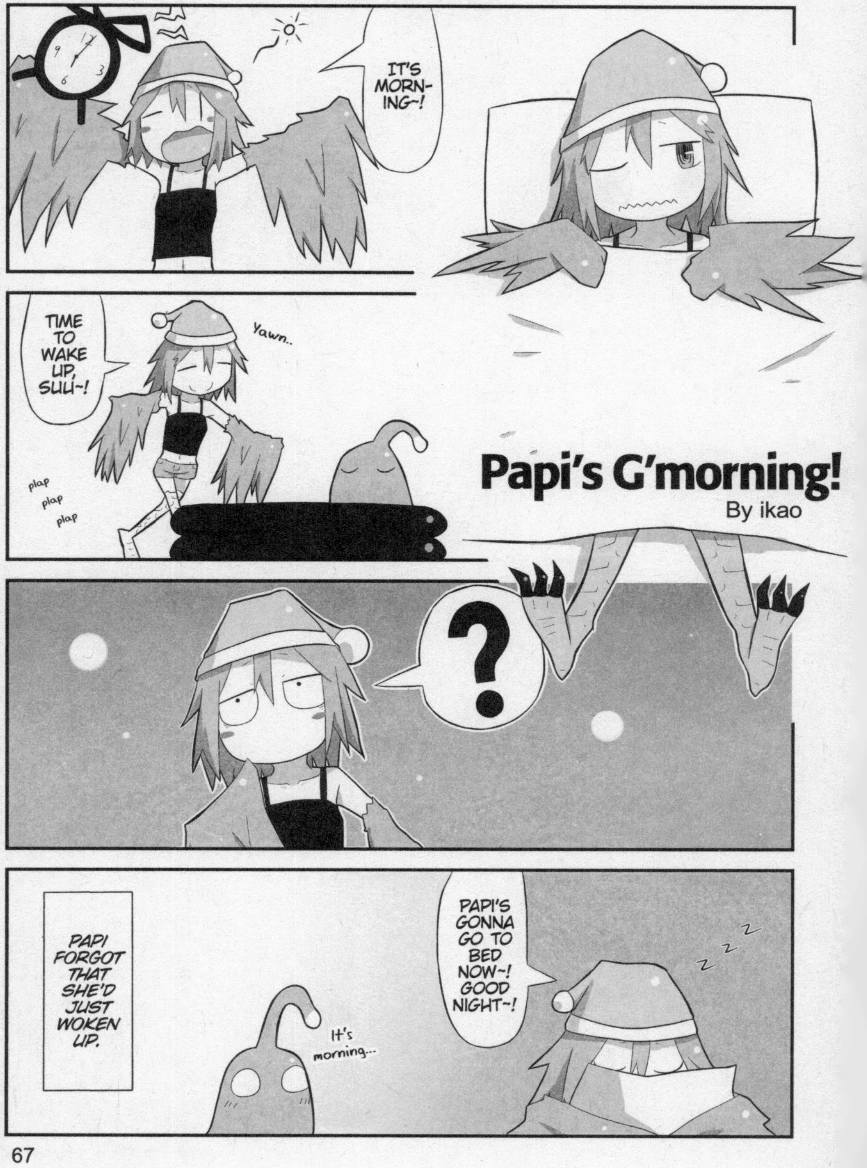
Papi's G'morning!
By ikao
IT'S MORNING~!
TIME TO WAKE UP, SUU~!
Yawn..
plap plap plap
?
PAPI'S GONNA GO TO BED NOW~! GOOD NIGHT~!
Z Z Z
It's morning...
PAPI FORGOT THAT SHE'D JUST WOKEN UP.

Almost a Good Idea

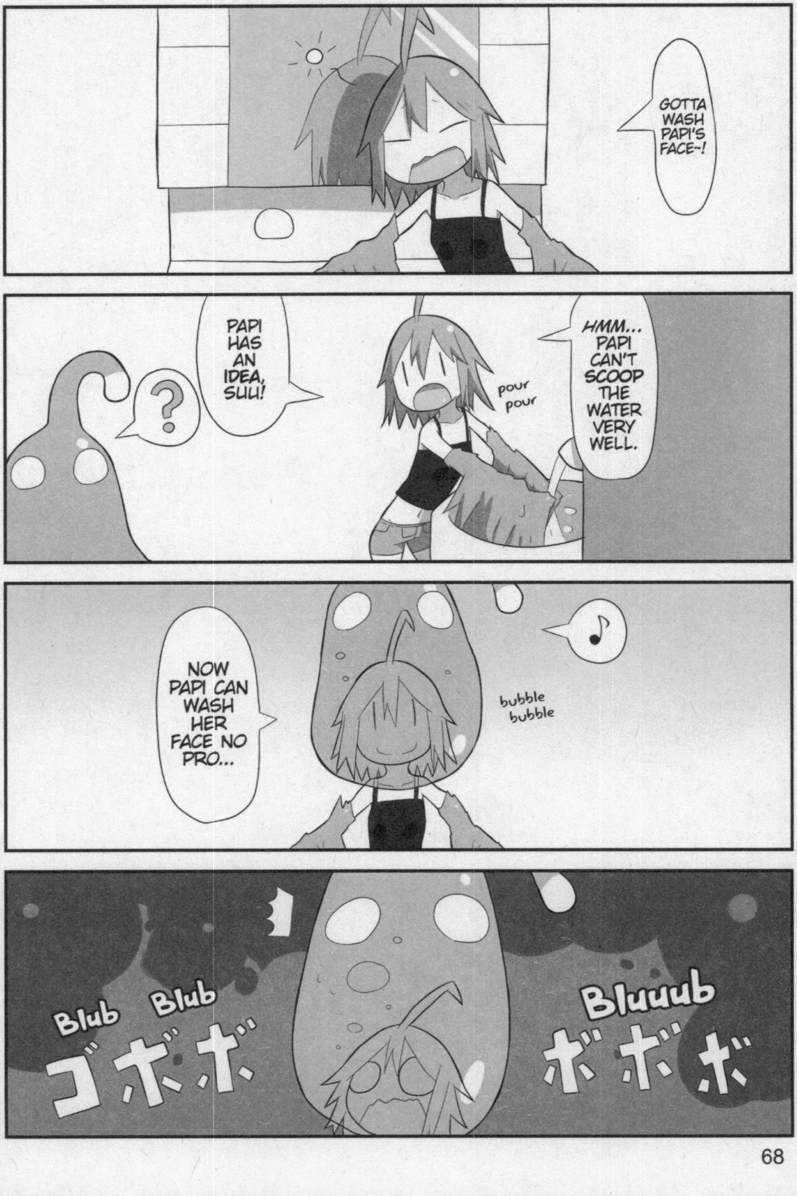

GOTTA WASH PAPI'S FACE~!
HMM... PAPI CAN'T SCOOP THE WATER VERY WELL.
pour pour
PAPI HAS AN IDEA, SUU!
?
♪
bubble bubble
NOW PAPI CAN WASH HER FACE NO PRO...
Bluuub
ボボボ
Blub Blub
ゴボボ

Egg-stravaganza

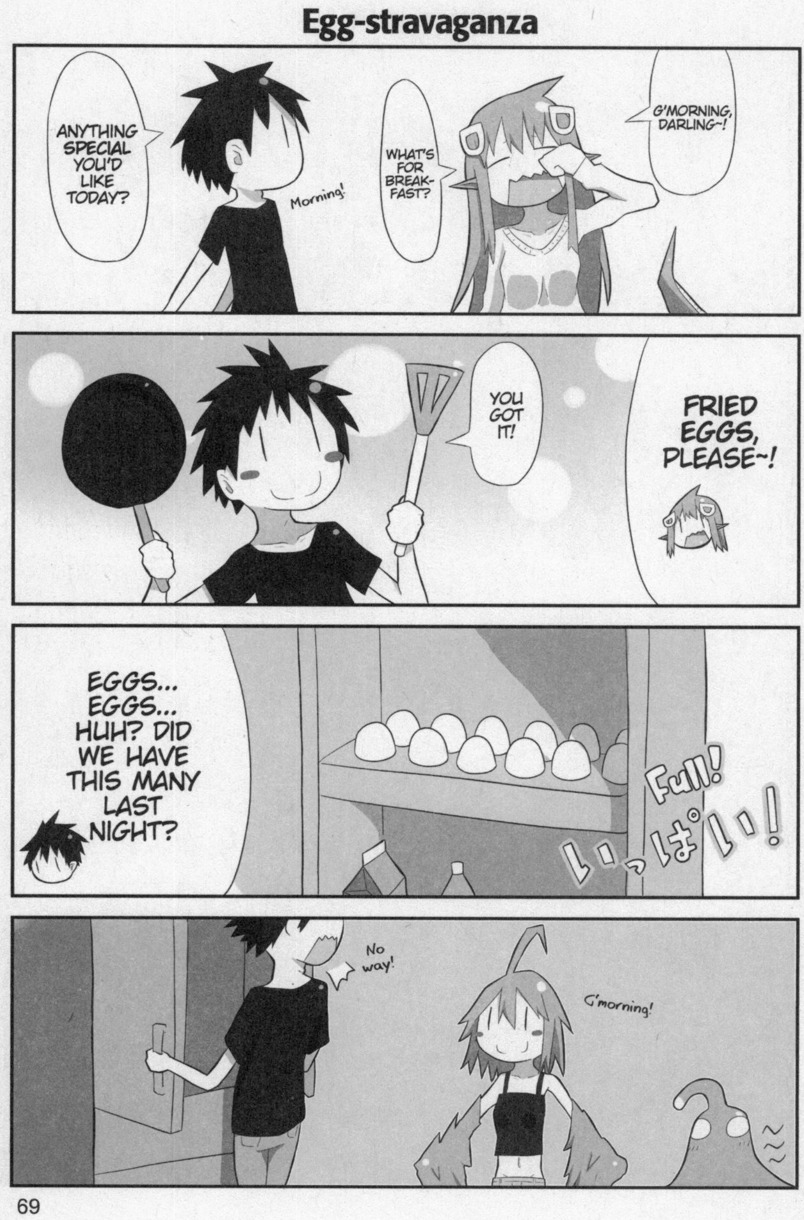
G'MORNING, DARLING~!
WHAT'S FOR BREAK-FAST?
Morning!
ANYTHING SPECIAL YOU'D LIKE TODAY?
FRIED EGGS, PLEASE~!
YOU GOT IT!
Full!
いっぱい！
EGGS... EGGS... HUH? DID WE HAVE THIS MANY LAST NIGHT?
G'morning!
No way!

Down the Hatch!

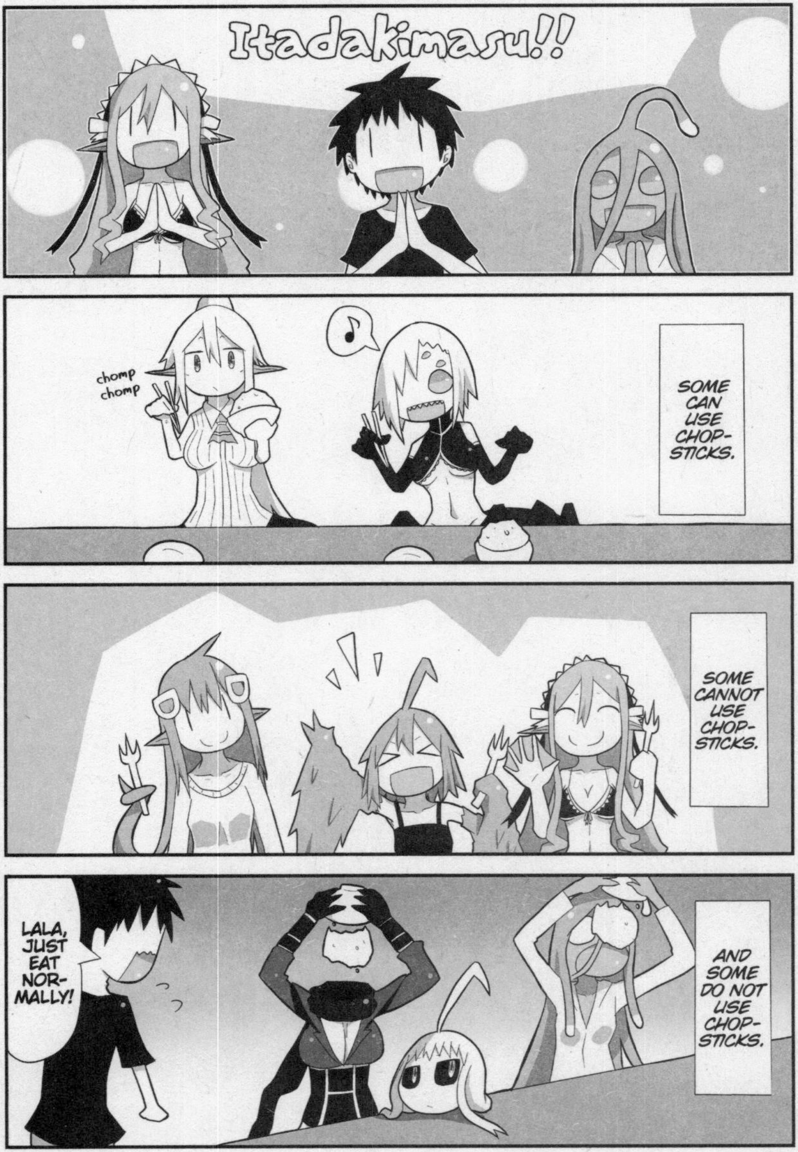
Itadakimasu!!
SOME CAN USE CHOPSTICKS.
♪
chomp chomp
SOME CANNOT USE CHOPSTICKS.
AND SOME DO NOT USE CHOPSTICKS.
LALA, JUST EAT NORMALLY!

Leave It To Me

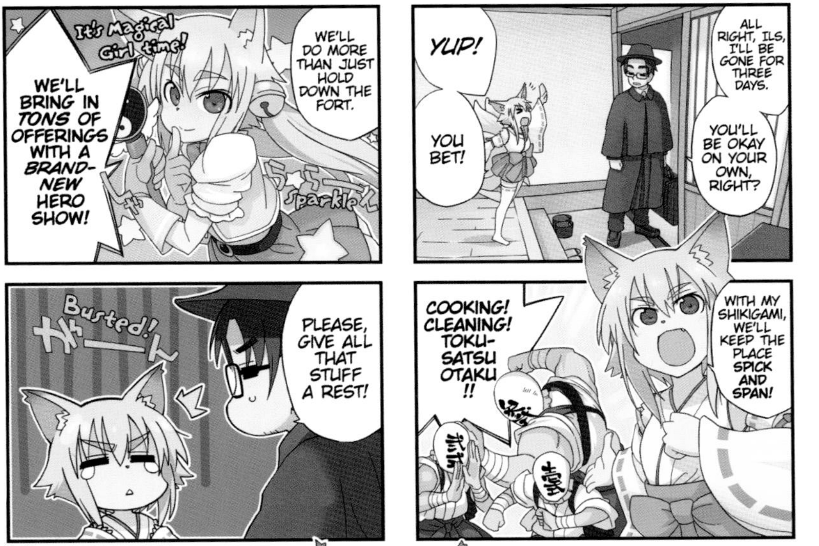
ALL RIGHT, ILS, I'LL BE GONE FOR THREE DAYS.
YOU'LL BE OKAY ON YOUR OWN, RIGHT?
YUP!
YOU BET!
WE'LL DO MORE THAN JUST HOLD DOWN THE FORT.
It's Magical Girl time!
WE'LL BRING IN TONS OF OFFERINGS WITH A BRAND-NEW HERO SHOW!
Sparkle
WITH MY SHIKIGAMI, WE'LL KEEP THE PLACE SPICK AND SPAN!
COOKING! CLEANING! TOKU-SATSU OTAKU!!
PLEASE, GIVE ALL THAT STUFF A REST!
Busted!

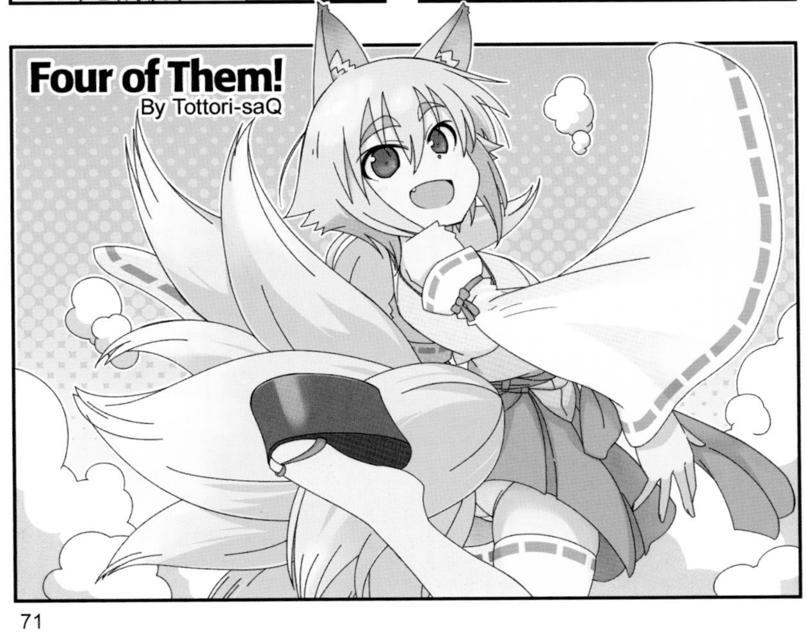
Four of Them!
By Tottori-saQ

Were There Always This Many?

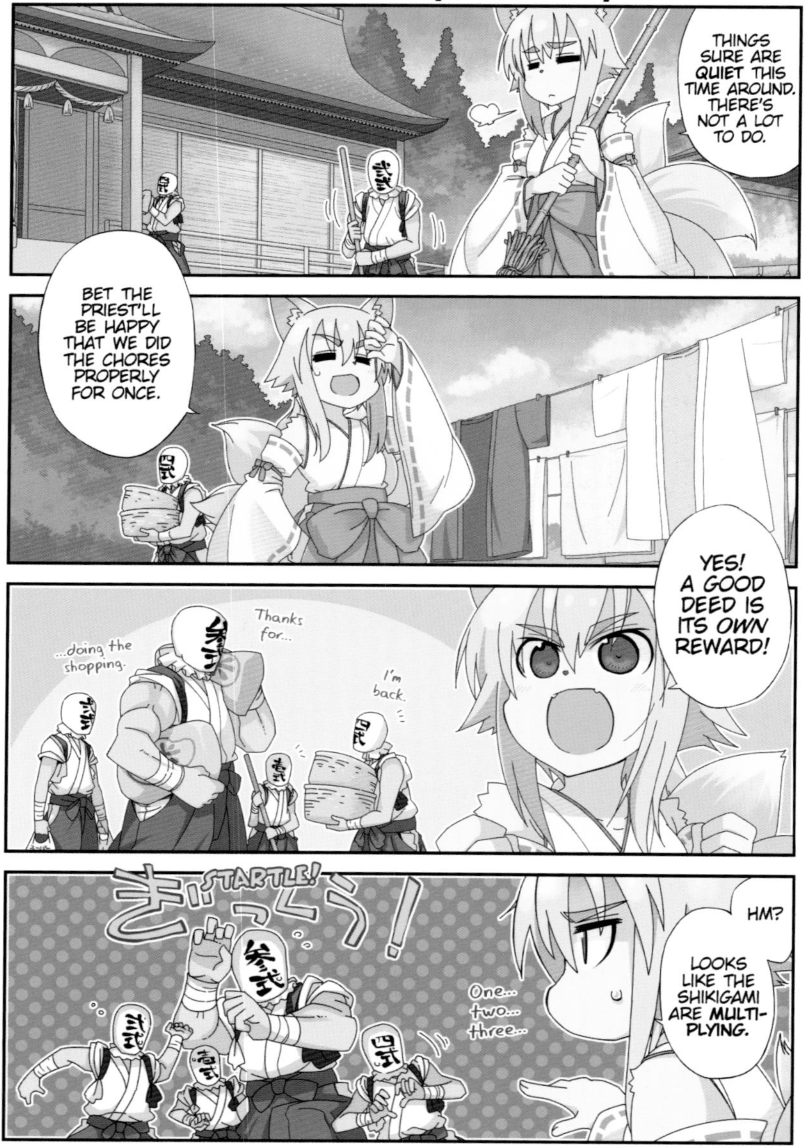
THINGS SURE ARE QUIET THIS TIME AROUND. THERE'S NOT A LOT TO DO.
BET THE PRIEST'LL BE HAPPY THAT WE DID THE CHORES PROPERLY FOR ONCE.
YES! A GOOD DEED IS ITS OWN REWARD!
Thanks for...
I'm back.
...doing the shopping.
HM?
LOOKS LIKE THE SHIKIGAMI ARE MULTI-PLYING.
STARTLE!
One... two... three...

Very Suspicious

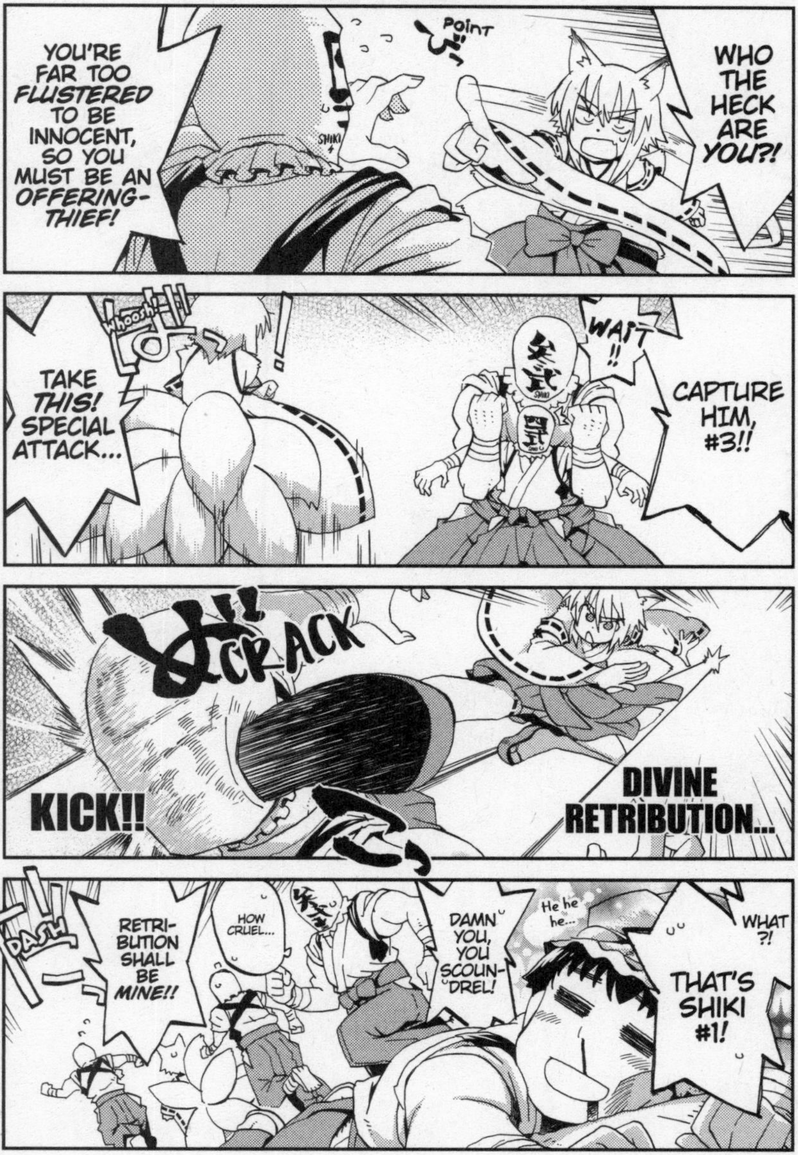
WHO THE HECK ARE YOU?!
Point
SHIKI 4
YOU'RE FAR TOO FLUSTERED TO BE INNOCENT, SO YOU MUST BE AN OFFERING-THIEF!
CAPTURE HIM, #3!!
WAIT!!
SHIKI
SHIKI 4
whoosh!
TAKE THIS! SPECIAL ATTACK...
DIVINE RETRIBUTION...
CRACK
KICK!!
WHAT?!
THAT'S SHIKI #1!
He he he...
DAMN YOU, YOU SCOUNDREL!
HOW CRUEL...
RETRIBUTION SHALL BE MINE!!
DASH

It's Because You Look So Similar

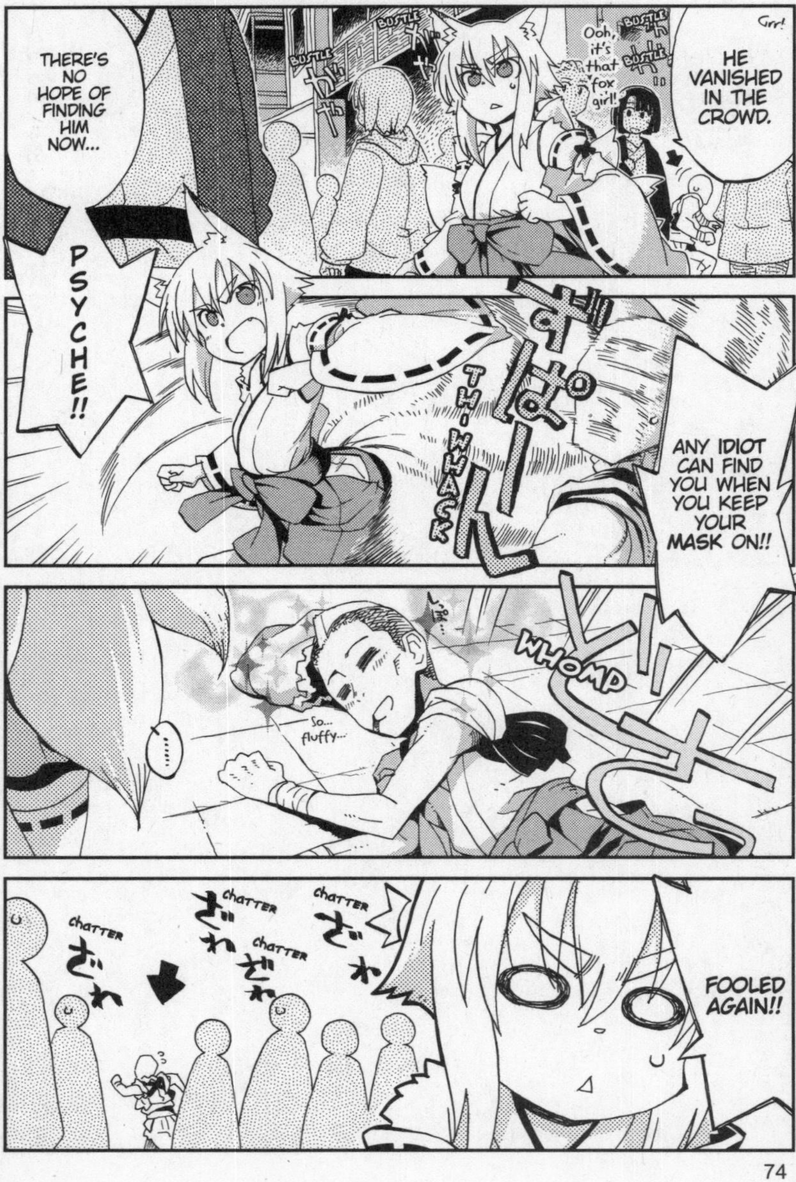

Grr!
HE VANISHED IN THE CROWD.
BUSTLE
Ooh, it's that fox girl!
BUSTLE
BUSTLE
BUSTLE
THERE'S NO HOPE OF FINDING HIM NOW...
ANY IDIOT CAN FIND YOU WHEN YOU KEEP YOUR MASK ON!!
THWHACK
PSYCHE!!
WHOMP
So... fluffy...
......
FOOLED AGAIN!!
CHATTER
CHATTER
CHATTER
CHATTER

Dubious Moves

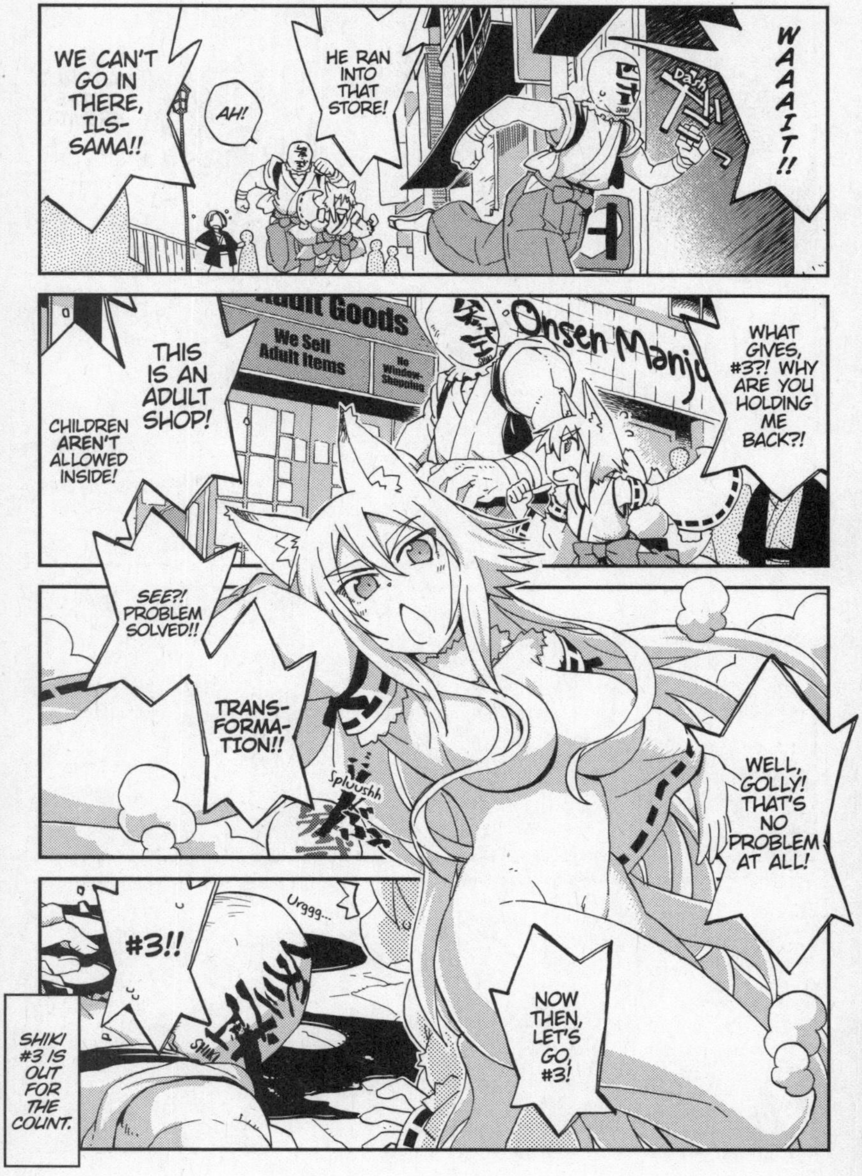
WAAAAIT!!
Dash
HE RAN INTO THAT STORE!
AH!
WE CAN'T GO IN THERE, ILS-SAMA!!
WHAT GIVES, #3?! WHY ARE YOU HOLDING ME BACK?!
Onsen Manju
Adult Goods
We Sell Adult Items
No Window-Shopping
THIS IS AN ADULT SHOP!
CHILDREN AREN'T ALLOWED INSIDE!
WELL, GOLLY! THAT'S NO PROBLEM AT ALL!
Spluushh
TRANSFORMATION!!
SEE?! PROBLEM SOLVED!!
NOW THEN, LET'S GO, #3!
Urggg...
#3!!
SHIKI #3 IS OUT FOR THE COUNT.

You Leave Me No Choice

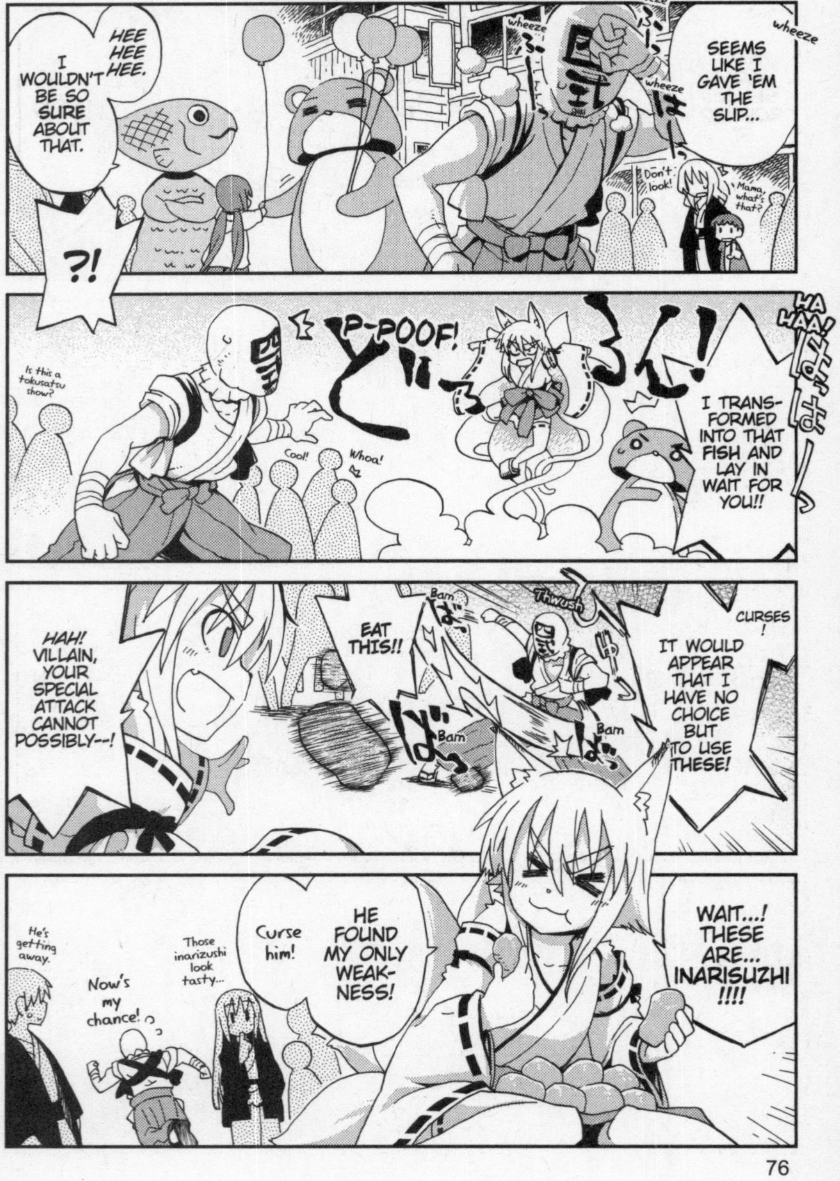
wheeze
wheeze
wheeze
wheeze
SEEMS LIKE I GAVE 'EM THE SLIP...
Mama, what's that?
Don't look!
HEE HEE HEE.
I WOULDN'T BE SO SURE ABOUT THAT.
?!
HA HAA!
I TRANSFORMED INTO THAT FISH AND LAY IN WAIT FOR YOU!!
P-POOF!
Whoa!
Cool!
Is this a tokusatsu show?
CURSES!
IT WOULD APPEAR THAT I HAVE NO CHOICE BUT TO USE THESE!
Thwush
Bam
Bam
EAT THIS!!
Bam
HAH! VILLAIN, YOUR SPECIAL ATTACK CANNOT POSSIBLY--!
WAIT...! THESE ARE... INARISUZHI !!!!
HE FOUND MY ONLY WEAK-NESS!
Curse him!
Those inarizushi look tasty...
Now's my chance!
He's getting away.

Villain or Not?

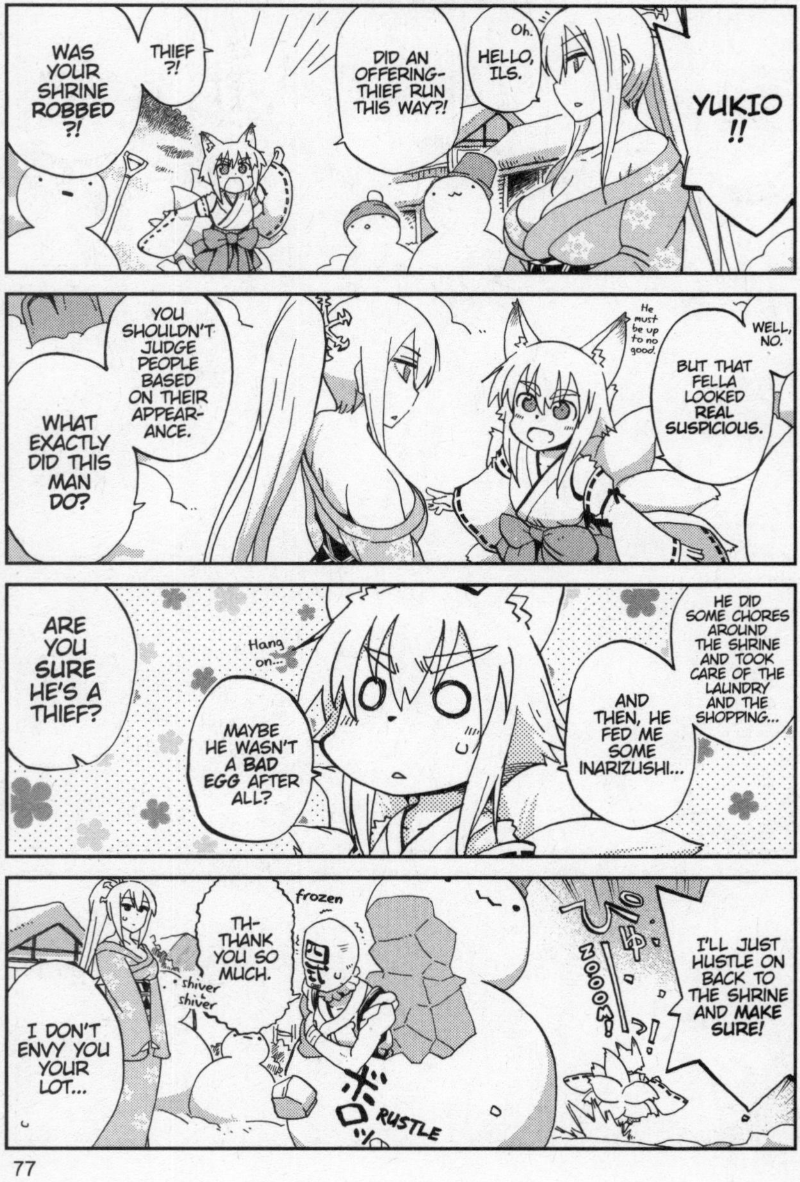
YUKIO!!
Oh.
HELLO, ILS.
DID AN OFFERING-THIEF RUN THIS WAY?!
THIEF?!
WAS YOUR SHRINE ROBBED?!
WELL, NO.
BUT THAT FELLA LOOKED REAL SUSPICIOUS.
He must be up to no good.
YOU SHOULDN'T JUDGE PEOPLE BASED ON THEIR APPEARANCE.
WHAT EXACTLY DID THIS MAN DO?
HE DID SOME CHORES AROUND THE SHRINE AND TOOK CARE OF THE LAUNDRY AND THE SHOPPING...
AND THEN, HE FED ME SOME INARIZUSHI...
Hang on...
MAYBE HE WASN'T A BAD EGG AFTER ALL?
ARE YOU SURE HE'S A THIEF?
I'LL JUST HUSTLE ON BACK TO THE SHRINE AND MAKE SURE!
frozen
TH-THANK YOU SO MUCH.
shiver shiver
RUSTLE
I DON'T ENVY YOU YOUR LOT...

The Priest Is A Worrywart

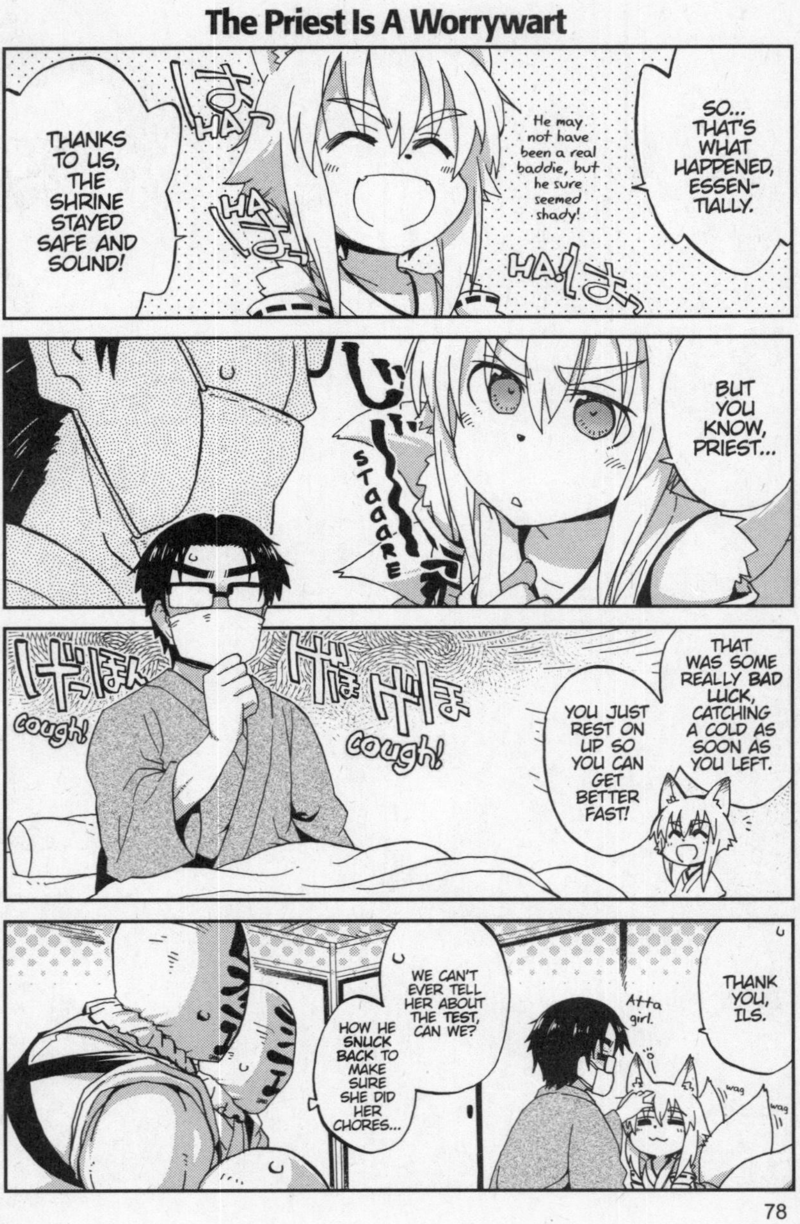
SO... THAT'S WHAT HAPPENED, ESSENTIALLY.
He may not have been a real baddie, but he sure seemed shady!
HA! はっ
HA
HA
THANKS TO US, THE SHRINE STAYED SAFE AND SOUND!
BUT YOU KNOW, PRIEST...
STAAARE
THAT WAS SOME REALLY BAD LUCK, CATCHING A COLD AS SOON AS YOU LEFT.
YOU JUST REST ON UP SO YOU CAN GET BETTER FAST!
cough!
cough!
THANK YOU, ILS.
Atta girl.
wag
wag
WE CAN'T EVER TELL HER ABOUT THE TEST, CAN WE?
HOW HE SNUCK BACK TO MAKE SURE SHE DID HER CHORES...

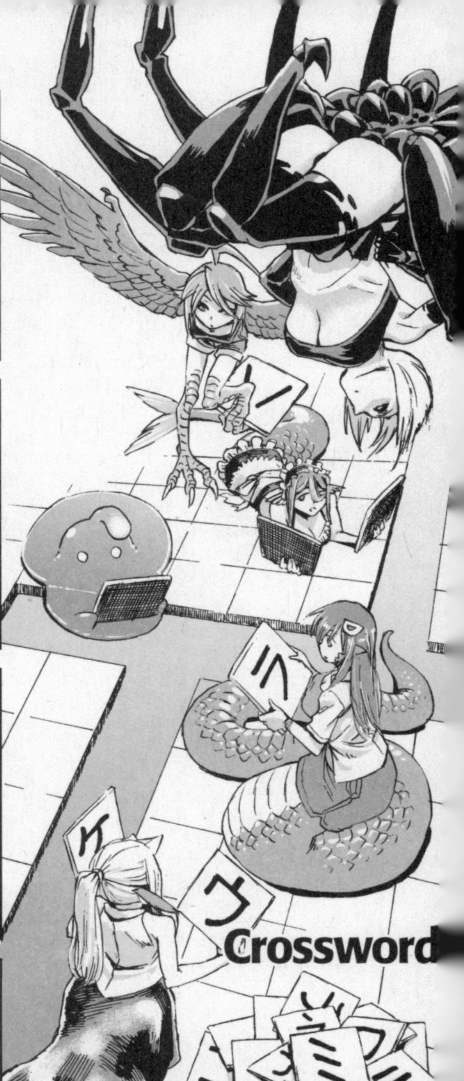

Crossword

By kanemaki thomas

Dangerous Knowledge

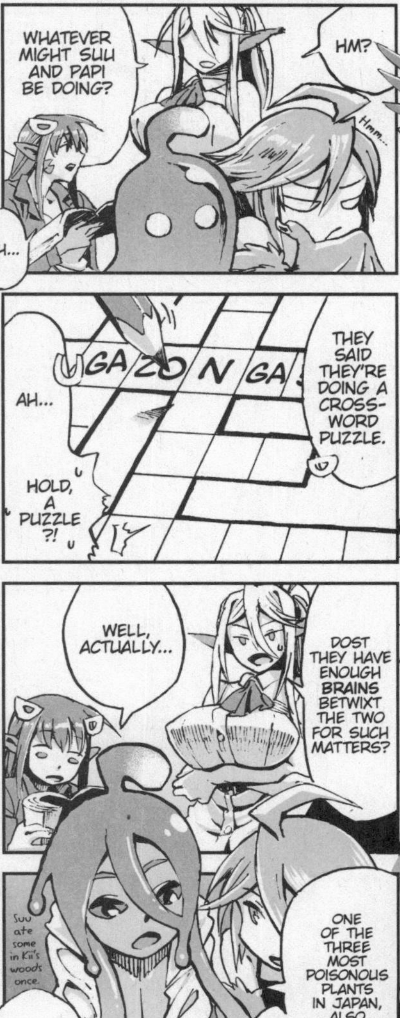

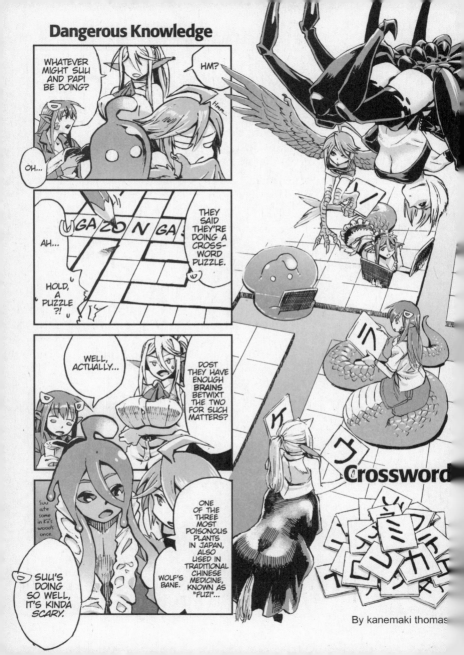

HM?
Hmm...
WHATEVER MIGHT SUU AND PAPI BE DOING?
OH...
THEY SAID THEY'RE DOING A CROSS-WORD PUZZLE.
AH...
HOLD, A PUZZLE?!
DOST THEY HAVE ENOUGH BRAINS BETWIXT THE TWO FOR SUCH MATTERS?
WELL, ACTUALLY...
ONE OF THE THREE MOST POISONOUS PLANTS IN JAPAN, ALSO USED IN TRADITIONAL CHINESE MEDICINE, KNOWN AS "FUZI"...
WOLF'S BANE.
Suu ate some in Kii's woods once.
SUU'S DOING SO WELL, IT'S KINDA SCARY.

Catching Crabs

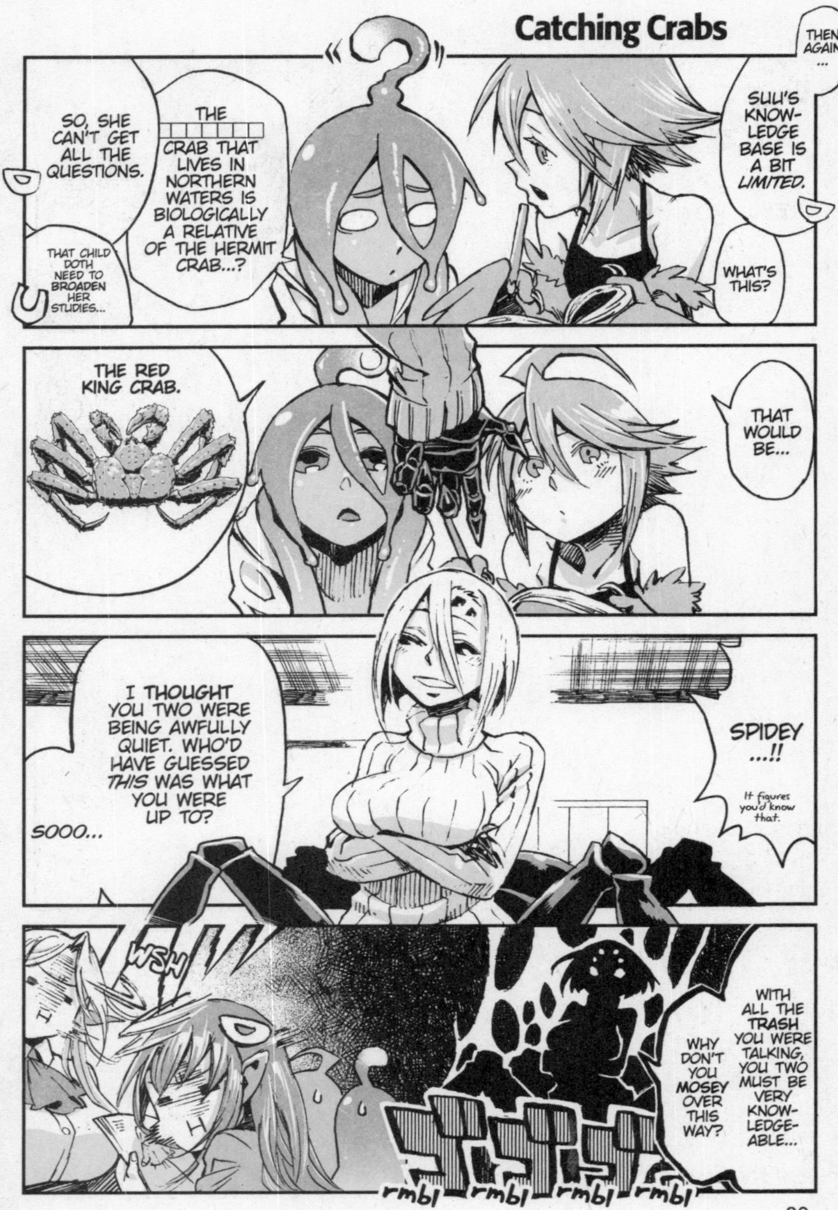

THEN AGAIN ...
SUU'S KNOW-LEDGE BASE IS A BIT *LIMITED.*
WHAT'S THIS?
THE □□□□□□□ CRAB THAT LIVES IN NORTHERN WATERS IS BIOLOGICALLY A RELATIVE OF THE HERMIT CRAB...?
SO, SHE CAN'T GET ALL THE QUESTIONS.
THAT CHILD DOTH NEED TO BROADEN HER STUDIES...
THAT WOULD BE...
THE RED KING CRAB.
SPIDEY ...!!
It figures you'd know that.
I THOUGHT YOU TWO WERE BEING AWFULLY QUIET. WHO'D HAVE GUESSED *THIS* WAS WHAT YOU WERE UP TO?
SOOO...
WITH ALL THE TRASH YOU WERE TALKING, YOU TWO MUST BE VERY KNOW-LEDGE-ABLE...
WHY DON'T YOU MOSEY OVER THIS WAY?
WSH
rmbl rmbl rmbl rmbl

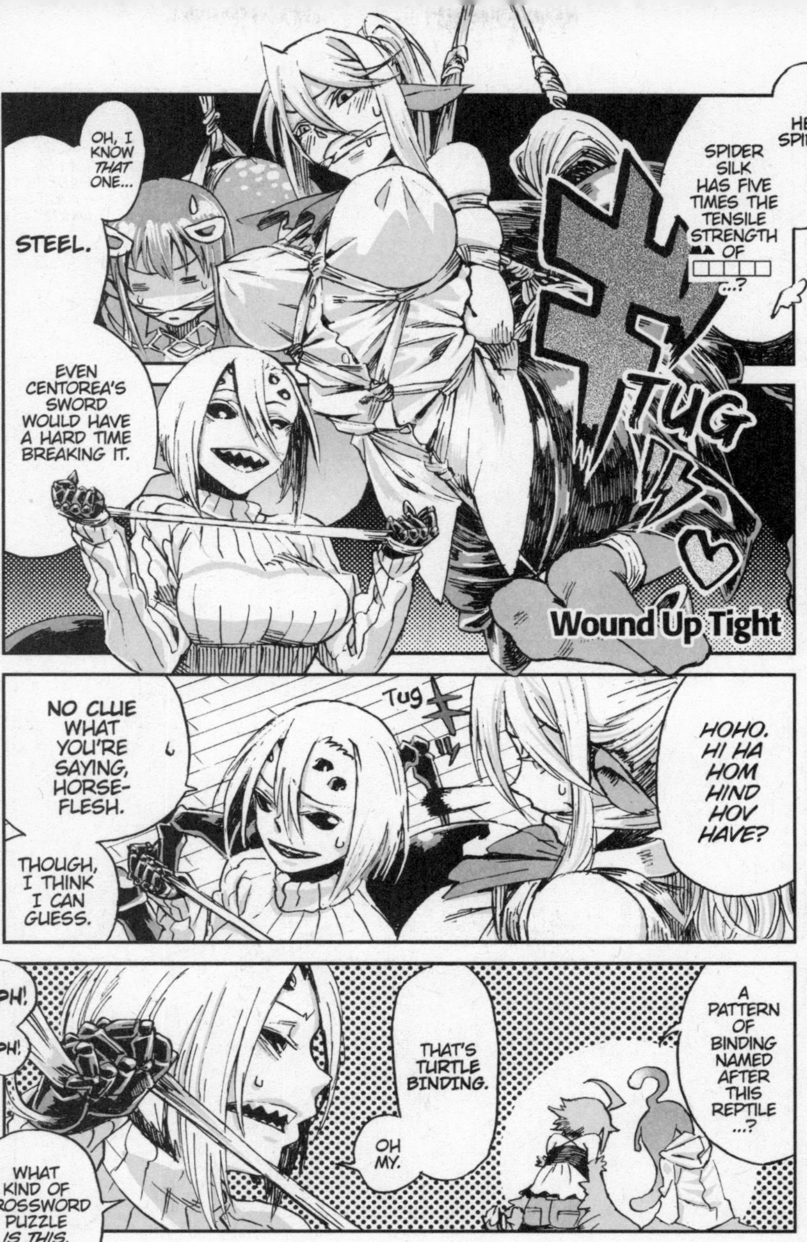
HEY, SPIDEY. SPIDER SILK HAS FIVE TIMES THE TENSILE STRENGTH OF □□□□□□...?
OH, I KNOW THAT ONE... STEEL.
TUG
EVEN CENTOREA'S SWORD WOULD HAVE A HARD TIME BREAKING IT.
Wound Up Tight
HOHO. HI HA HOM HIND HOV HAVE?
Tug
NO CLUE WHAT YOU'RE SAYING, HORSE-FLESH.
THOUGH, I THINK I CAN GUESS.
A PATTERN OF BINDING NAMED AFTER THIS REPTILE ...?
THAT'S TURTLE BINDING.
OH MY.
MPH! MPH!
WHAT KIND OF CROSSWORD PUZZLE IS THIS, ANYWAY?

Isn't It More Exciting This Way?

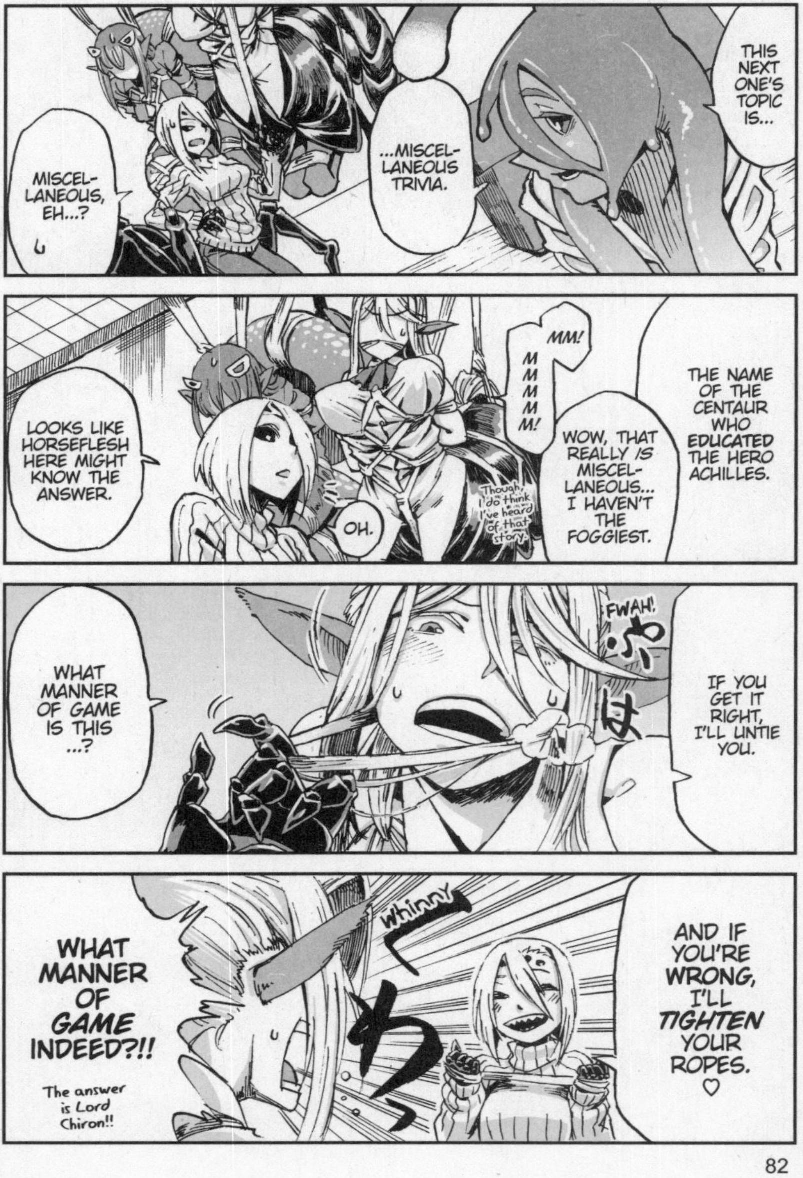
THIS NEXT ONE'S TOPIC IS...
...MISCEL-LANEOUS TRIVIA.
MISCEL-LANEOUS, EH...?
THE NAME OF THE CENTAUR WHO EDUCATED THE HERO ACHILLES.
MM! MMMMMM!
WOW, THAT REALLY *IS* MISCEL-LANEOUS... I HAVEN'T THE FOGGIEST.
Though, I do think I've heard of that story.
OH.
LOOKS LIKE HORSEFLESH HERE MIGHT KNOW THE ANSWER.
IF YOU GET IT RIGHT, I'LL UNTIE YOU.
FWAH!
WHAT MANNER OF GAME IS THIS ...?
AND IF YOU'RE WRONG, I'LL *TIGHTEN* YOUR ROPES. ♡
Whinny
WHAT MANNER OF *GAME* INDEED?!!
The answer is Lord Chiron!!

History Lesson

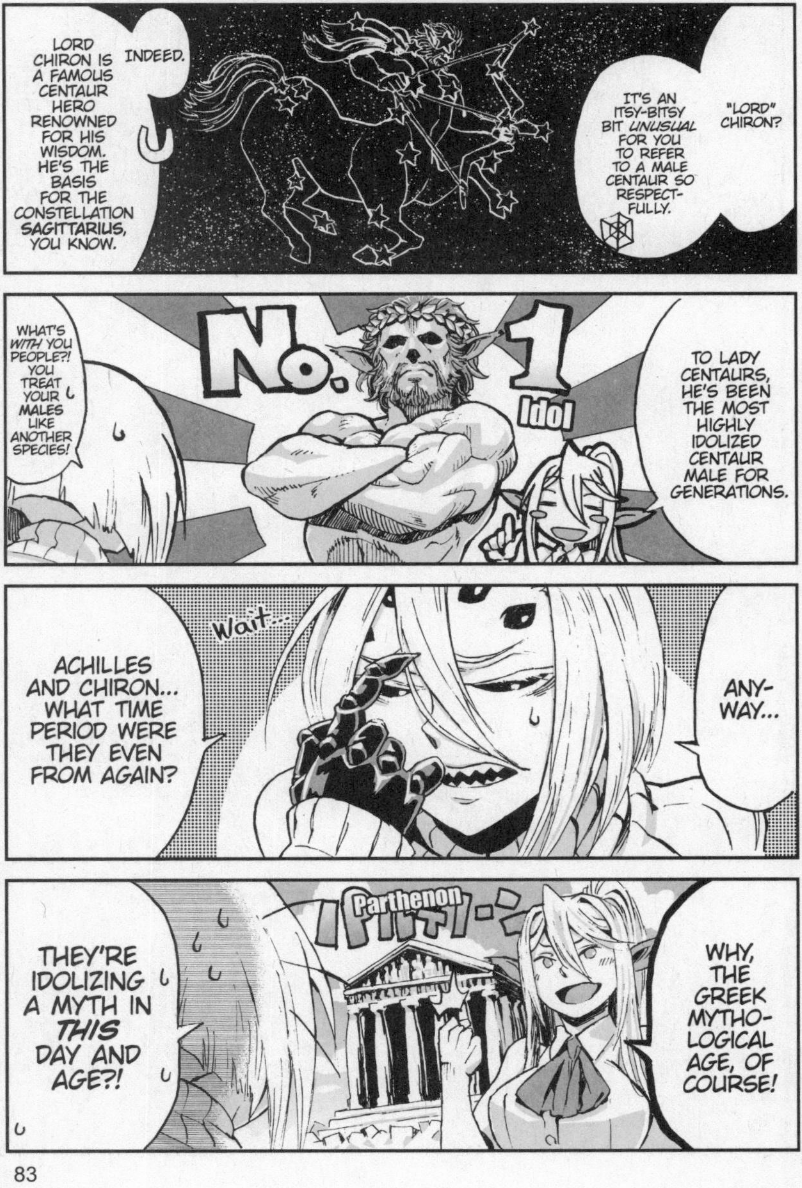
"LORD" CHIRON?
IT'S AN ITSY-BITSY BIT *UNUSUAL* FOR YOU TO REFER TO A MALE CENTAUR SO RESPECT-FULLY.
INDEED.
LORD CHIRON IS A FAMOUS CENTAUR HERO RENOWNED FOR HIS WISDOM. HE'S THE BASIS FOR THE CONSTELLATION SAGITTARIUS, YOU KNOW.
TO LADY CENTAURS, HE'S BEEN THE MOST HIGHLY IDOLIZED CENTAUR MALE FOR GENERATIONS.
No. 1
Idol
WHAT'S *WITH* YOU PEOPLE?! YOU TREAT YOUR MALES LIKE ANOTHER SPECIES!
ANY-WAY...
Wait...
ACHILLES AND CHIRON... WHAT TIME PERIOD WERE THEY EVEN FROM AGAIN?
WHY, THE GREEK MYTHO-LOGICAL AGE, OF COURSE!
Parthenon
THEY'RE IDOLIZING A MYTH IN *THIS* DAY AND AGE?!

The Serpent's Temptation

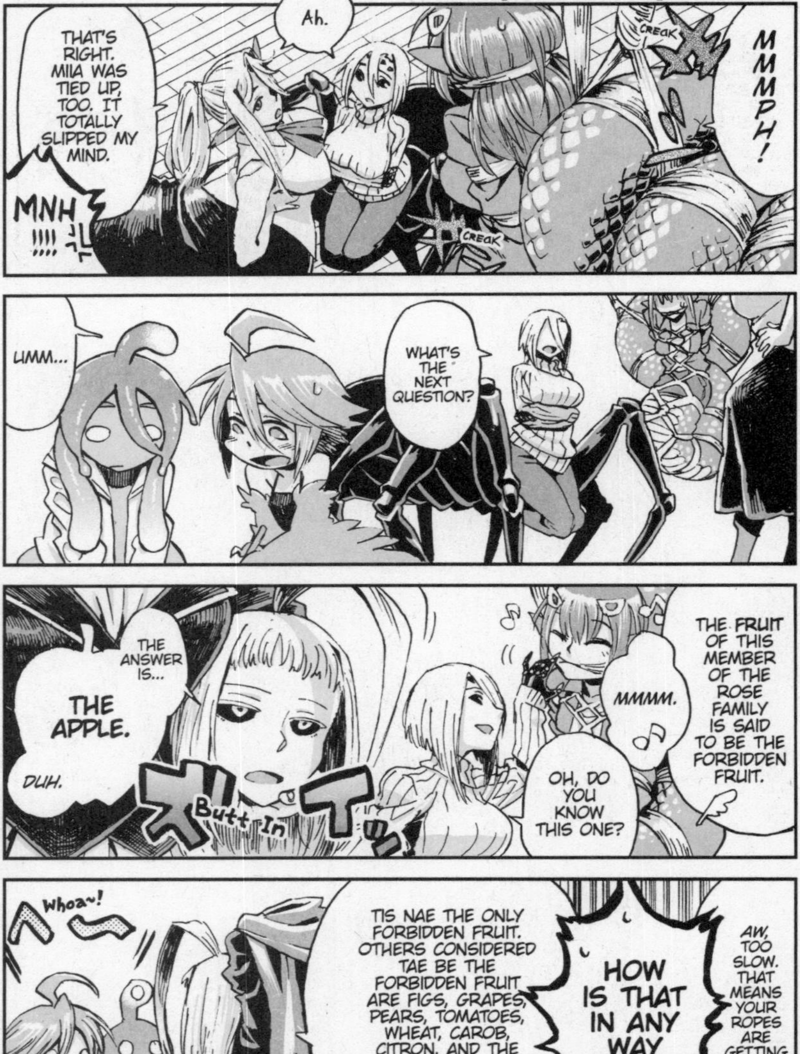

MMMPH!
CREAK
Ah.
THAT'S RIGHT. MIIA WAS TIED UP, TOO. IT TOTALLY SLIPPED MY MIND.
CREAK
MNH!!!!
WHAT'S THE NEXT QUESTION?
UMM...
THE FRUIT OF THIS MEMBER OF THE ROSE FAMILY IS SAID TO BE THE FORBIDDEN FRUIT.
MMMM.
OH, DO YOU KNOW THIS ONE?
THE ANSWER IS... THE APPLE. DUH.
Butt In
AW, TOO SLOW. THAT MEANS YOUR ROPES ARE GETTING TIGHTENED.
HOW IS THAT IN ANY WAY FAIR?!!
TIS NAE THE ONLY FORBIDDEN FRUIT. OTHERS CONSIDERED TAE BE THE FORBIDDEN FRUIT ARE FIGS, GRAPES, PEARS, TOMATOES, WHEAT, CAROB, CITRON, AND THE FRUIT OF THE DATURA... TAE NAME BUT A FEW...
Whoa~!

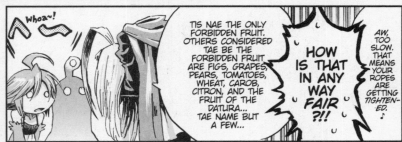

Basic Chuunibyou Education

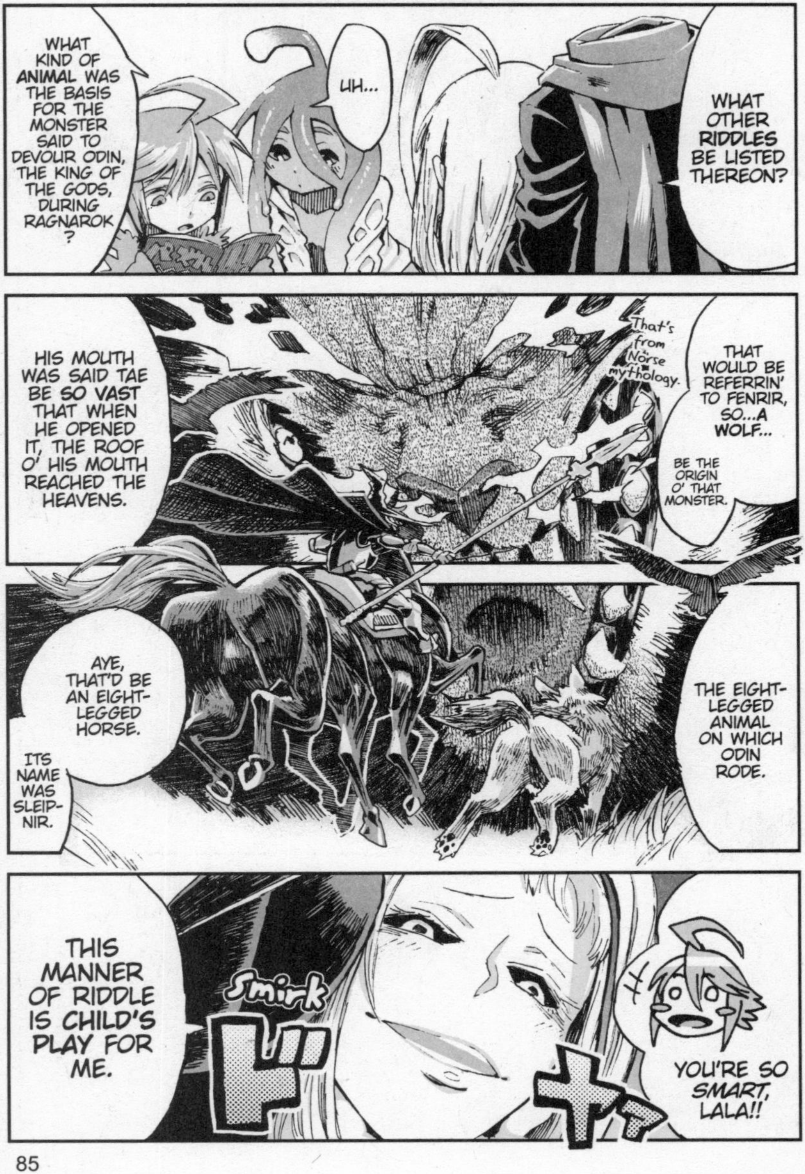
WHAT OTHER RIDDLES BE LISTED THEREON?
UH...
WHAT KIND OF ANIMAL WAS THE BASIS FOR THE MONSTER SAID TO DEVOUR ODIN, THE KING OF THE GODS, DURING RAGNAROK?
THAT WOULD BE REFERRIN' TO FENRIR, SO...A WOLF...
That's from Norse mythology.
BE THE ORIGIN O' THAT MONSTER.
HIS MOUTH WAS SAID TAE BE SO VAST THAT WHEN HE OPENED IT, THE ROOF O' HIS MOUTH REACHED THE HEAVENS.
THE EIGHT-LEGGED ANIMAL ON WHICH ODIN RODE.
AYE, THAT'D BE AN EIGHT-LEGGED HORSE.
ITS NAME WAS SLEIPNIR.
YOU'RE SO SMART, LALA!!
Smirk
ドヤ
THIS MANNER OF RIDDLE IS CHILD'S PLAY FOR ME.

A Question of Life or Death

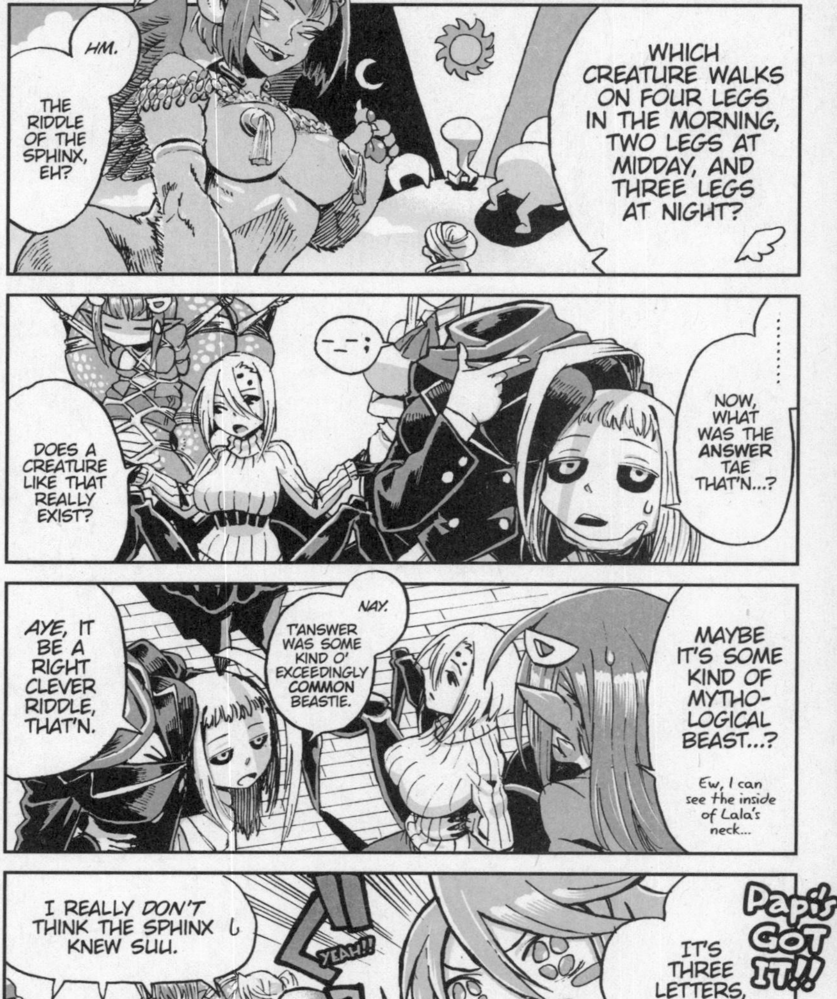
WHICH CREATURE WALKS ON FOUR LEGS IN THE MORNING, TWO LEGS AT MIDDAY, AND THREE LEGS AT NIGHT?
HM.
THE RIDDLE OF THE SPHINX, EH?
......
NOW, WHAT WAS THE ANSWER TAE THAT'N...?
DOES A CREATURE LIKE THAT REALLY EXIST?
MAYBE IT'S SOME KIND OF MYTHOLOGICAL BEAST...?
Ew, I can see the inside of Lala's neck...
NAY.
T'ANSWER WAS SOME KIND O' EXCEEDINGLY COMMON BEASTIE.
AYE, IT BE A RIGHT CLEVER RIDDLE, THAT'N.
Papi's GOT IT!!
IT'S THREE LETTERS, SO THE ANSWER'S GOTTA BE... SUU! PAPI KNOWS IT!!
YEAH!!
I REALLY DON'T THINK THE SPHINX KNEW SUU.

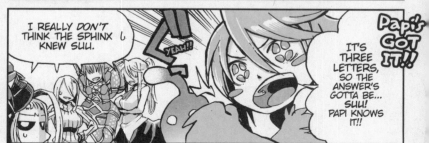

Metamorphosis?

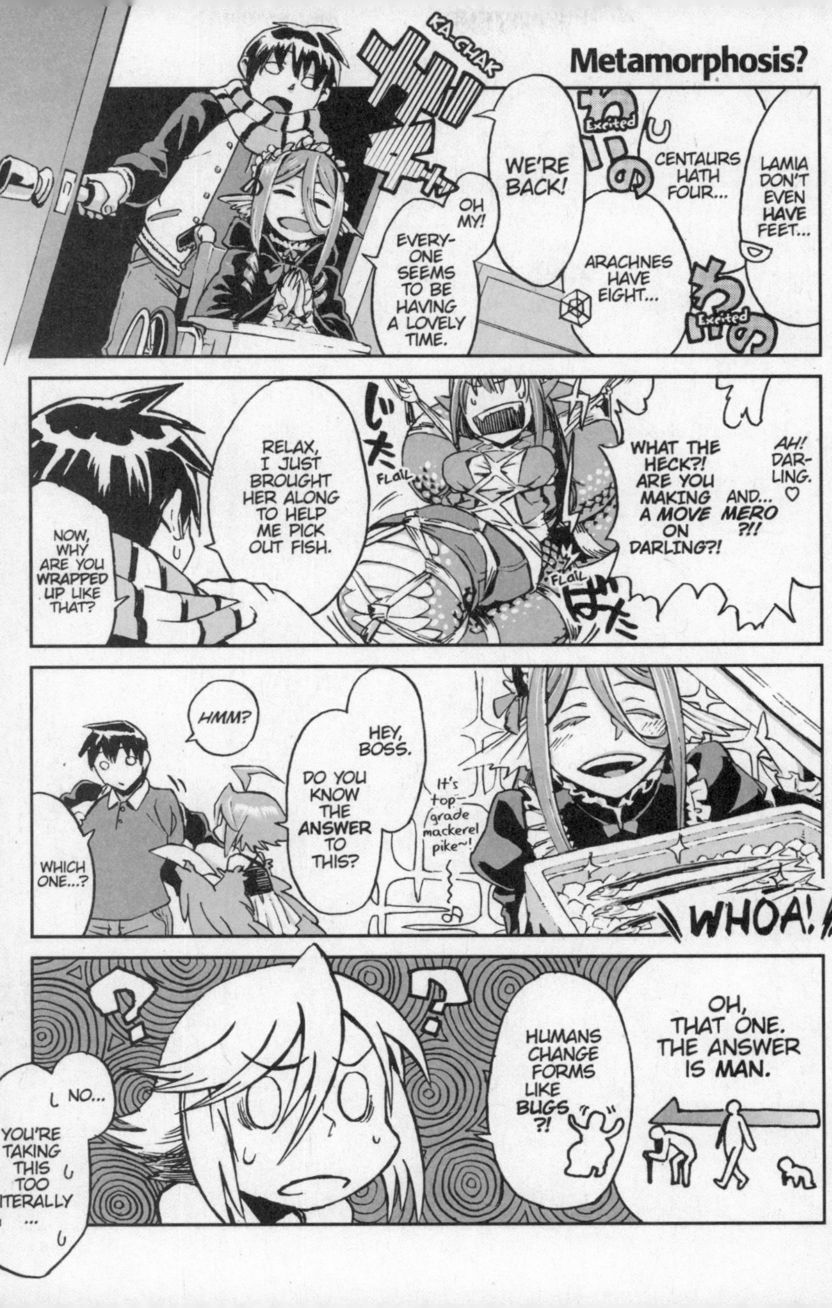
LAMIA DON'T EVEN HAVE FEET...
CENTAURS HATH FOUR...
ARACHNES HAVE EIGHT...
Excited
Excited
WE'RE BACK!
KA-CHAK
OH MY!
EVERY-ONE SEEMS TO BE HAVING A LOVELY TIME.
AH! DARLING. ♡
WHAT THE HECK?! ARE YOU MAKING A MOVE ON DARLING?!
AND... MERO ?!!
FLAIL
FLAIL
RELAX, I JUST BROUGHT HER ALONG TO HELP ME PICK OUT FISH.
NOW, WHY ARE YOU WRAPPED UP LIKE THAT?
WHOA!
It's top-grade mackerel pike~!
HEY, BOSS.
DO YOU KNOW THE ANSWER TO THIS?
HMM?
WHICH ONE...?
OH, THAT ONE. THE ANSWER IS MAN.
HUMANS CHANGE FORMS LIKE BUGS ?!
NO...
YOU'RE TAKING THIS TOO LITERALLY ...

The Grand Prize

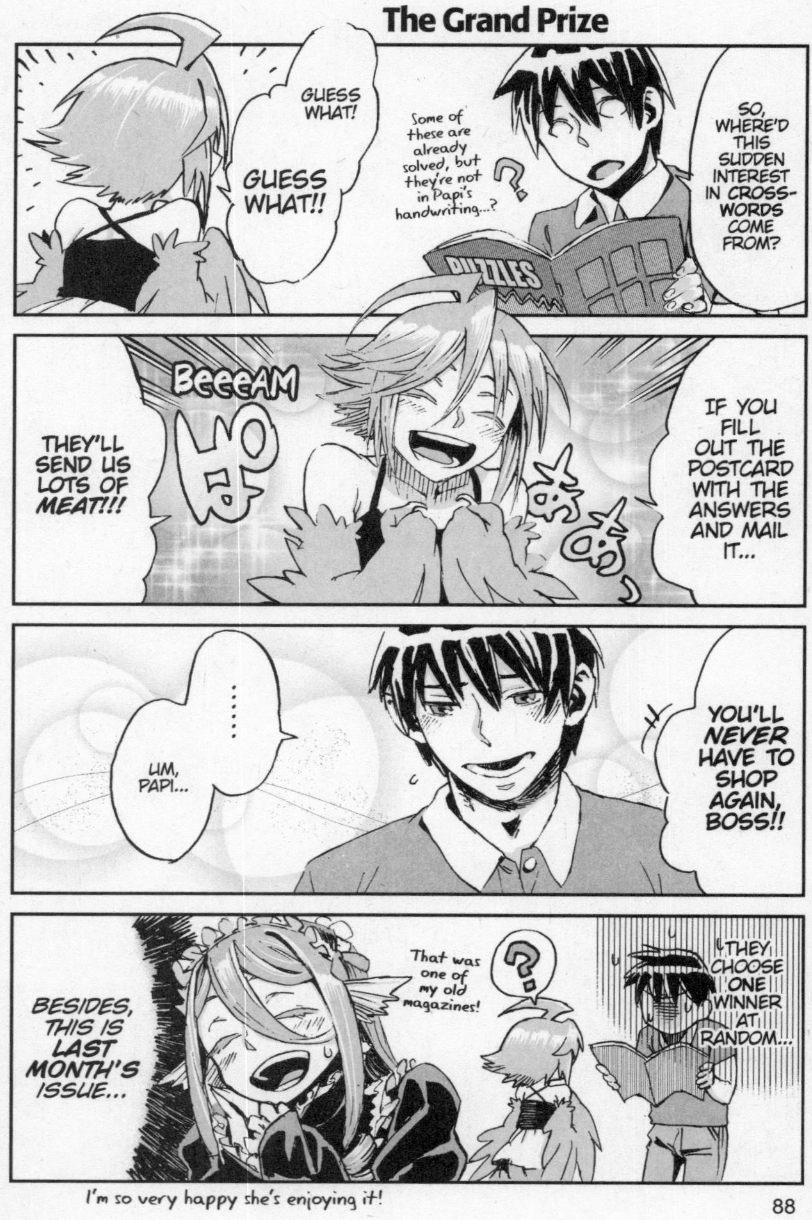
SO, WHERE'D THIS SUDDEN INTEREST IN CROSS-WORDS COME FROM?
PUZZLES
Some of these are already solved, but they're not in Papi's handwriting...?
GUESS WHAT!
GUESS WHAT!!
IF YOU FILL OUT THE POSTCARD WITH THE ANSWERS AND MAIL IT...
BeeeAM
THEY'LL SEND US LOTS OF *MEAT*!!!
YOU'LL *NEVER* HAVE TO SHOP AGAIN, BOSS!!
......
UM, PAPI...
THEY CHOOSE ONE WINNER AT RANDOM...
That was one of my old magazines!
BESIDES, THIS IS LAST MONTH'S ISSUE...

I'm so very happy she's enjoying it!

モンスター娘のいる日常
4コマアンソロジー

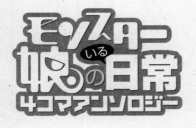

Warm-up Exercises

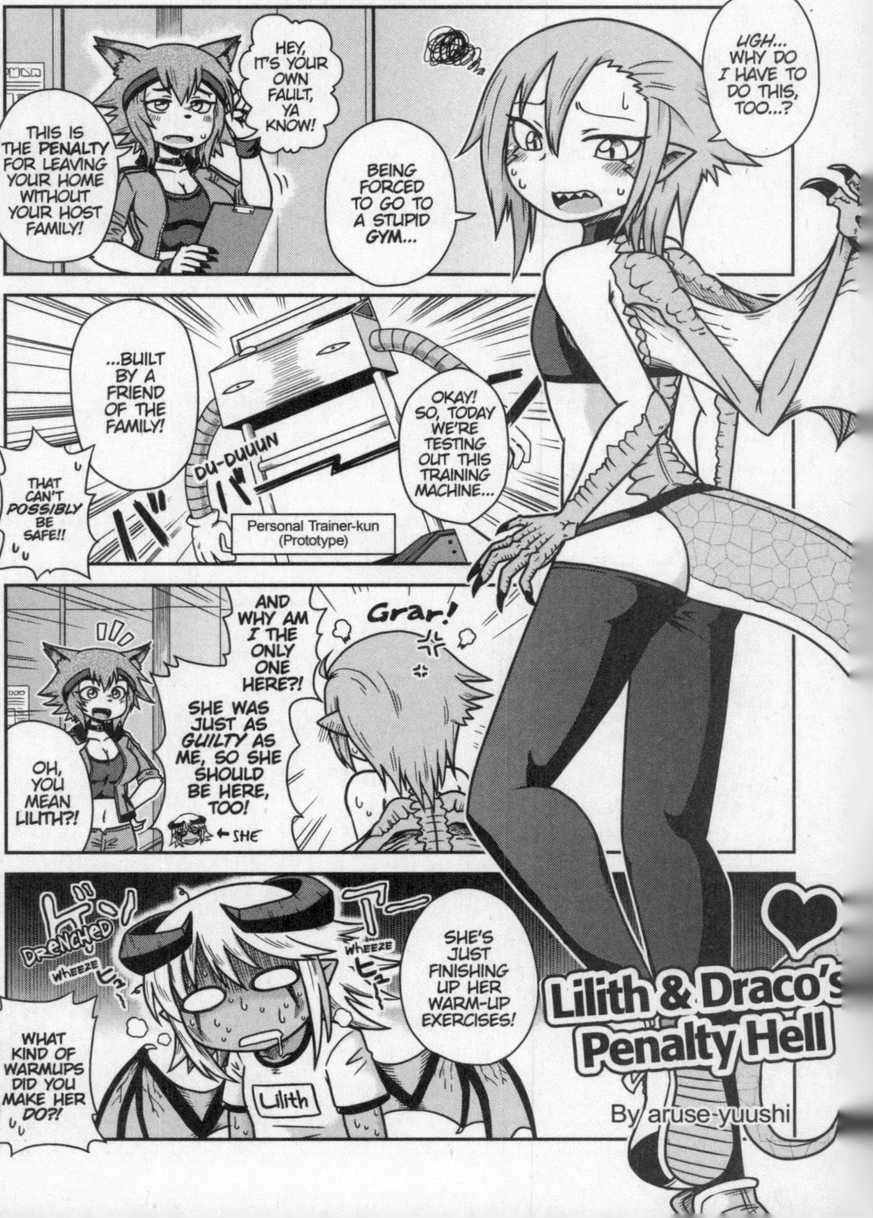
UGH... WHY DO I HAVE TO DO THIS, TOO...?
BEING FORCED TO GO TO A STUPID GYM...
HEY, IT'S YOUR OWN FAULT, YA KNOW!
THIS IS THE PENALTY FOR LEAVING YOUR HOME WITHOUT YOUR HOST FAMILY!
OKAY! SO, TODAY WE'RE TESTING OUT THIS TRAINING MACHINE...
DU-DUUUN
Personal Trainer-kun (Prototype)
...BUILT BY A FRIEND OF THE FAMILY!
THAT CAN'T POSSIBLY BE SAFE!!
Grar!
AND WHY AM I THE ONLY ONE HERE?!
SHE WAS JUST AS GUILTY AS ME, SO SHE SHOULD BE HERE, TOO!
OH, YOU MEAN LILITH?!
← SHE
SHE'S JUST FINISHING UP HER WARM-UP EXERCISES!
WHEEZE
DRENCHED
WHEEZE
Lilith
WHAT KIND OF WARMUPS DID YOU MAKE HER DO?!
Lilith & Draco's Penalty Hell
By aruse-yuushi

Trap

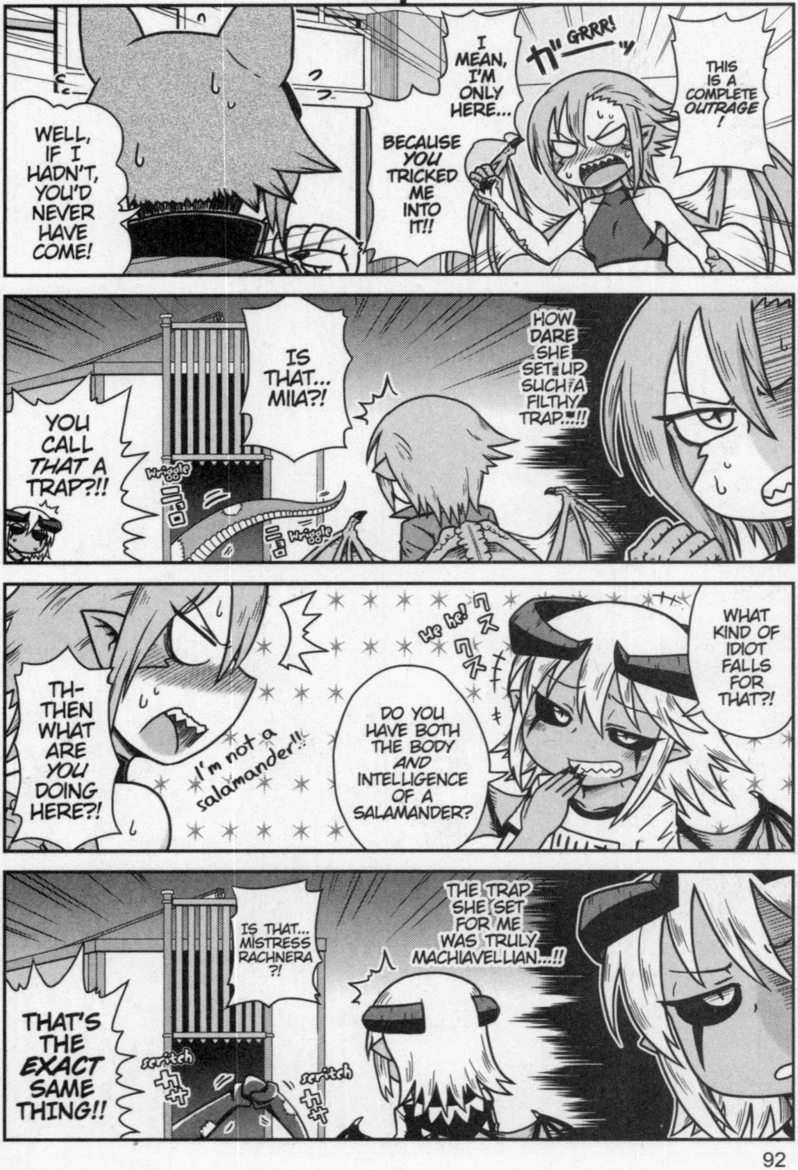
THIS IS A COMPLETE *OUTRAGE*!
GRRR!
I MEAN, I'M ONLY HERE...
BECAUSE *YOU* TRICKED ME INTO IT!!
WELL, IF I HADN'T, YOU'D NEVER HAVE COME!
HOW DARE SHE SET UP SUCH A FILTHY TRAP...!!!
IS THAT... MIIA?!
wriggle
wriggle
YOU CALL *THAT* A TRAP?!!
WHAT KIND OF IDIOT FALLS FOR THAT?!
He he!
DO YOU HAVE BOTH THE BODY *AND* INTELLIGENCE OF A SALAMANDER?
I'm not a salamander!!
TH-THEN WHAT ARE *YOU* DOING HERE?!
THE TRAP SHE SET FOR ME WAS TRULY MACHIAVELLIAN...!!
IS THAT... MISTRESS RACHNERA?!
scritch
scritch
THAT'S THE *EXACT* SAME THING!!

Run Away

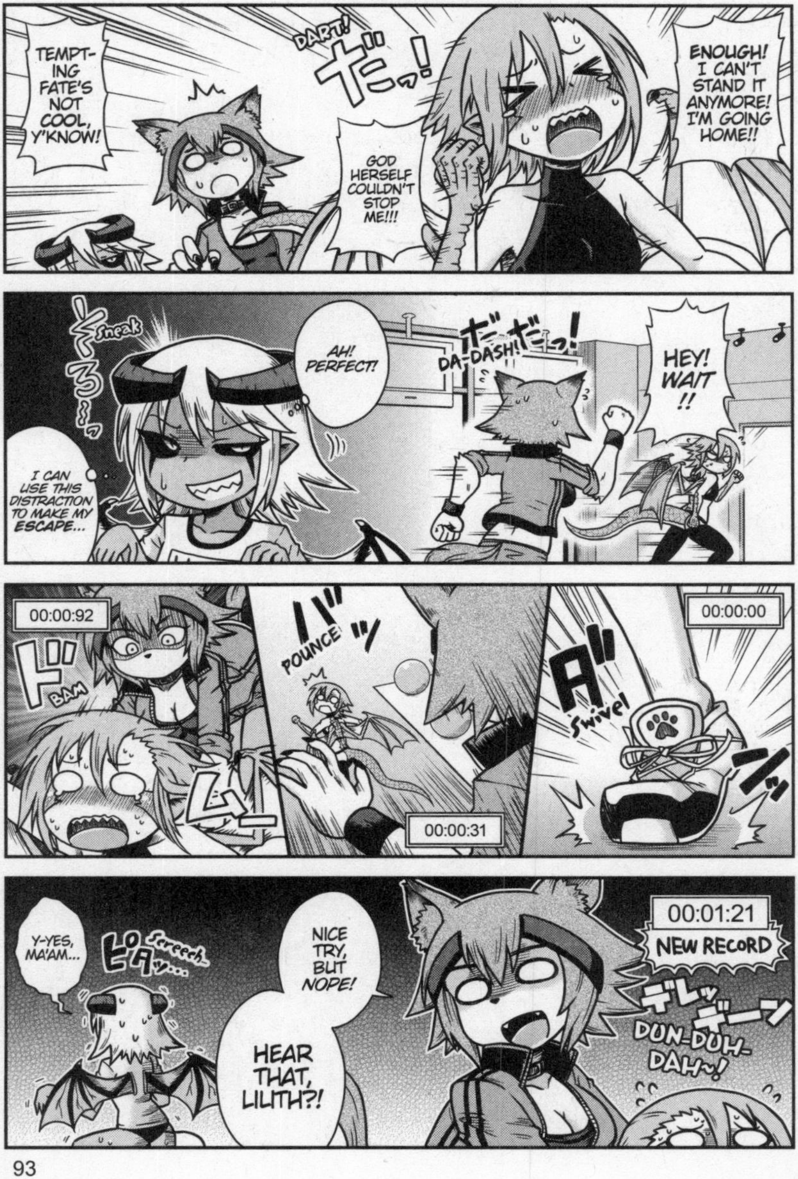
ENOUGH! I CAN'T STAND IT ANYMORE! I'M GOING HOME!!
GOD HERSELF COULDN'T STOP ME!!!
DART!
TEMPTING FATE'S NOT COOL, Y'KNOW!
HEY! WAIT!!
DA-DASH!
AH! PERFECT!
sneak
I CAN USE THIS DISTRACTION TO MAKE MY ESCAPE...
00:00:00
Swivel
POUNCE
00:00:31
00:00:92
BAM
00:01:21
NEW RECORD
DUN-DUH-DAH~!
NICE TRY, BUT NOPE!
HEAR THAT, LILITH?!
Screeech
Y-YES, MA'AM...

Choices

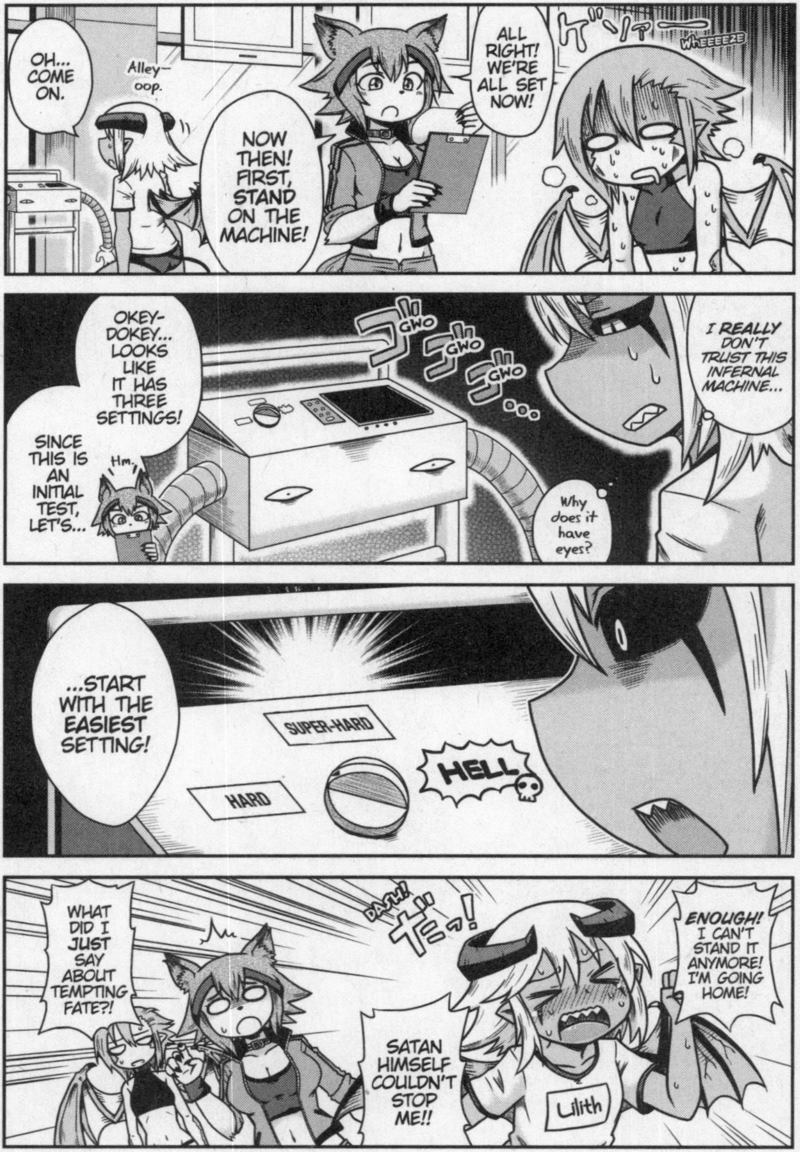
WhEEEEZE
ALL RIGHT! WE'RE ALL SET NOW!
NOW THEN! FIRST, STAND ON THE MACHINE!
Alley-oop.
OH... COME ON.
I REALLY DON'T TRUST THIS INFERNAL MACHINE...
GWO
GWO
GWO
Why does it have eyes?
OKEY-DOKEY... LOOKS LIKE IT HAS THREE SETTINGS!
Hm.
SINCE THIS IS AN INITIAL TEST, LET'S...
HELL
SUPER-HARD
...START WITH THE EASIEST SETTING!
HARD
ENOUGH! I CAN'T STAND IT ANYMORE! I'M GOING HOME!
DASH!
SATAN HIMSELF COULDN'T STOP ME!!
Lilith
WHAT DID I JUST SAY ABOUT TEMPTING FATE?!

Hypnosis

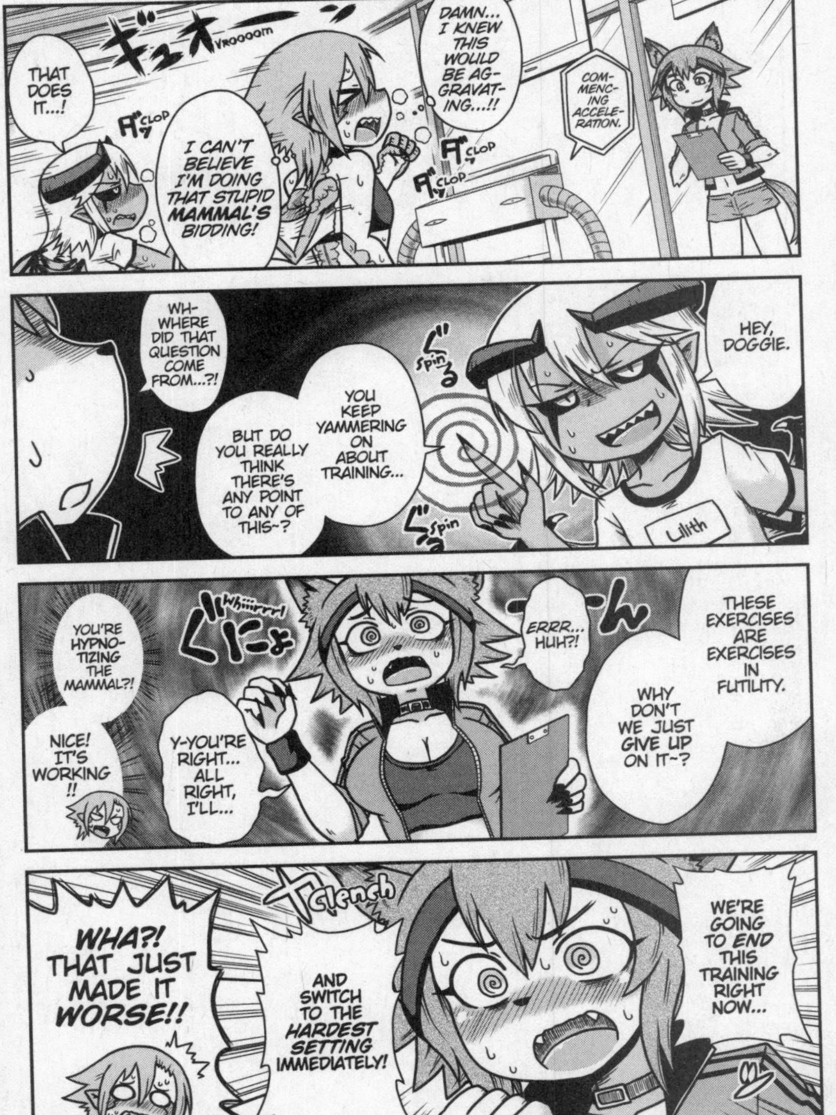
VROOOOM
COMMENCING ACCELERATION.
DAMN... I KNEW THIS WOULD BE AGGRAVATING...!!
CLOP
CLOP
I CAN'T BELIEVE I'M DOING THAT STUPID MAMMAL'S BIDDING!
CLOP
THAT DOES IT...!
HEY, DOGGIE.
SPIN
YOU KEEP YAMMERING ON ABOUT TRAINING...
BUT DO YOU REALLY THINK THERE'S ANY POINT TO ANY OF THIS~?
SPIN
WH-WHERE DID THAT QUESTION COME FROM...?!
Ulith
THESE EXERCISES ARE EXERCISES IN FUTILITY.
WHY DON'T WE JUST GIVE UP ON IT~?
ERRR... HUH?!
WHIIIRRRL
YOU'RE HYPNOTIZING THE MAMMAL?!
Y-YOU'RE RIGHT... ALL RIGHT, I'LL...
NICE! IT'S WORKING!!
CLENCH
WE'RE GOING TO END THIS TRAINING RIGHT NOW...
AND SWITCH TO THE HARDEST SETTING IMMEDIATELY!
WHA?! THAT JUST MADE IT WORSE!!

Hypnosis: Round 2

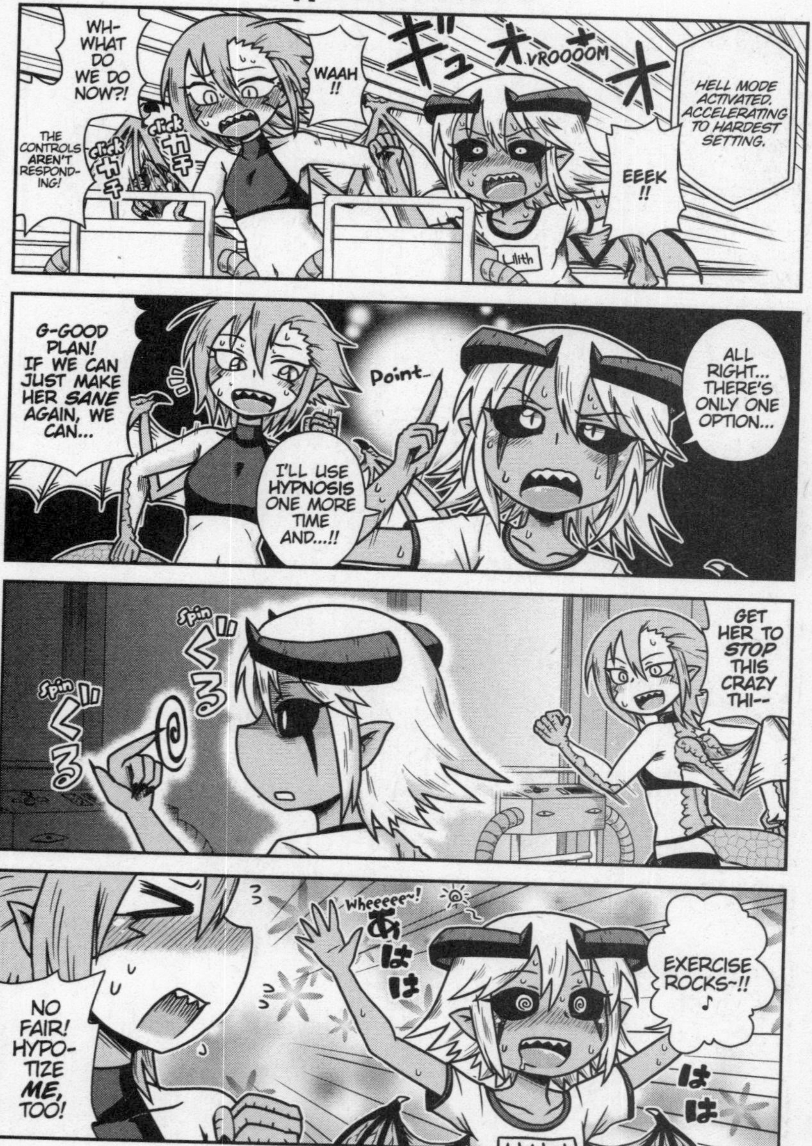

HELL MODE ACTIVATED. ACCELERATING TO HARDEST SETTING.
ギュオオオ VROOOOM
EEEK!!
WAAH!!
WH-WHAT DO WE DO NOW?!
click カチ
click カチ
THE CONTROLS AREN'T RESPONDING!
ALL RIGHT... THERE'S ONLY ONE OPTION...
Point..
I'LL USE HYPNOSIS ONE MORE TIME AND...!!
G-GOOD PLAN! IF WE CAN JUST MAKE HER SANE AGAIN, WE CAN...
GET HER TO STOP THIS CRAZY THI--
spin ぐるぐる
spin ぐるぐる
EXERCISE ROCKS~!! ♪
wheeeee~! あはは
はは
NO FAIR! HYPOTIZE ME, TOO!

Compulsory Mode

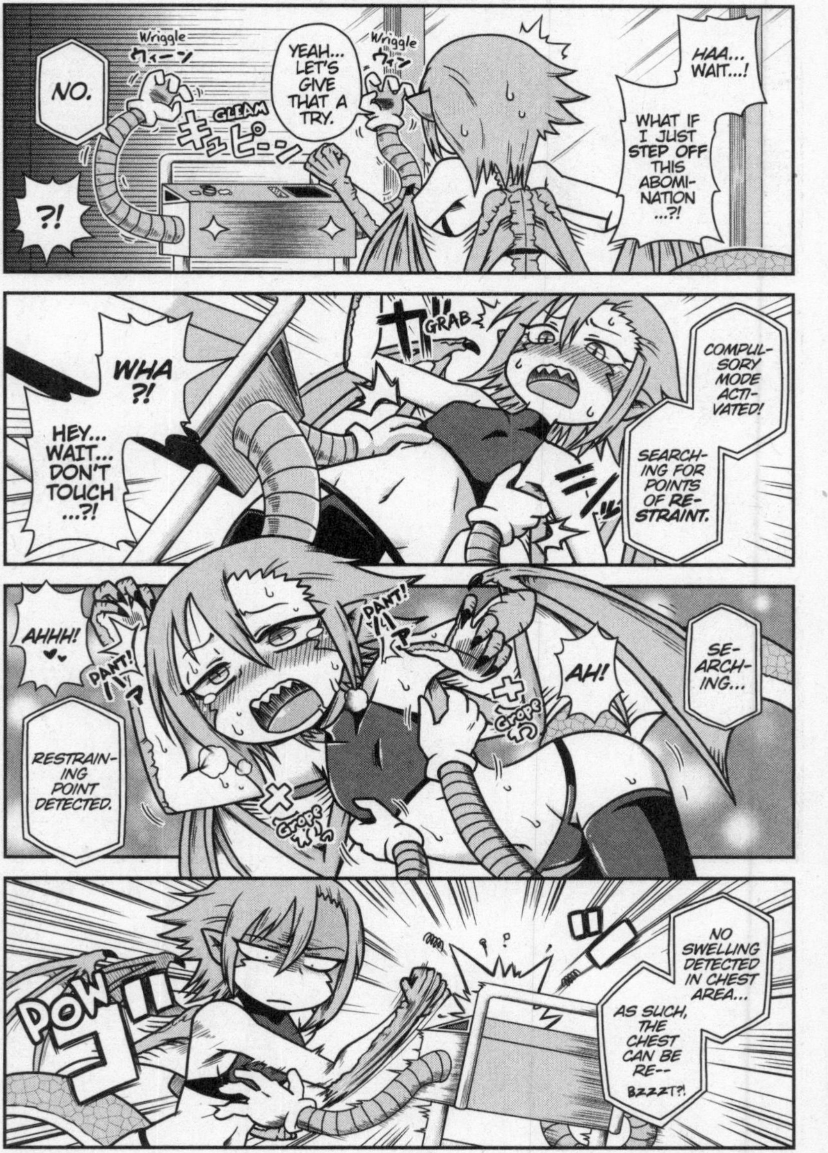

HAA... WAIT...!
WHAT IF I JUST STEP OFF THIS ABOMINATION ...?!
Wriggle ウィン
YEAH... LET'S GIVE THAT A TRY.
GLEAM キュピーン
Wriggle ウィーン
NO.
?!
COMPULSORY MODE ACTIVATED!
GRAB
SEARCHING FOR POINTS OF RESTRAINT.
WHA ?!
HEY... WAIT... DON'T TOUCH ...?!
SEARCHING...
AH!
Grope
PANT!
AHHH! ♥♥
PANT!
RESTRAINING POINT DETECTED.
Grope
NO SWELLING DETECTED IN CHEST AREA...
AS SUCH, THE CHEST CAN BE RE-- BZZZT?!
POW!!

Points

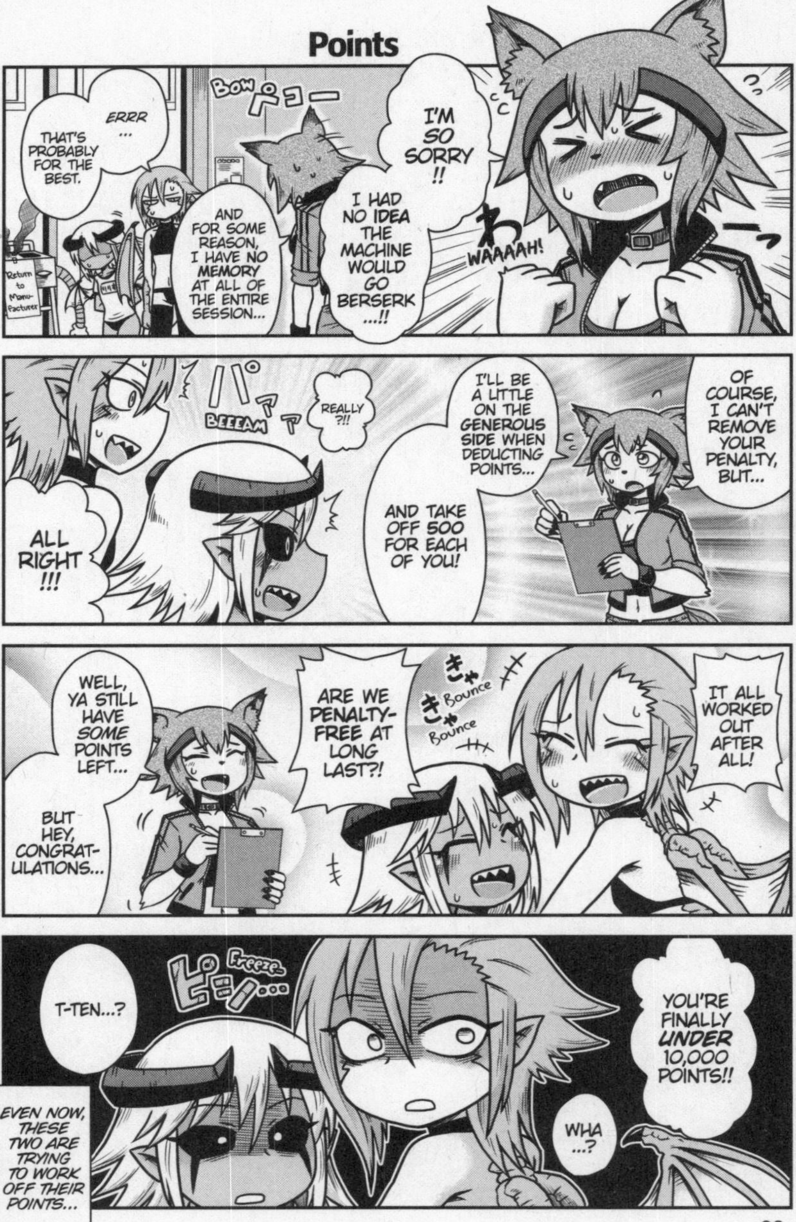
I'M SO SORRY!!
わ
WAAAAH!
I HAD NO IDEA THE MACHINE WOULD GO BERSERK...!!
Bow
AND FOR SOME REASON, I HAVE NO MEMORY AT ALL OF THE ENTIRE SESSION...
ERRR...
THAT'S PROBABLY FOR THE BEST.
Return to Manu-facturer
OF COURSE, I CAN'T REMOVE YOUR PENALTY, BUT...
I'LL BE A LITTLE ON THE GENEROUS SIDE WHEN DEDUCTING POINTS...
AND TAKE OFF 500 FOR EACH OF YOU!
REALLY?!!
パ
BEEEAM
ALL RIGHT!!!
IT ALL WORKED OUT AFTER ALL!
きゃ Bounce
きゃ Bounce
ARE WE PENALTY-FREE AT LONG LAST?!
WELL, YA STILL HAVE SOME POINTS LEFT...
BUT HEY, CONGRATULATIONS...
YOU'RE FINALLY UNDER 10,000 POINTS!!
WHA...?
Freeze
T-TEN...?
EVEN NOW, THESE TWO ARE TRYING TO WORK OFF THEIR POINTS...

モンスター娘のいる日常
4コマアンソロジー

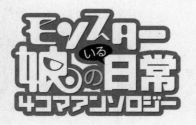

DASH!
ダッ!
SATAN HIMSELF COULDN'T STOP ME!!
Lilith

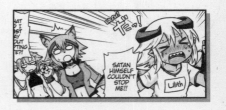

Pool Lanes with Monster Girls

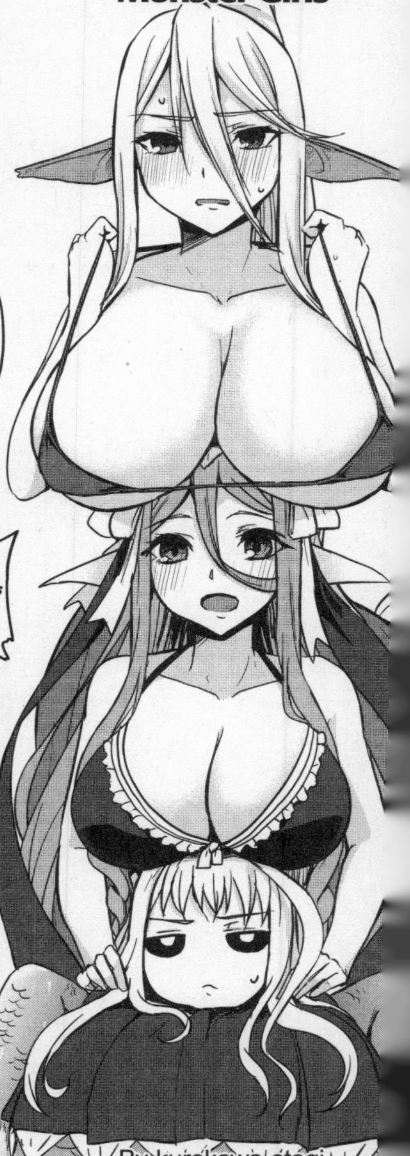

By kurokawa otogi

Return to the Gym

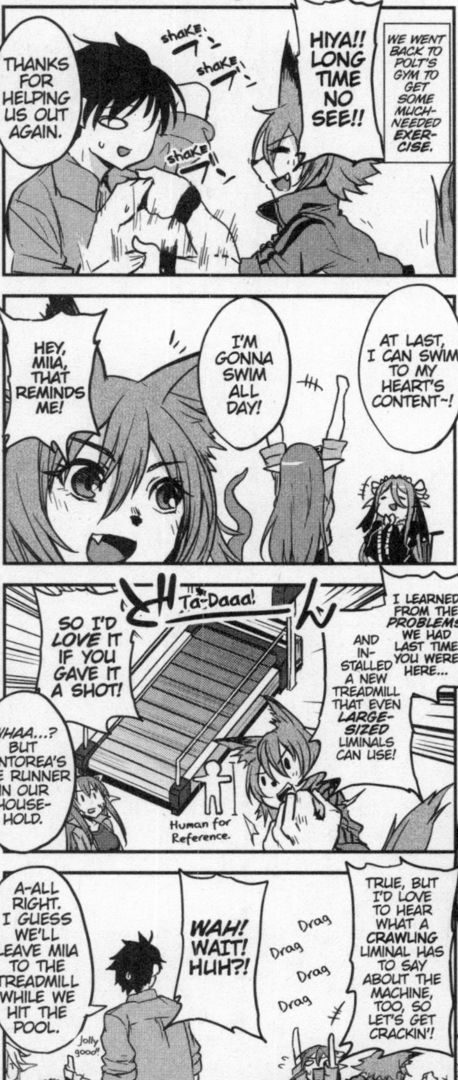
WE WENT BACK TO POLT'S GYM TO GET SOME MUCH-NEEDED EXERCISE.
HIYA!! LONG TIME NO SEE!!
shaKE
shaKE
shaKE
THANKS FOR HELPING US OUT AGAIN.
AT LAST, I CAN SWIM TO MY HEART'S CONTENT~!
I'M GONNA SWIM ALL DAY!
HEY, MIIA, THAT REMINDS ME!
I LEARNED FROM THE PROBLEMS WE HAD LAST TIME YOU WERE HERE...
AND INSTALLED A NEW TREADMILL THAT EVEN LARGE-SIZED LIMINALS CAN USE!
Ta-Daaa!
SO I'D LOVE IT IF YOU GAVE IT A SHOT!
WHAA...? BUT CENTOREA'S THE RUNNER IN OUR HOUSEHOLD.
Human for Reference.
TRUE, BUT I'D LOVE TO HEAR WHAT A CRAWLING LIMINAL HAS TO SAY ABOUT THE MACHINE, TOO, SO LET'S GET CRACKIN'!
Drag
Drag
Drag
Drag
WAH! WAIT! HUH?!
A-ALL RIGHT. I GUESS WE'LL LEAVE MIIA TO THE TREADMILL WHILE WE HIT THE POOL.
Jolly good!

Doing the ~~Dog~~ Horse Paddle

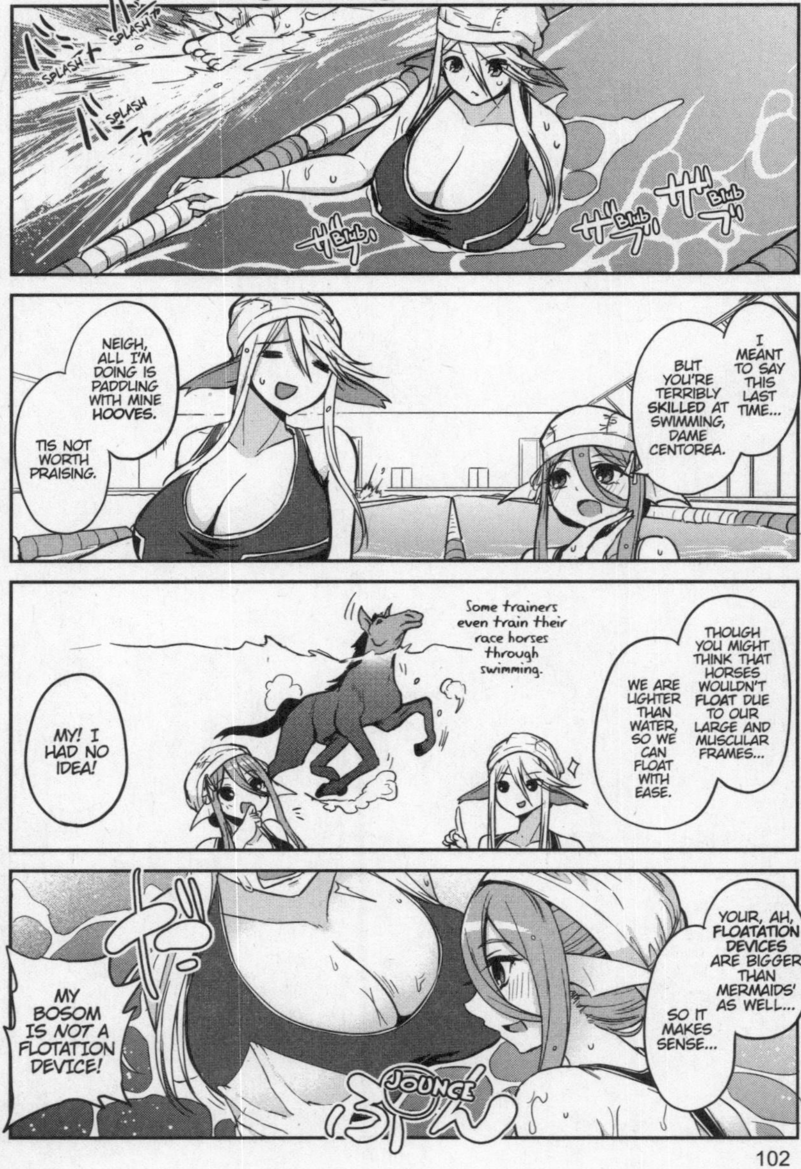

Blub
Blub
Blub
SPLASH
SPLASH
SPLASH
I MEANT TO SAY THIS LAST TIME...
BUT YOU'RE TERRIBLY SKILLED AT SWIMMING, DAME CENTOREA.
NEIGH, ALL I'M DOING IS PADDLING WITH MINE HOOVES.
TIS NOT WORTH PRAISING.
THOUGH YOU MIGHT THINK THAT HORSES WOULDN'T FLOAT DUE TO OUR LARGE AND MUSCULAR FRAMES...
WE ARE LIGHTER THAN WATER, SO WE CAN FLOAT WITH EASE.
Some trainers even train their race horses through swimming.
MY! I HAD NO IDEA!
YOUR, AH, FLOATATION DEVICES ARE BIGGER THAN MERMAIDS' AS WELL...
SO IT MAKES SENSE...
JOUNCE
MY BOSOM IS NOT A FLOTATION DEVICE!

Buoyancy

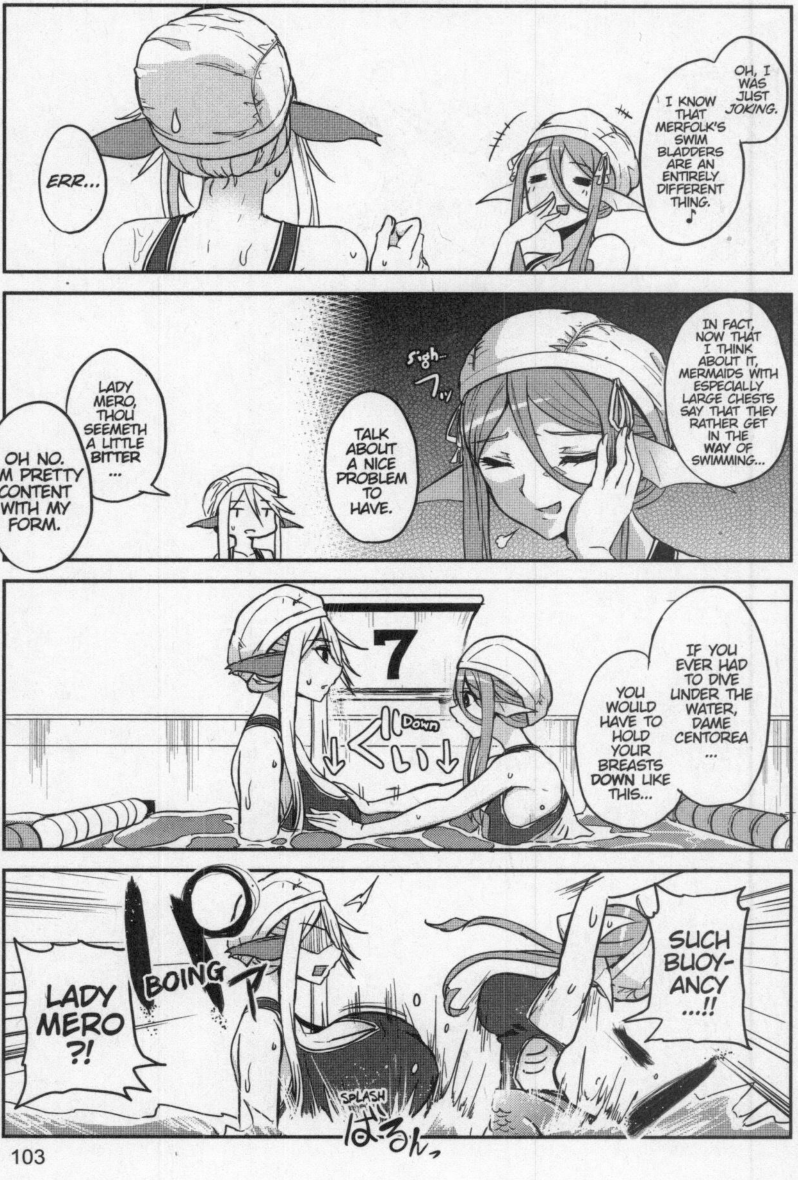
OH, I WAS JUST JOKING.
I KNOW THAT MERFOLK'S SWIM BLADDERS ARE AN ENTIRELY DIFFERENT THING. ♪
ERR...
IN FACT, NOW THAT I THINK ABOUT IT, MERMAIDS WITH ESPECIALLY LARGE CHESTS SAY THAT THEY RATHER GET IN THE WAY OF SWIMMING...
Sigh...
TALK ABOUT A NICE PROBLEM TO HAVE.
LADY MERO, THOU SEEMETH A LITTLE BITTER ...
OH NO. I'M PRETTY CONTENT WITH MY FORM.
7
IF YOU EVER HAD TO DIVE UNDER THE WATER, DAME CENTOREA ...
YOU WOULD HAVE TO HOLD YOUR BREASTS DOWN LIKE THIS...
Down
SUCH BUOY-ANCY ...!!
BOING
LADY MERO ?!
SPLASH
ばるんっ

Breathing Technique

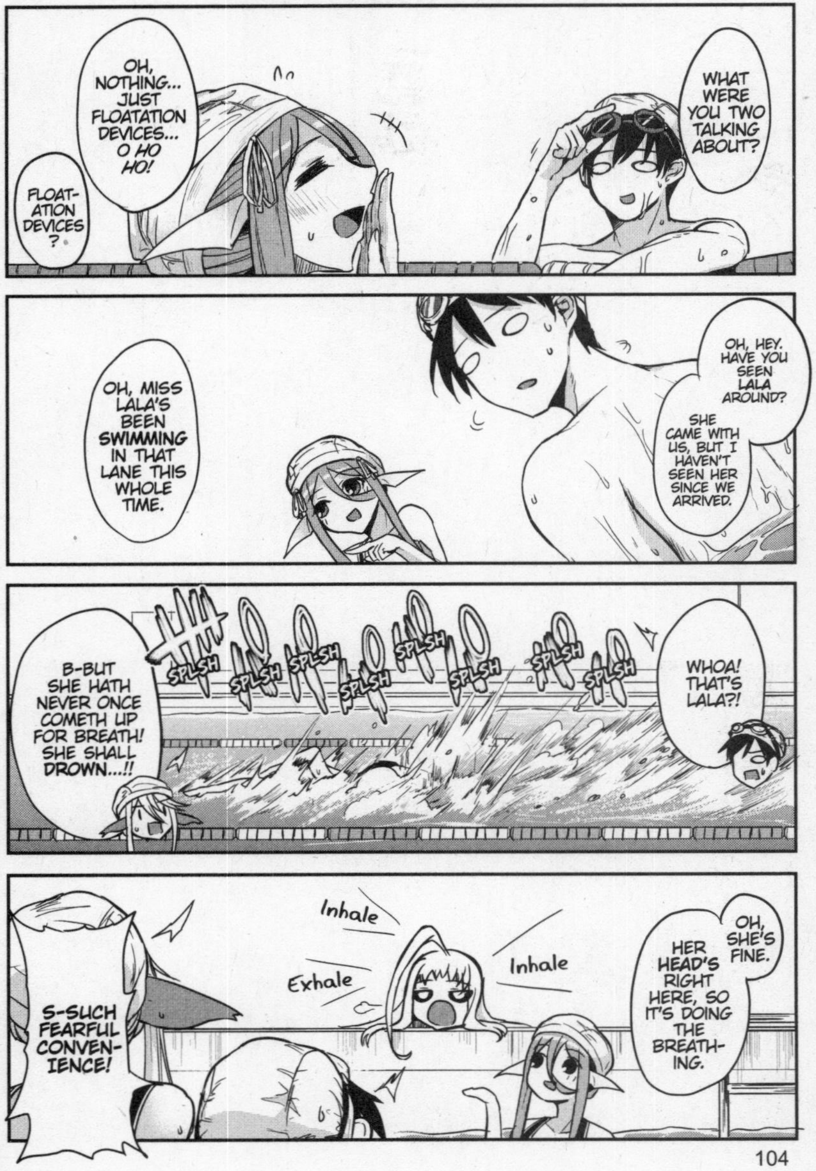
WHAT WERE YOU TWO TALKING ABOUT?
OH, NOTHING... JUST FLOATATION DEVICES... O HO HO!
FLOAT-ATION DEVICES?
OH, HEY. HAVE YOU SEEN LALA AROUND?
SHE CAME WITH US, BUT I HAVEN'T SEEN HER SINCE WE ARRIVED.
OH, MISS LALA'S BEEN SWIMMING IN THAT LANE THIS WHOLE TIME.
WHOA! THAT'S LALA?!
SPLSH
SPLSH
SPLSH
SPLSH
SPLSH
SPLSH
SPLSH
SPLSH
B-BUT SHE HATH NEVER ONCE COMETH UP FOR BREATH! SHE SHALL DROWN...!!
OH, SHE'S FINE.
HER HEAD'S RIGHT HERE, SO IT'S DOING THE BREATH-ING.
Inhale
Inhale
Exhale
S-SUCH FEARFUL CONVEN-IENCE!

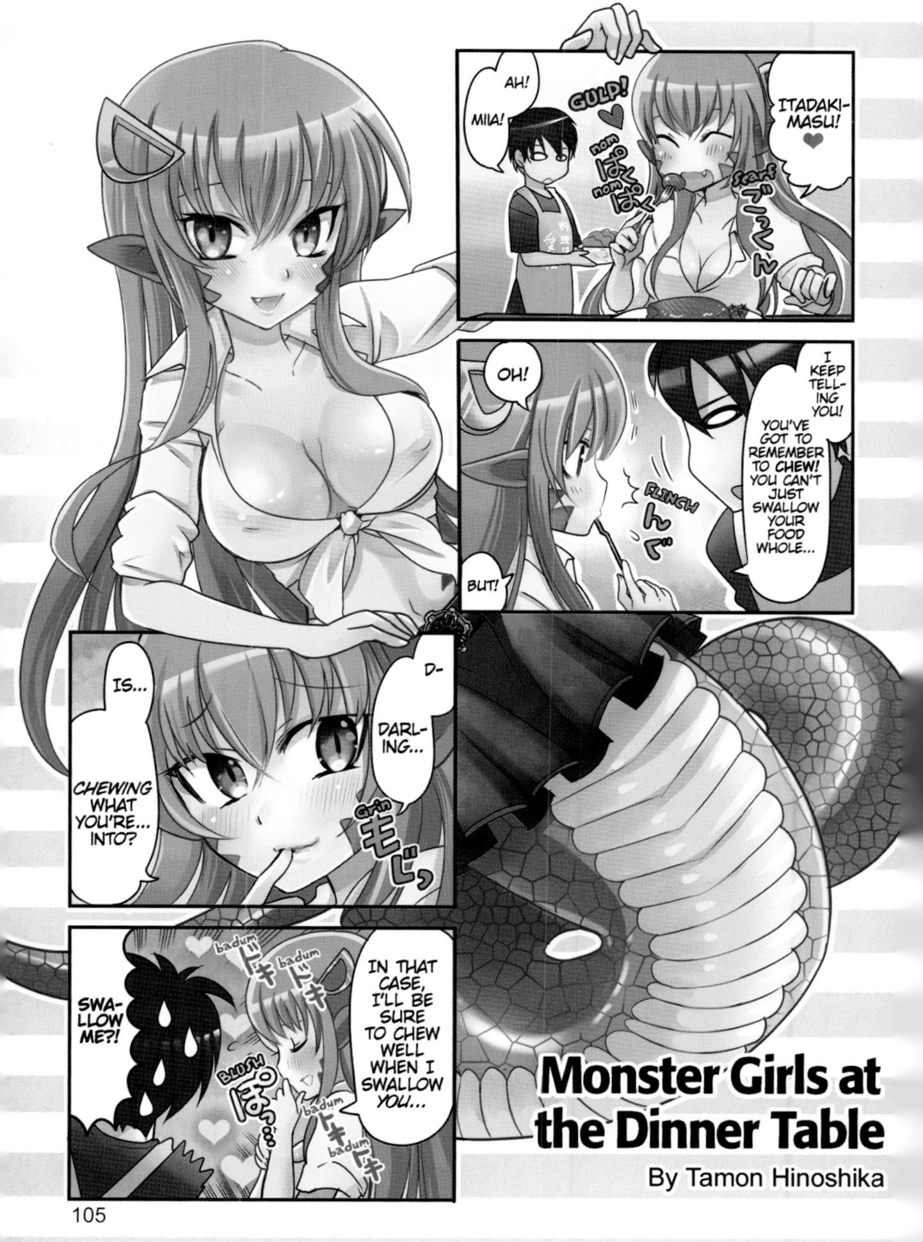
ITADAKI-MASU! ♥
Scarf
GULP! ♥
nom nom
AH!
MIIA!
I KEEP TELLING YOU! YOU'VE GOT TO REMEMBER TO CHEW! YOU CAN'T JUST SWALLOW YOUR FOOD WHOLE...
OH!
FLINCH
BUT!
D-DARLING...
Grin
IS...
CHEWING WHAT YOU'RE... INTO?
IN THAT CASE, I'LL BE SURE TO CHEW WELL WHEN I SWALLOW YOU...
badum badum
BLUSH
badum badum
SWALLOW ME?!

Monster Girls at the Dinner Table

By Tamon Hinoshika

Dullahan at Dinner

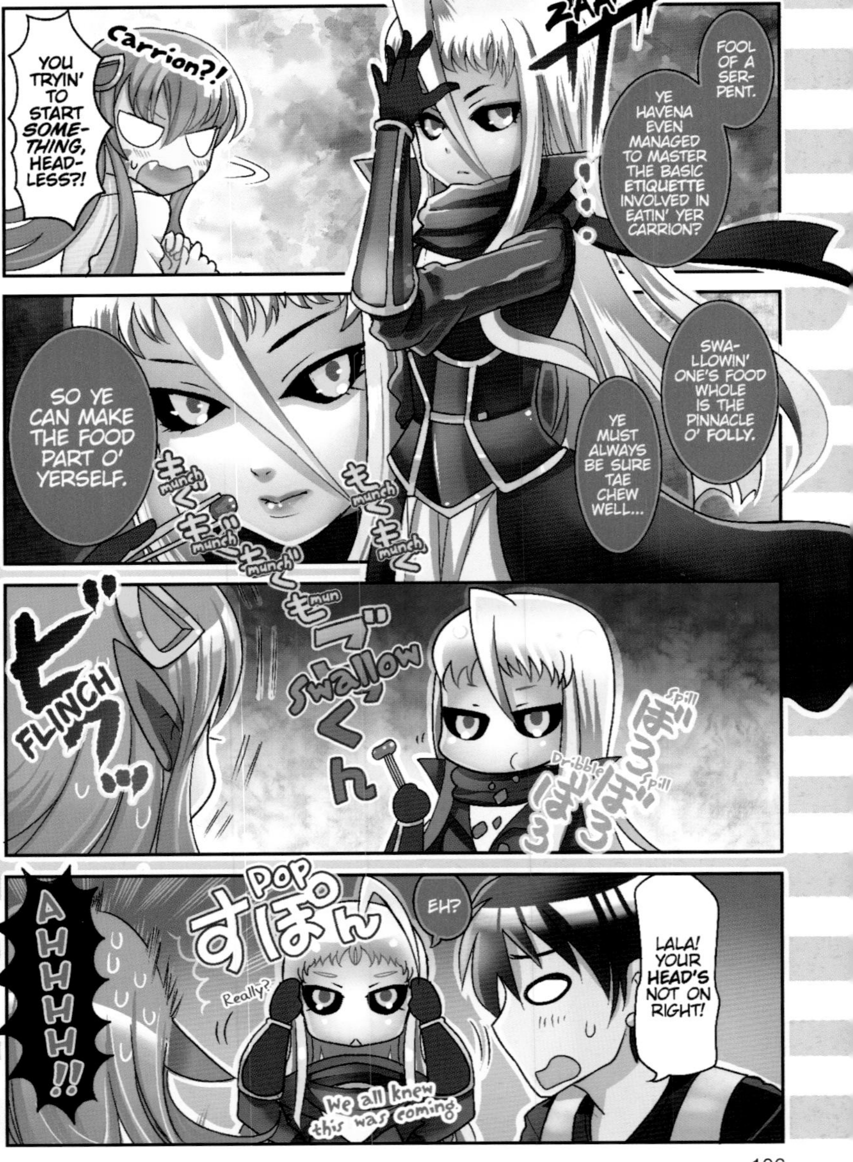
Z'AA!
FOOL OF A SERPENT.
YE HAVENA EVEN MANAGED TO MASTER THE BASIC ETIQUETTE INVOLVED IN EATIN' YER CARRION?
Carrion?!
YOU TRYIN' TO START SOMETHING, HEADLESS?!
SWALLOWIN' ONE'S FOOD WHOLE IS THE PINNACLE O' FOLLY.
YE MUST ALWAYS BE SURE TAE CHEW WELL...
munch munch
munch munch
SO YE CAN MAKE THE FOOD PART O' YERSELF.
spill
Dribble
spill
swallow
mun
FLINCH
LALA! YOUR HEAD'S NOT ON RIGHT!
EH?
POP
Really?
We all knew this was coming.
AHHHHH!!

No Going Back

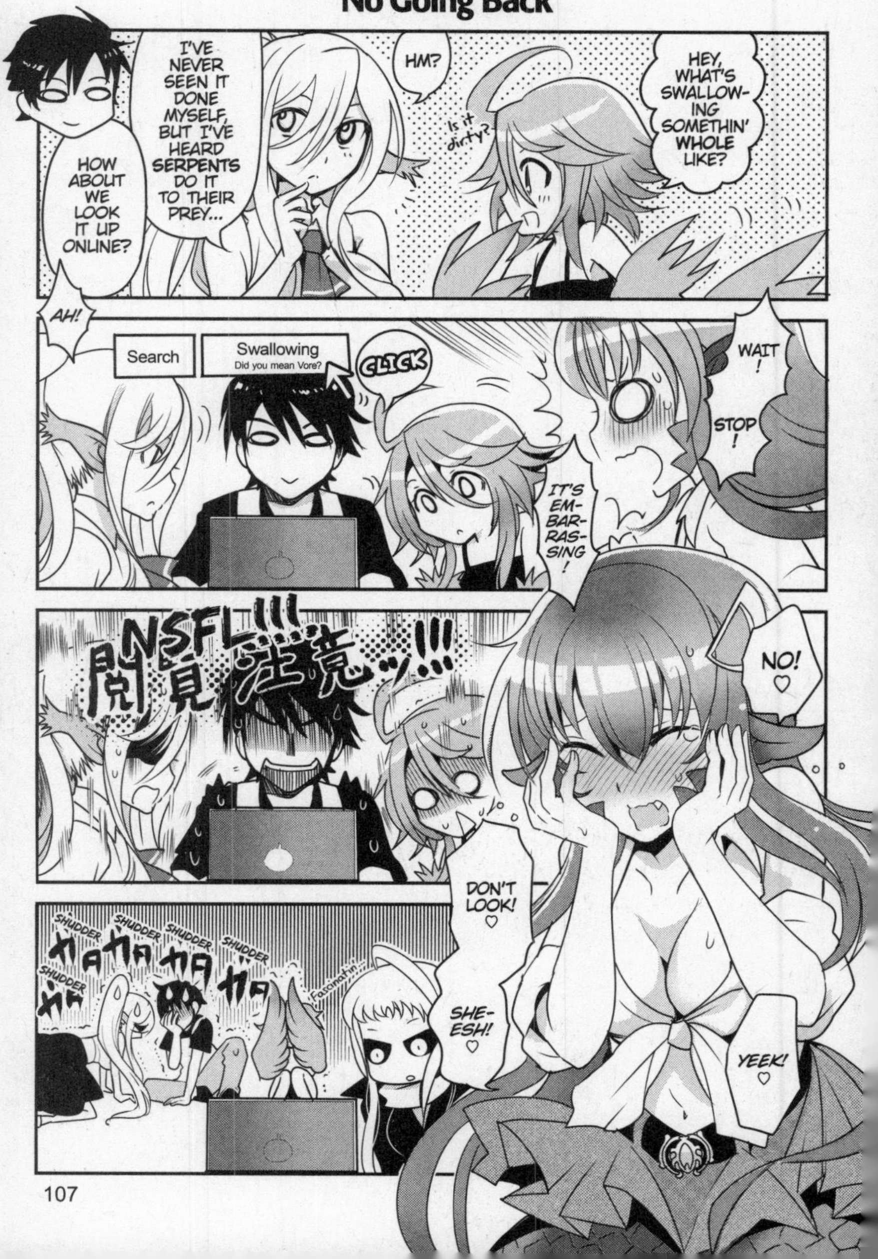

HEY, WHAT'S SWALLOWING SOMETHIN' WHOLE LIKE?
Is it dirty?
HM?
I'VE NEVER SEEN IT DONE MYSELF, BUT I'VE HEARD SERPENTS DO IT TO THEIR PREY...
HOW ABOUT WE LOOK IT UP ONLINE?
WAIT! STOP!
IT'S EMBARRASSING!
CLICK
Swallowing
Did you mean Vore?
Search
AH!
NO! ♡
NSFL!!!
閲覧注意ッ!!!
DON'T LOOK! ♡
YEEK! ♡
SHEESH! ♡
Fascinatin'...
SHUDDER
SHUDDER
SHUDDER
SHUDDER
SHUDDER

Cute, But No

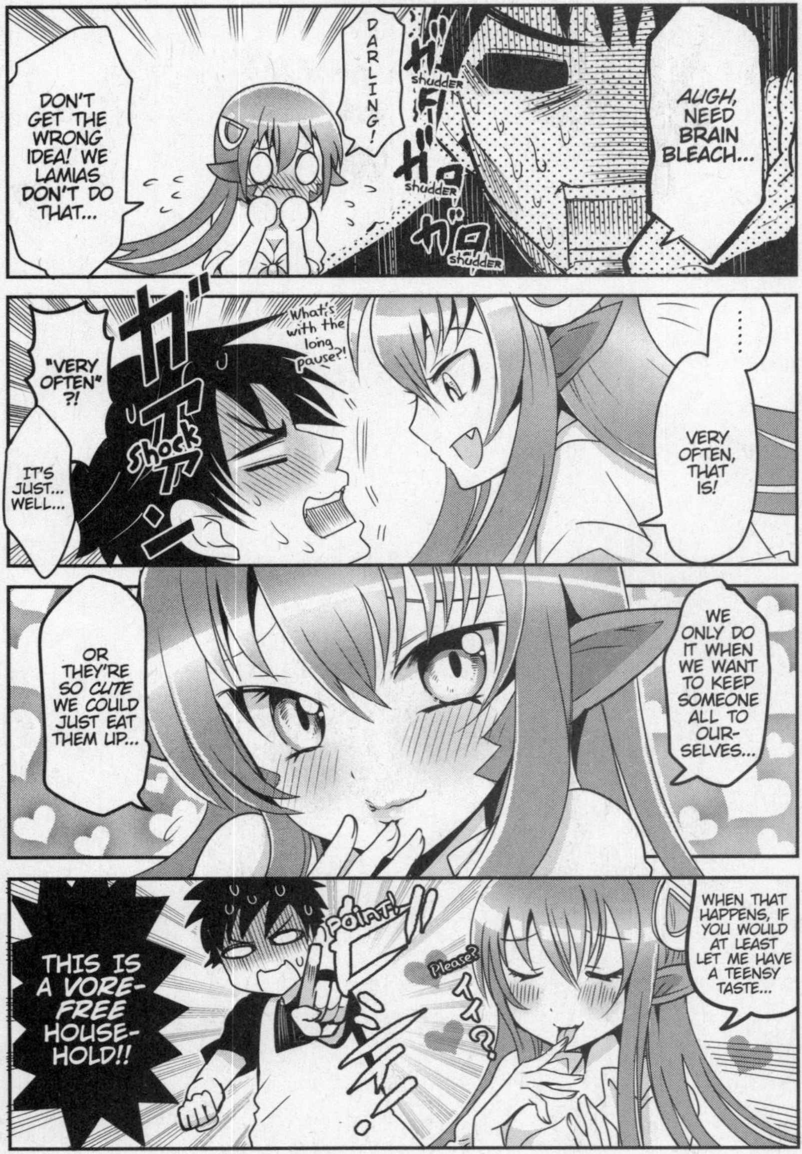
AUGH, NEED BRAIN BLEACH...
shudder
shudder
shudder
DARLING!
DON'T GET THE WRONG IDEA! WE LAMIAS DON'T DO THAT...
......
VERY OFTEN, THAT IS!
What's with the long pause?!
shock
"VERY OFTEN"?!
IT'S JUST... WELL...
WE ONLY DO IT WHEN WE WANT TO KEEP SOMEONE ALL TO OUR-SELVES...
OR THEY'RE SO CUTE WE COULD JUST EAT THEM UP...
WHEN THAT HAPPENS, IF YOU WOULD AT LEAST LET ME HAVE A TEENSY TASTE...
Please?
POINT!
THIS IS A VORE-FREE HOUSE-HOLD!!

Independent Study

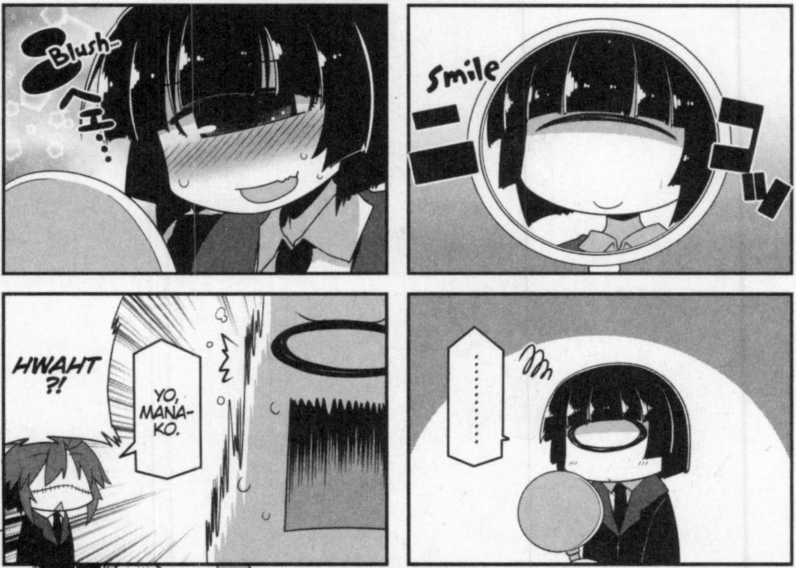
Smile
ニコッ
Blush...
へエ…
......
HWAHT ?!
YO, MANAKO.

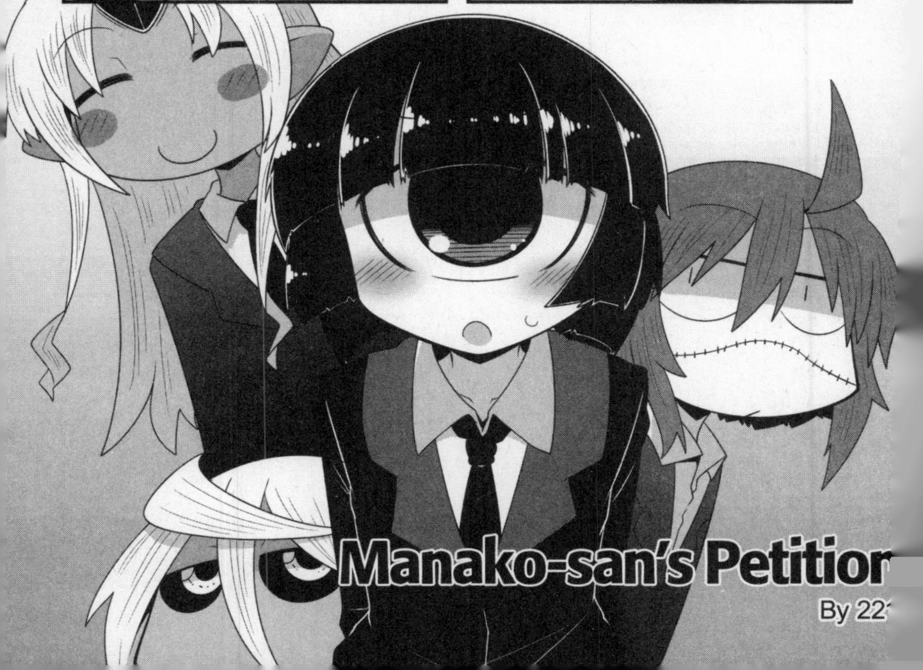
Manako-san's Petition
By 22

What Happened The Other Day

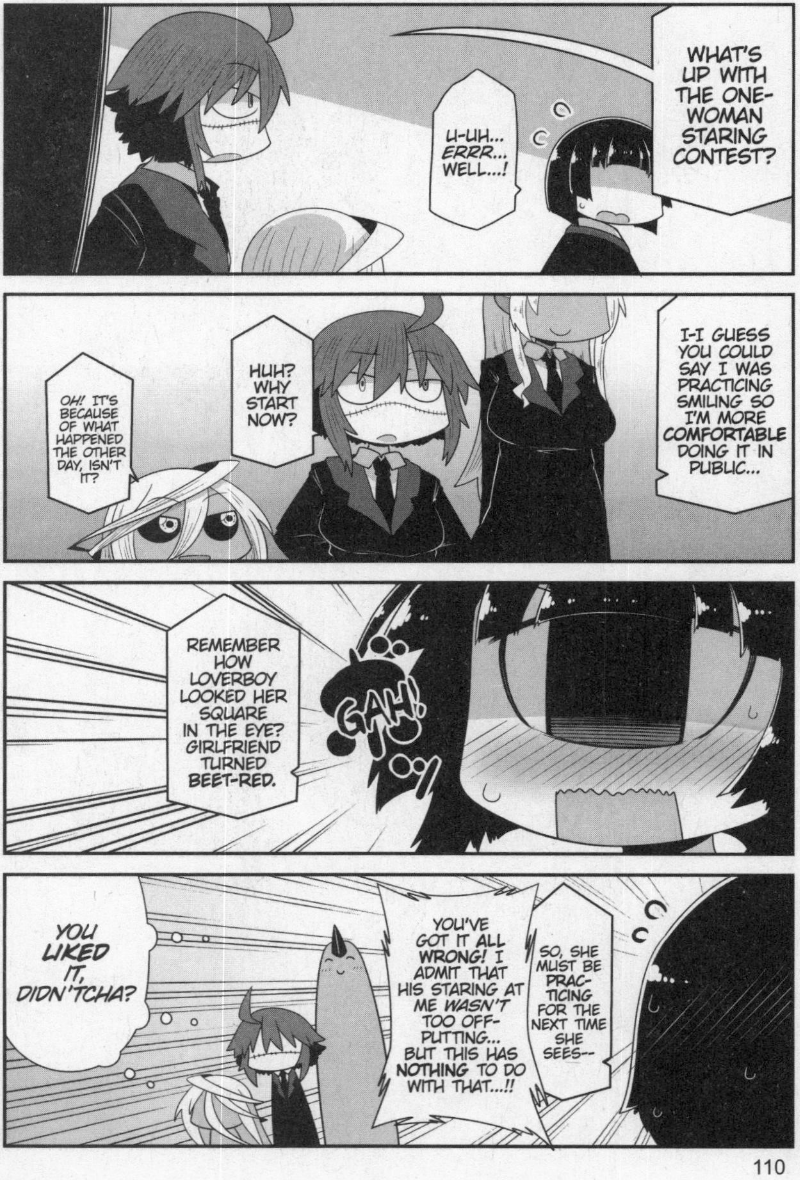
WHAT'S UP WITH THE ONE-WOMAN STARING CONTEST?
U-UH... ERRR... WELL...!
I-I GUESS YOU COULD SAY I WAS PRACTICING SMILING SO I'M MORE COMFORTABLE DOING IT IN PUBLIC...
HUH? WHY START NOW?
OH! IT'S BECAUSE OF WHAT HAPPENED THE OTHER DAY, ISN'T IT?
GAH!
REMEMBER HOW LOVERBOY LOOKED HER SQUARE IN THE EYE? GIRLFRIEND TURNED BEET-RED.
SO, SHE MUST BE PRAC-TICING FOR THE NEXT TIME SHE SEES--
YOU'VE GOT IT ALL WRONG! I ADMIT THAT HIS STARING AT ME WASN'T TOO OFF-PUTTING... BUT THIS HAS NOTHING TO DO WITH THAT...!!
YOU LIKED IT, DIDN'TCHA?

Impressions

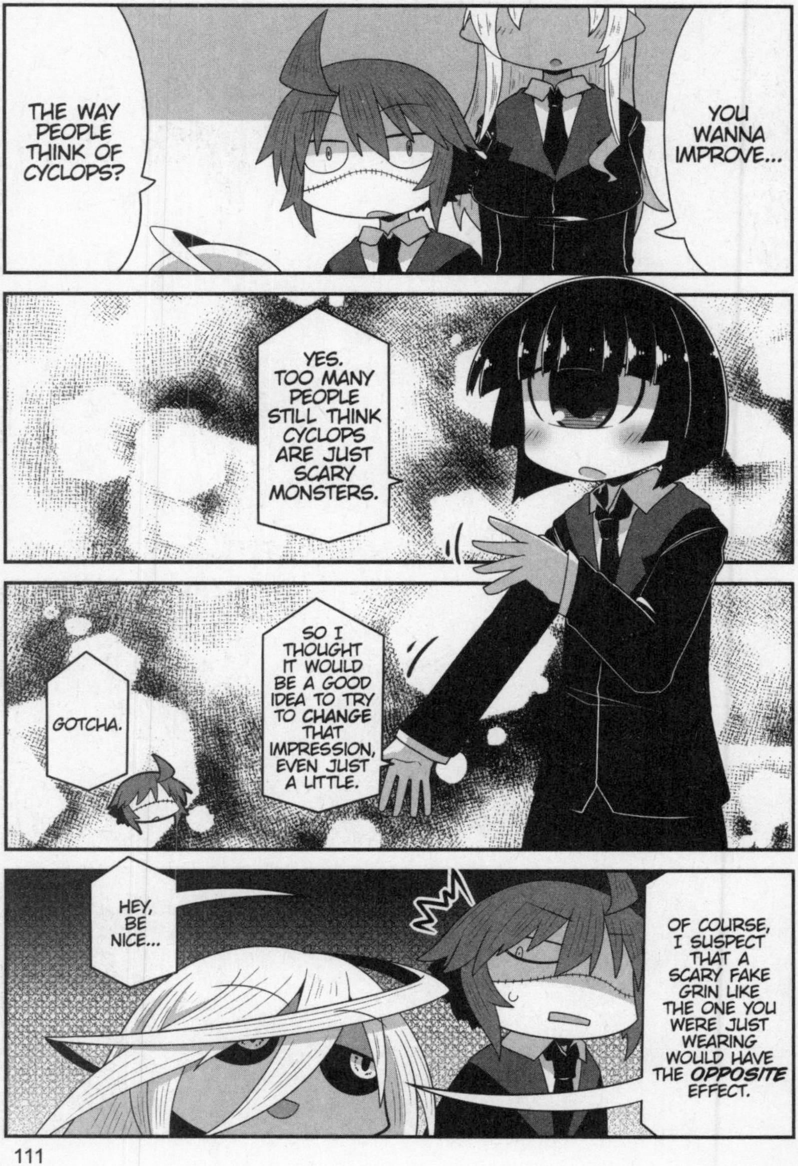
YOU WANNA IMPROVE...
THE WAY PEOPLE THINK OF CYCLOPS?
YES. TOO MANY PEOPLE STILL THINK CYCLOPS ARE JUST SCARY MONSTERS.
SO I THOUGHT IT WOULD BE A GOOD IDEA TO TRY TO CHANGE THAT IMPRESSION, EVEN JUST A LITTLE.
GOTCHA.
OF COURSE, I SUSPECT THAT A SCARY FAKE GRIN LIKE THE ONE YOU WERE JUST WEARING WOULD HAVE THE OPPOSITE EFFECT.
HEY, BE NICE...

Wardrobe Malfunction

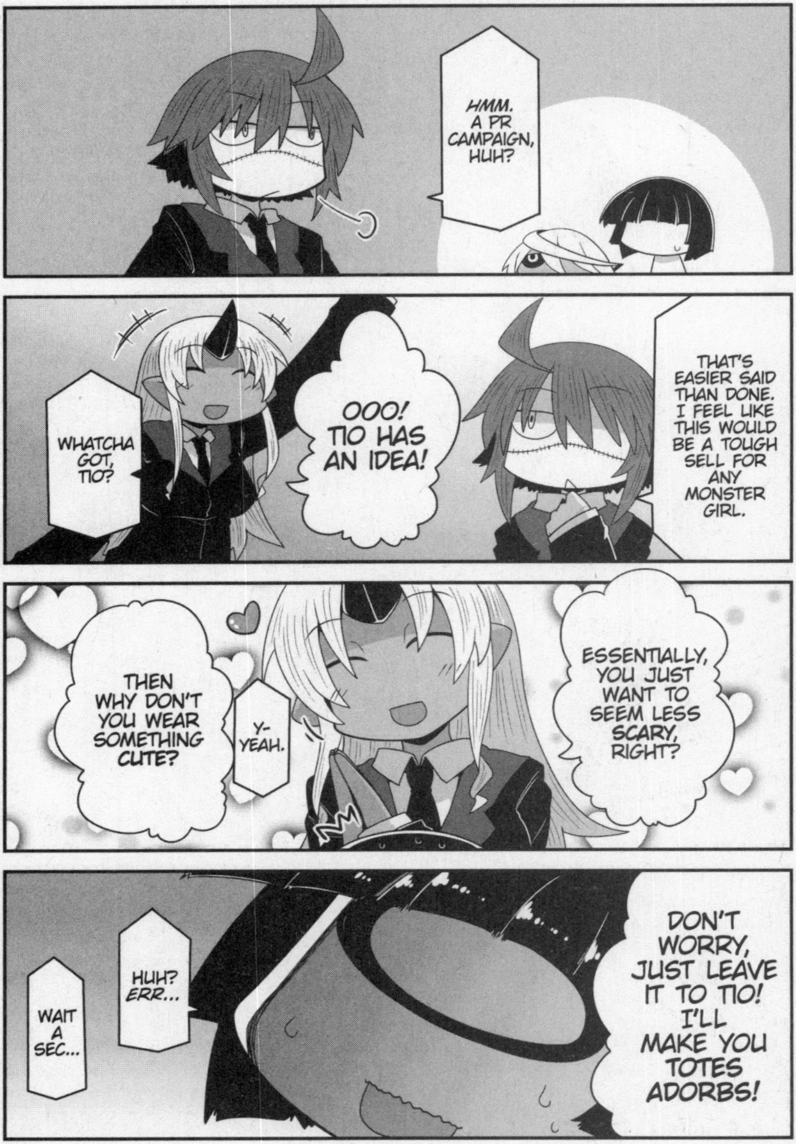
HMM. A PR CAMPAIGN, HUH?
THAT'S EASIER SAID THAN DONE. I FEEL LIKE THIS WOULD BE A TOUGH SELL FOR ANY MONSTER GIRL.
OOO! TIO HAS AN IDEA!
WHATCHA GOT, TIO?
ESSENTIALLY, YOU JUST WANT TO SEEM LESS SCARY, RIGHT?
Y-YEAH.
THEN WHY DON'T YOU WEAR SOMETHING CUTE?
DON'T WORRY, JUST LEAVE IT TO TIO! I'LL MAKE YOU TOTES ADORBS!
HUH? ERR...
WAIT A SEC...

I'll Be Gentle

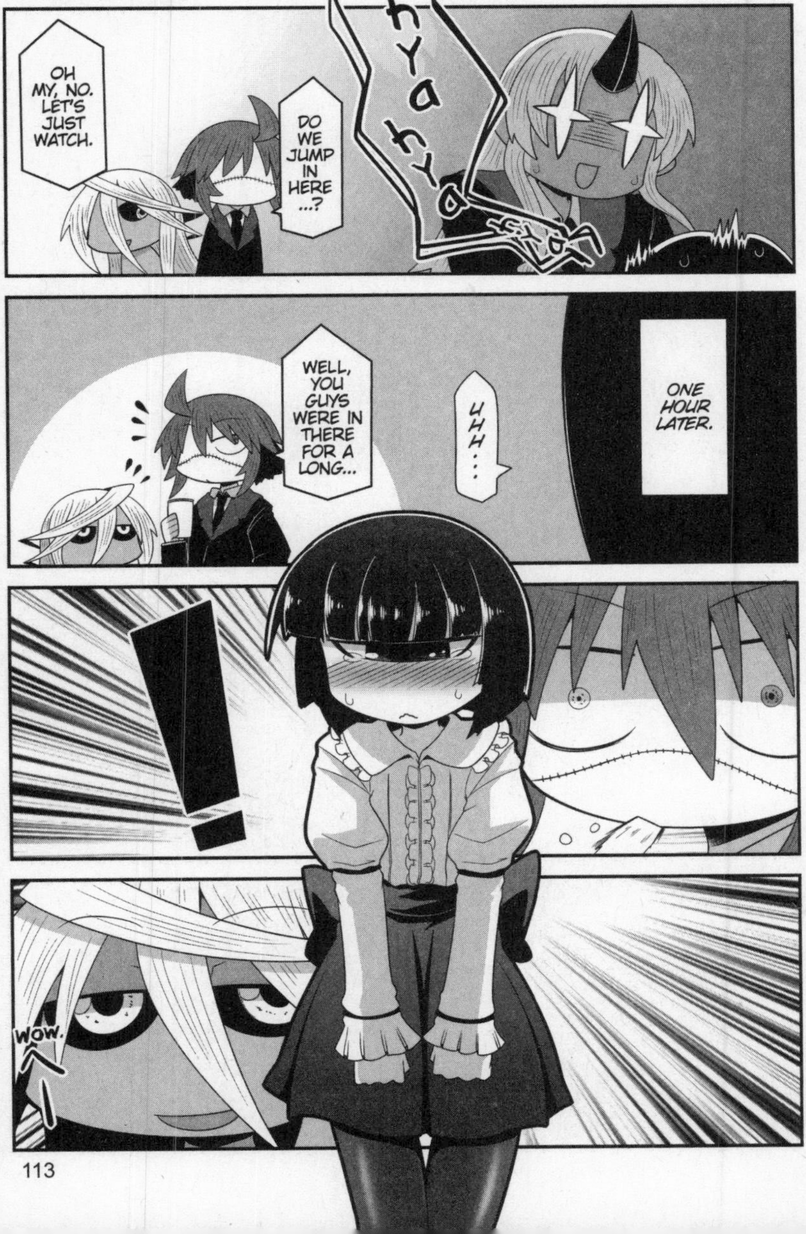
Ahyahya
DO WE JUMP IN HERE ...?
OH MY, NO. LET'S JUST WATCH.
ONE HOUR LATER.
UHH...
WELL, YOU GUYS WERE IN THERE FOR A LONG...
!
WOW.

Looking Good

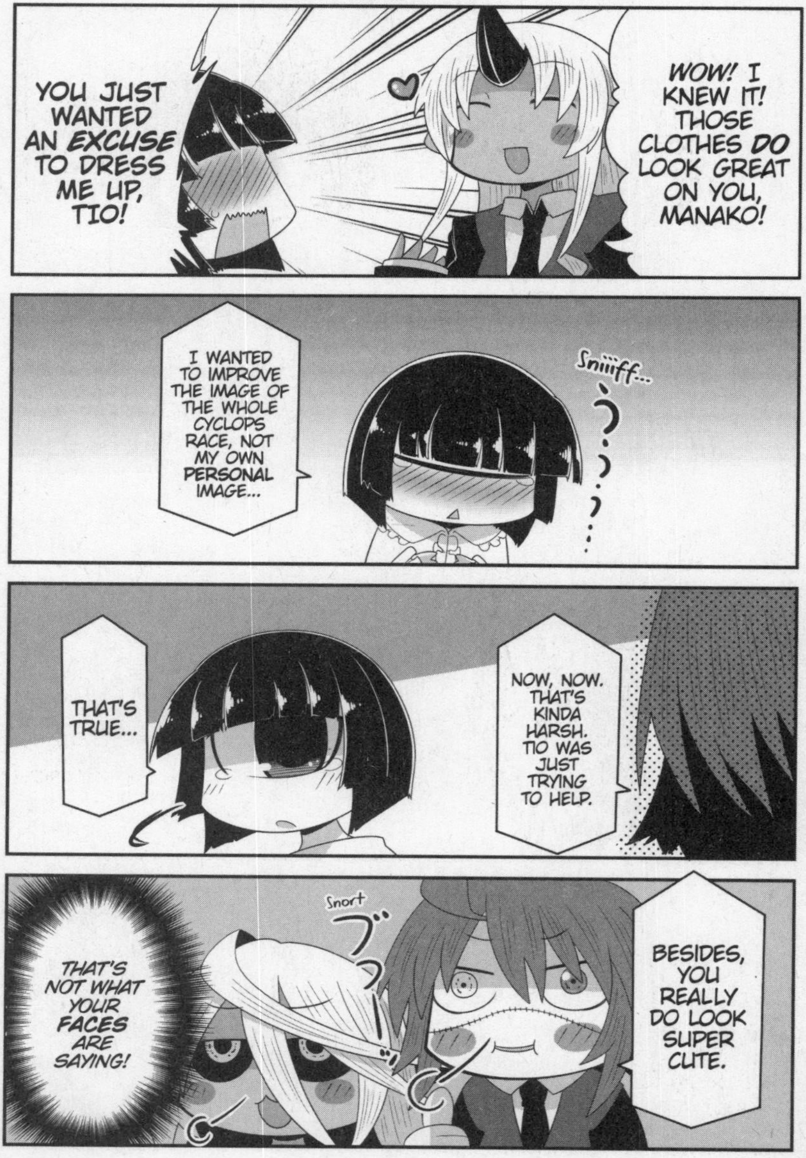
WOW! I KNEW IT! THOSE CLOTHES DO LOOK GREAT ON YOU, MANAKO!
YOU JUST WANTED AN EXCUSE TO DRESS ME UP, TIO!
Sniiiff...
I WANTED TO IMPROVE THE IMAGE OF THE WHOLE CYCLOPS RACE, NOT MY OWN PERSONAL IMAGE...
NOW, NOW. THAT'S KINDA HARSH. TIO WAS JUST TRYING TO HELP.
THAT'S TRUE...
BESIDES, YOU REALLY DO LOOK SUPER CUTE.
Snort
THAT'S NOT WHAT YOUR FACES ARE SAYING!

Emergency Dispatch

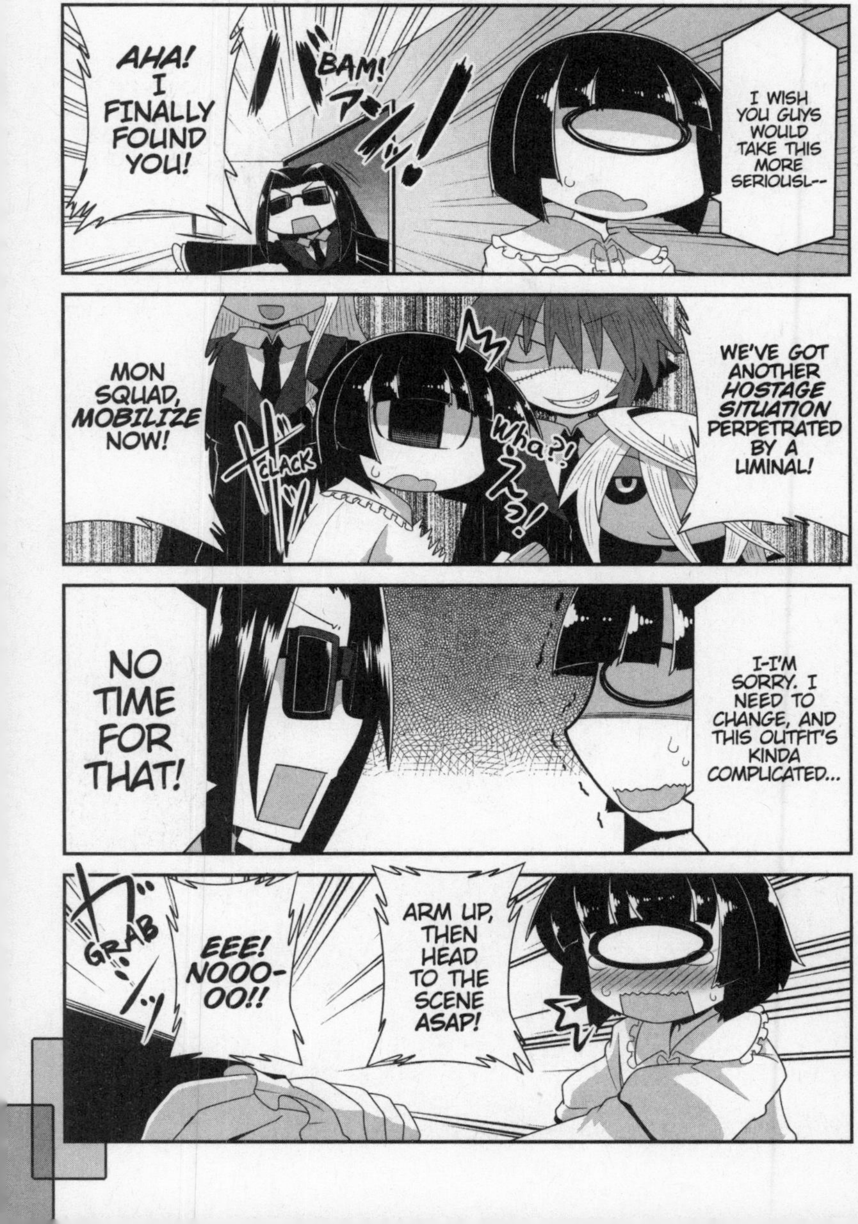
I WISH YOU GUYS WOULD TAKE THIS MORE SERIOUSL--
BAM!
AHA! I FINALLY FOUND YOU!
WE'VE GOT ANOTHER HOSTAGE SITUATION PERPETRATED BY A LIMINAL!
Wha?!
CLACK
MON SQUAD, MOBILIZE NOW!
I-I'M SORRY. I NEED TO CHANGE, AND THIS OUTFIT'S KINDA COMPLICATED...
NO TIME FOR THAT!
ARM UP, THEN HEAD TO THE SCENE ASAP!
EEE! NOOO-OO!!
GRAB

All's Well That Ends Well

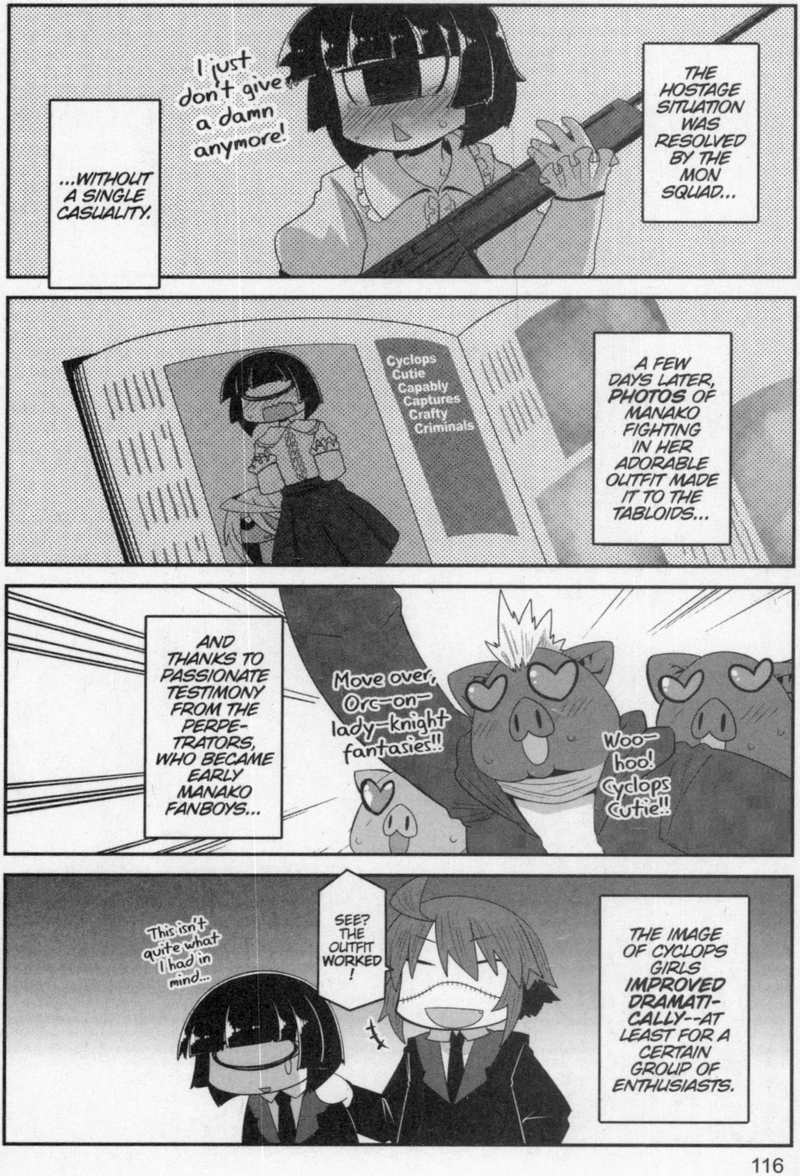
THE HOSTAGE SITUATION WAS RESOLVED BY THE MON SQUAD...
I just don't give a damn anymore!
...WITHOUT A SINGLE CASUALITY.
A FEW DAYS LATER, PHOTOS OF MANAKO FIGHTING IN HER ADORABLE OUTFIT MADE IT TO THE TABLOIDS...
Cyclops Cutie Capably Captures Crafty Criminals
Woo-hoo! Cyclops Cutie!!
Move over, Orc-on-lady-knight fantasies!!
AND THANKS TO PASSIONATE TESTIMONY FROM THE PERPETRATORS, WHO BECAME EARLY MANAKO FANBOYS...
THE IMAGE OF CYCLOPS GIRLS IMPROVED DRAMATICALLY--AT LEAST FOR A CERTAIN GROUP OF ENTHUSIASTS.
SEE? THE OUTFIT WORKED!
This isn't quite what I had in mind...

モンスター娘のいる日常
4コマアンソロジー

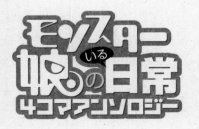

NSFL...
閲覧注意ッ!!!

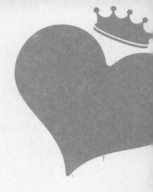

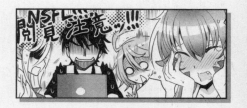

A Day in the Life of Tio-chan

By zank

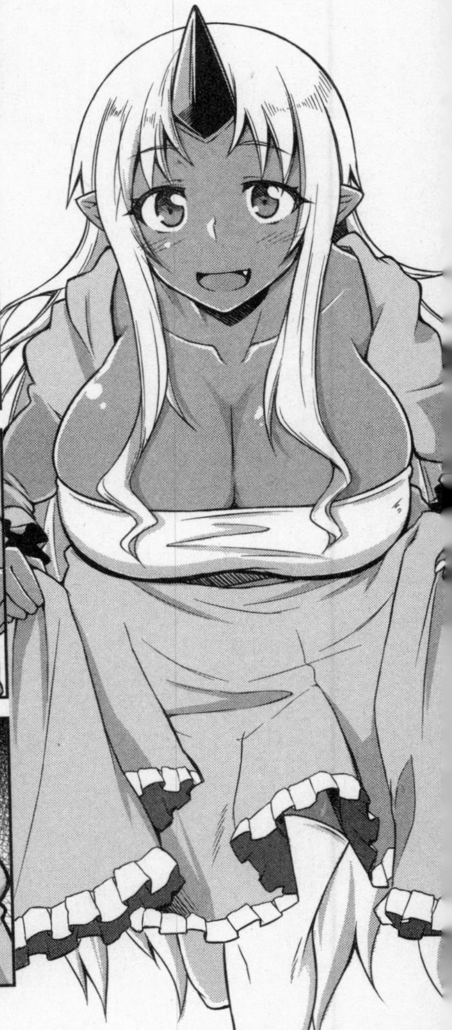

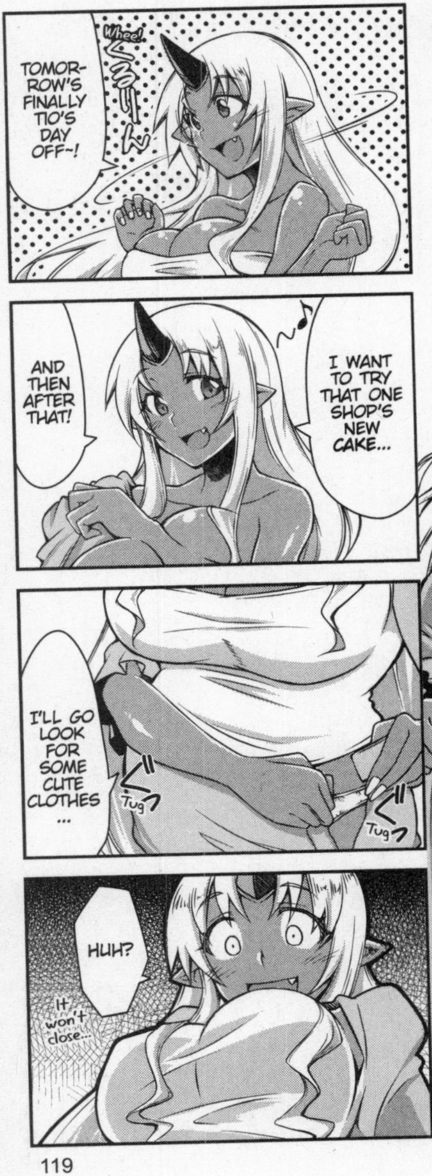
Whee!
TOMOR-ROW'S FINALLY TIO'S DAY OFF~!
I WANT TO TRY THAT ONE SHOP'S NEW CAKE...
AND THEN AFTER THAT!
Tug
Tug
I'LL GO LOOK FOR SOME CUTE CLOTHES ...
HUH?
It won't close...

Altered States

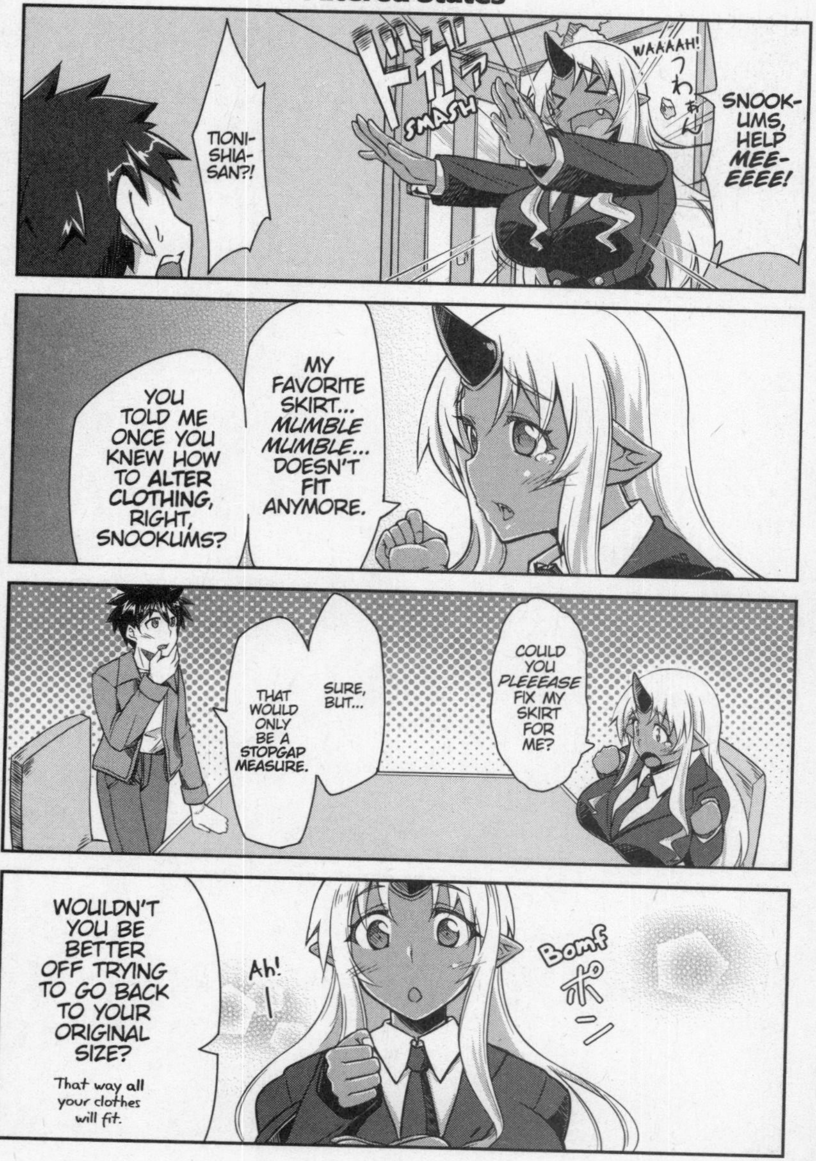
SNOOKUMS, HELP MEE-EEEE!
WAAAAH!
ドガァ
SMASH
TIONISHIA-SAN?!
MY FAVORITE SKIRT... MUMBLE MUMBLE... DOESN'T FIT ANYMORE.
YOU TOLD ME ONCE YOU KNEW HOW TO ALTER CLOTHING, RIGHT, SNOOKUMS?
COULD YOU PLEEEASE FIX MY SKIRT FOR ME?
SURE, BUT...
THAT WOULD ONLY BE A STOPGAP MEASURE.
Bomf
ポーン
Ah!
WOULDN'T YOU BE BETTER OFF TRYING TO GO BACK TO YOUR ORIGINAL SIZE?
That way all your clothes will fit.

Running Scared

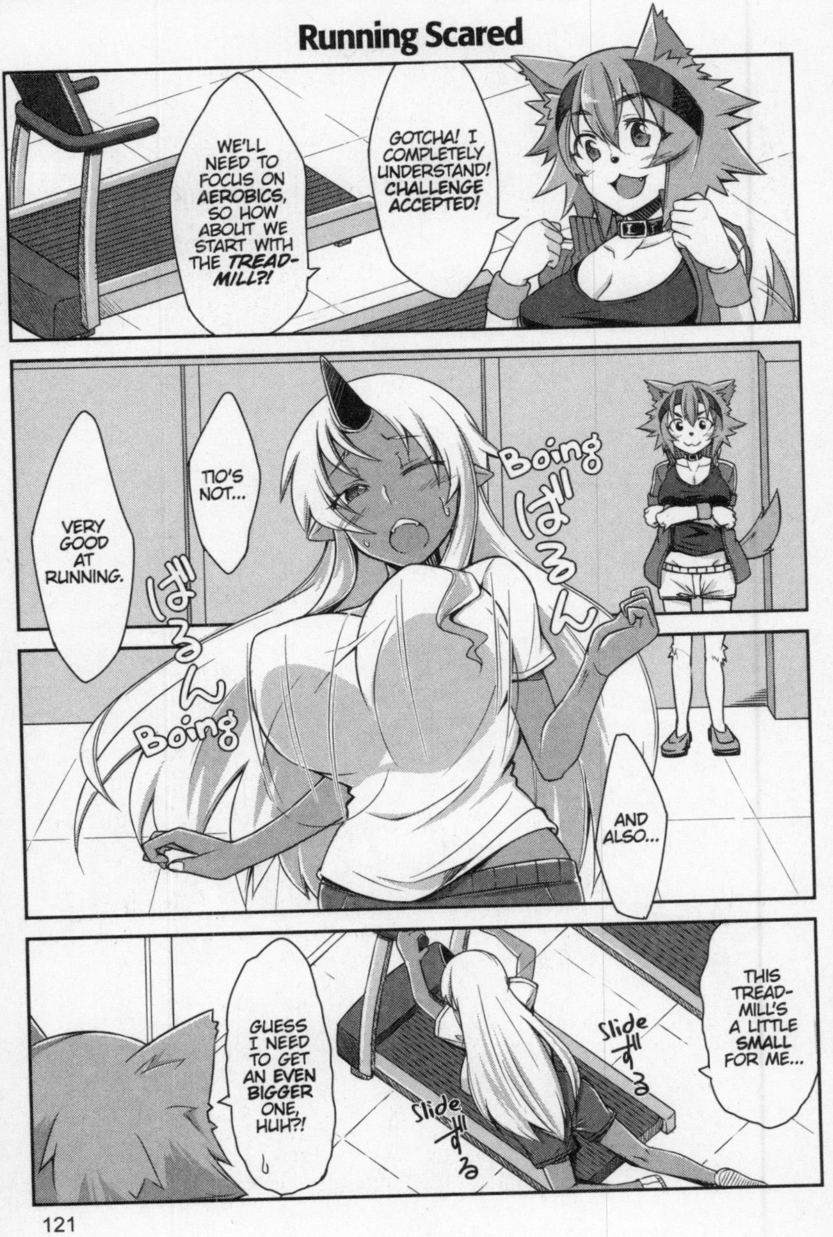
GOTCHA! I COMPLETELY UNDERSTAND! CHALLENGE ACCEPTED!
WE'LL NEED TO FOCUS ON AEROBICS, SO HOW ABOUT WE START WITH THE *TREAD-MILL*?!
Boing ばるん
TIO'S NOT...
VERY GOOD AT RUNNING.
ばるん Boing
AND ALSO...
THIS TREAD-MILL'S A LITTLE SMALL FOR ME...
Slide ずる
Slide ずる
GUESS I NEED TO GET AN EVEN BIGGER ONE, HUH?!

Pump It Up

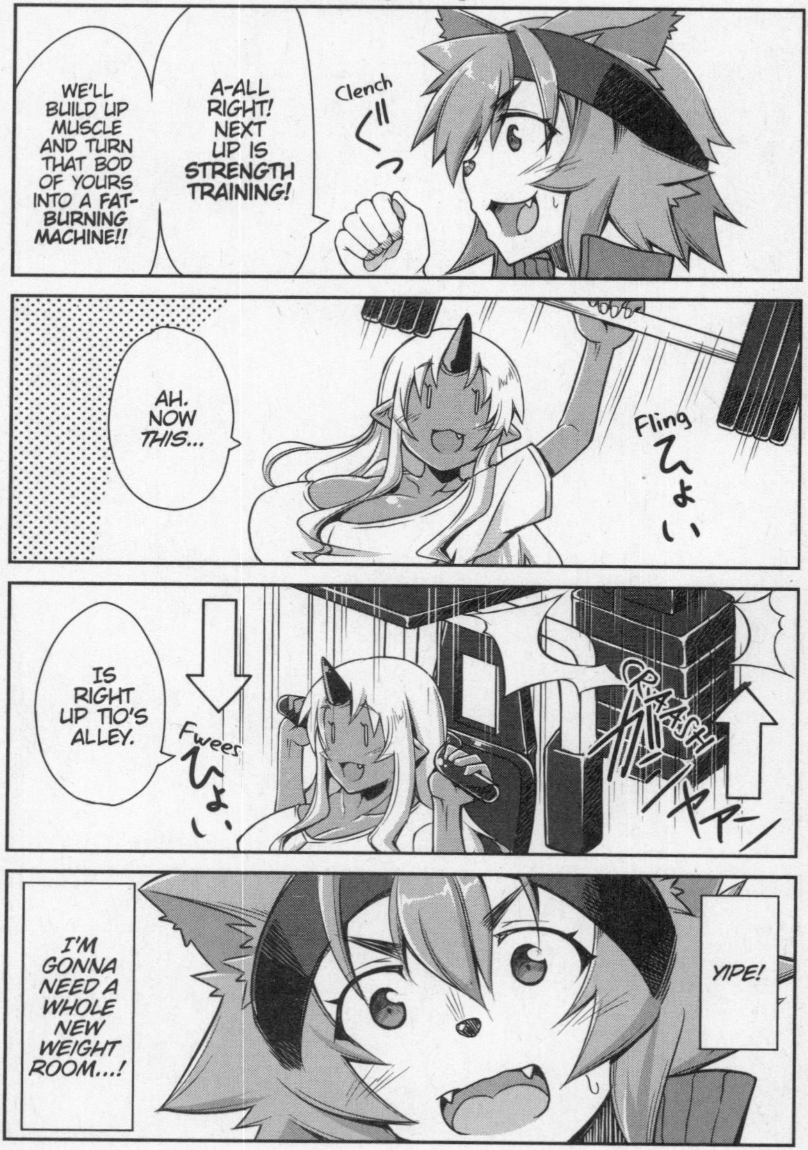
Clench
くっ
A-ALL RIGHT! NEXT UP IS STRENGTH TRAINING!
WE'LL BUILD UP MUSCLE AND TURN THAT BOD OF YOURS INTO A FAT-BURNING MACHINE!!
Fling
ひょい
AH. NOW *THIS*...
CRAASH
Fwees
ひょい
IS RIGHT UP TIO'S ALLEY.
YIPE!
I'M GONNA NEED A WHOLE NEW WEIGHT ROOM...!

Getting On Swimmingly

AWRIGHT, HERE'S THE POOL! PERFECT FOR FULL-BODY EXERCISE!!

WE'VE GOT SWIMSUITS FOR ALL BODY TYPES! HERE YA GO!

This is a bit embarrassing...

stroke

LOOKS LIKE WE FINALLY FOUND A WINNER...

Crack

Crack

WHAAA?!

OWW...

Smack

Everyday Solution

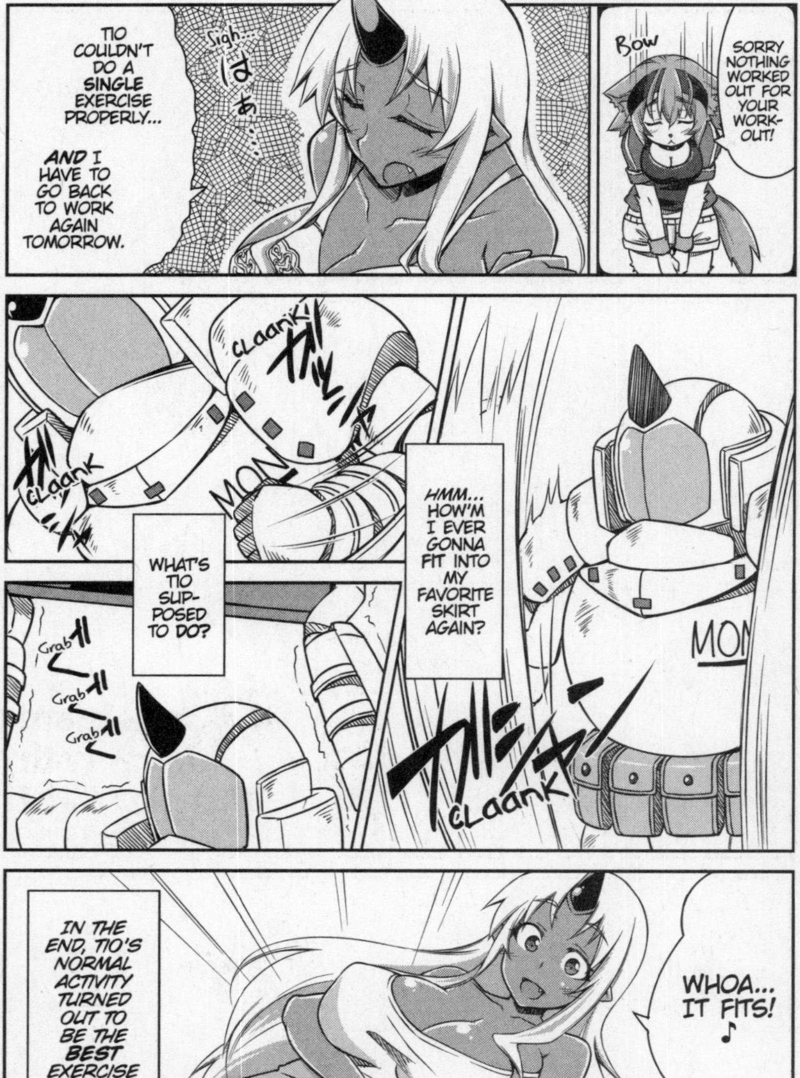

Bow
SORRY NOTHING WORKED OUT FOR YOUR WORK-OUT!
Sigh...
はぁ...
TIO COULDN'T DO A SINGLE EXERCISE PROPERLY...
AND I HAVE TO GO BACK TO WORK AGAIN TOMORROW.
HMM... HOW'M I EVER GONNA FIT INTO MY FAVORITE SKIRT AGAIN?
MON
Claank
Claank
Claank
MON
WHAT'S TIO SUP-POSED TO DO?
Grab
Grab
Grab
WHOA... IT FITS! ♪
IN THE END, TIO'S NORMAL ACTIVITY TURNED OUT TO BE THE BEST EXERCISE OF ALL.

Idioms

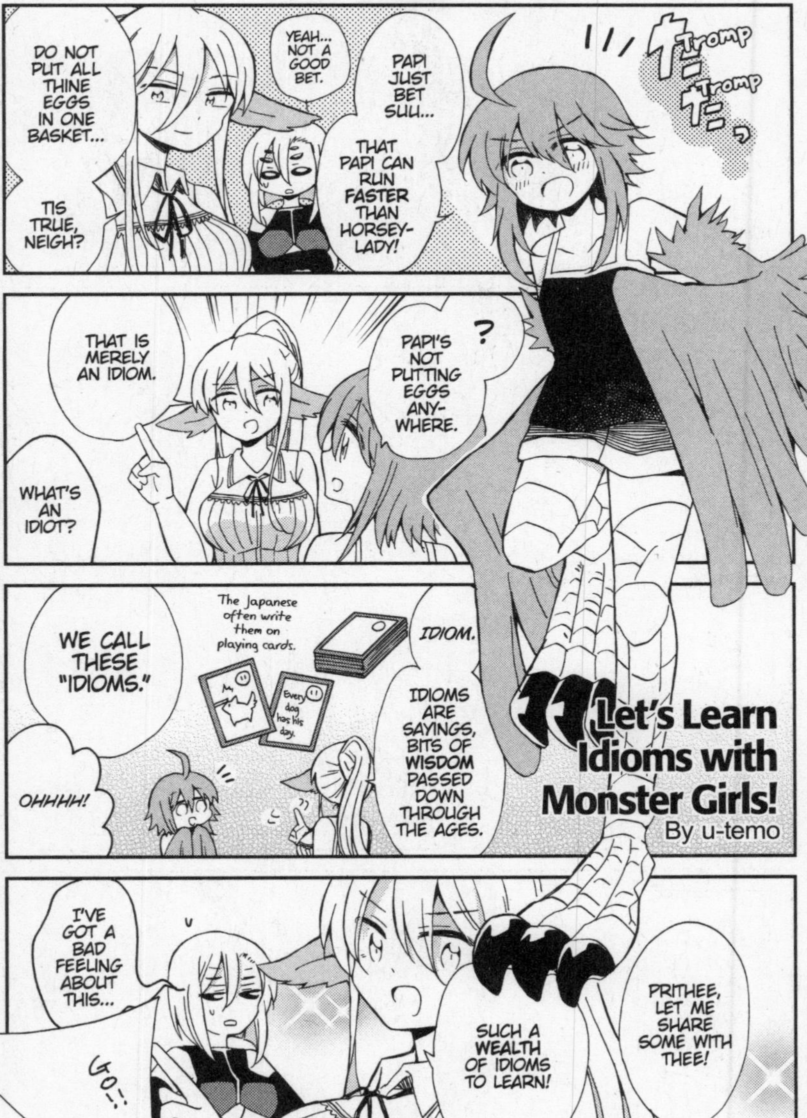
Tromp
Tromp
PAPI JUST BET SUU...
THAT PAPI CAN RUN FASTER THAN HORSEY-LADY!
YEAH... NOT A GOOD BET.
DO NOT PUT ALL THINE EGGS IN ONE BASKET...
TIS TRUE, NEIGH?
?
PAPI'S NOT PUTTING EGGS ANYWHERE.
THAT IS MERELY AN IDIOM.
WHAT'S AN IDIOT?
Let's Learn Idioms with Monster Girls!
By u-temo
IDIOM.
IDIOMS ARE SAYINGS, BITS OF WISDOM PASSED DOWN THROUGH THE AGES.
The Japanese often write them on playing cards.
Every dog has his day.
WE CALL THESE "IDIOMS."
OHHHH!
PRITHEE, LET ME SHARE SOME WITH THEE!
SUCH A WEALTH OF IDIOMS TO LEARN!
I'VE GOT A BAD FEELING ABOUT THIS...
GO!!

Snake in the Grass

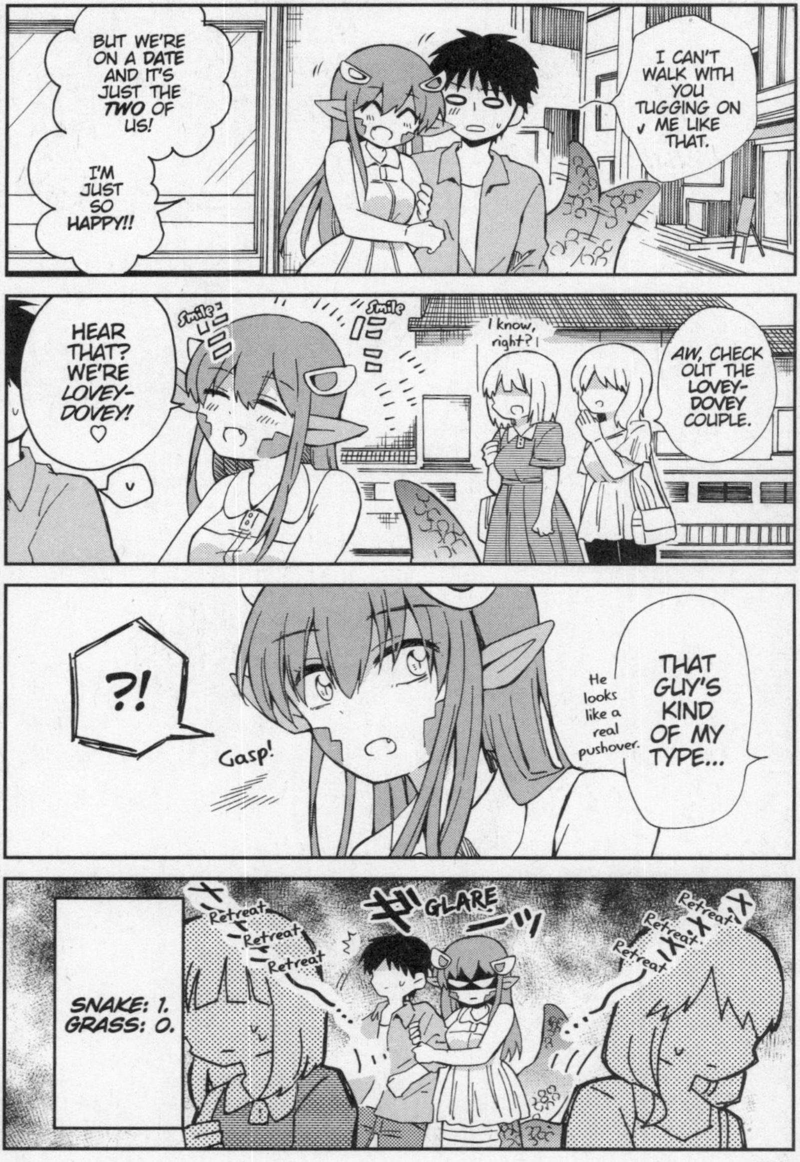
I CAN'T WALK WITH YOU TUGGING ON ME LIKE THAT.
BUT WE'RE ON A DATE AND IT'S JUST THE TWO OF US!
I'M JUST SO HAPPY!!
AW, CHECK OUT THE LOVEY-DOVEY COUPLE.
I know, right?!
Smile
Smile
HEAR THAT? WE'RE LOVEY-DOVEY! ♡
THAT GUY'S KIND OF MY TYPE...
He looks like a real pushover.
?!
Gasp!
Retreat
Retreat
Retreat
GLARE
Retreat
Retreat
Retreat
SNAKE: 1. GRASS: 0.

You Should Have Seen the One That Got Away

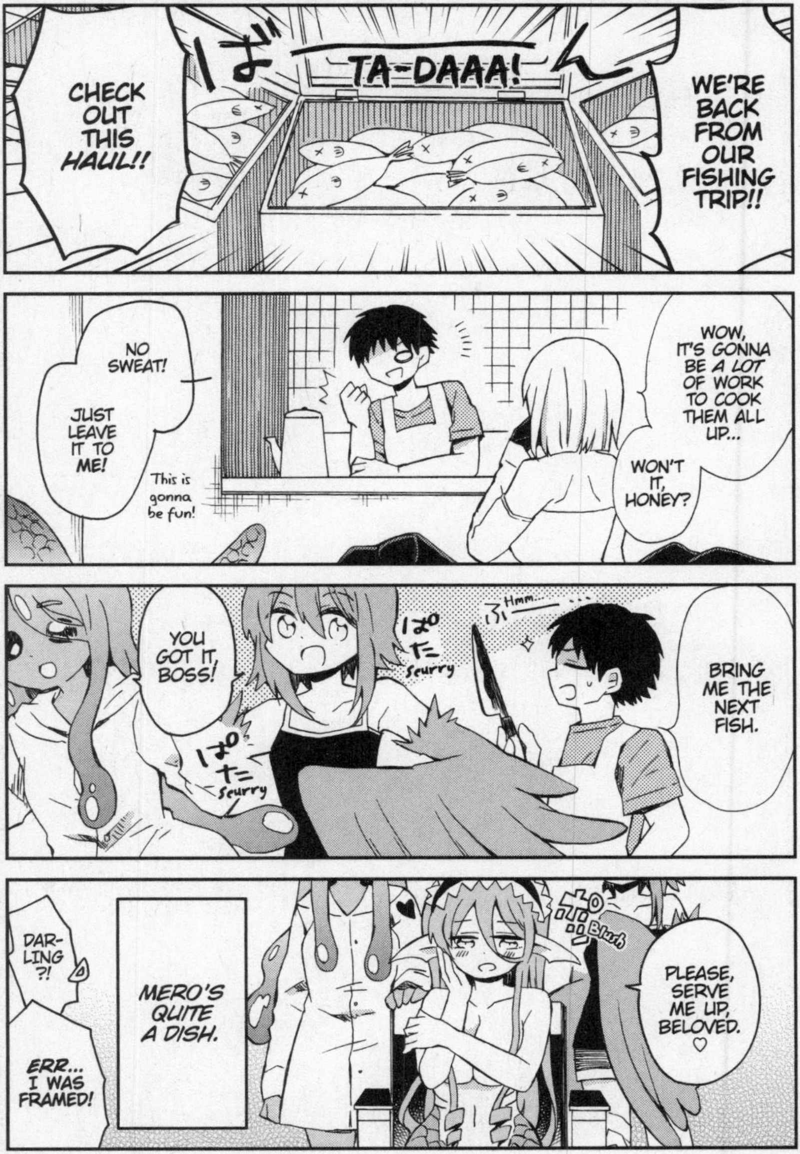

WE'RE BACK FROM OUR FISHING TRIP!!
ば TA-DAAA! ん
CHECK OUT THIS HAUL!!
WOW, IT'S GONNA BE A LOT OF WORK TO COOK THEM ALL UP...
WON'T IT, HONEY?
NO SWEAT!
JUST LEAVE IT TO ME!
This is gonna be fun!
BRING ME THE NEXT FISH.
Hmm...
Scurry
YOU GOT IT, BOSS!
Scurry
PLEASE, SERVE ME UP, BELOVED. ♡
Blush
MERO'S QUITE A DISH.
DARLING?!
ERR... I WAS FRAMED!

Never Look a Gift Horse in the Mouth

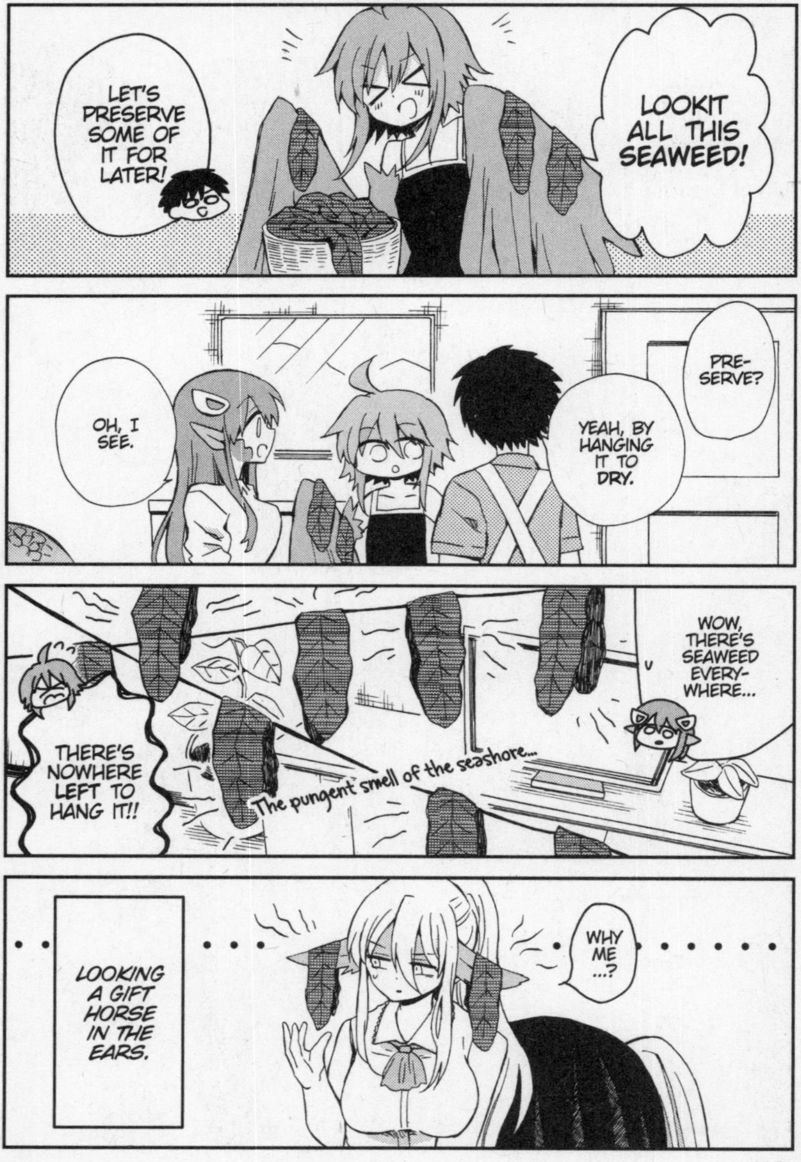
LOOKIT ALL THIS SEAWEED!
LET'S PRESERVE SOME OF IT FOR LATER!
PRE-SERVE?
YEAH, BY HANGING IT TO DRY.
OH, I SEE.
WOW, THERE'S SEAWEED EVERY-WHERE...
The pungent smell of the seashore...
THERE'S NOWHERE LEFT TO HANG IT!!
WHY ME ...?
LOOKING A GIFT HORSE IN THE EARS.

Speak of the Devil...

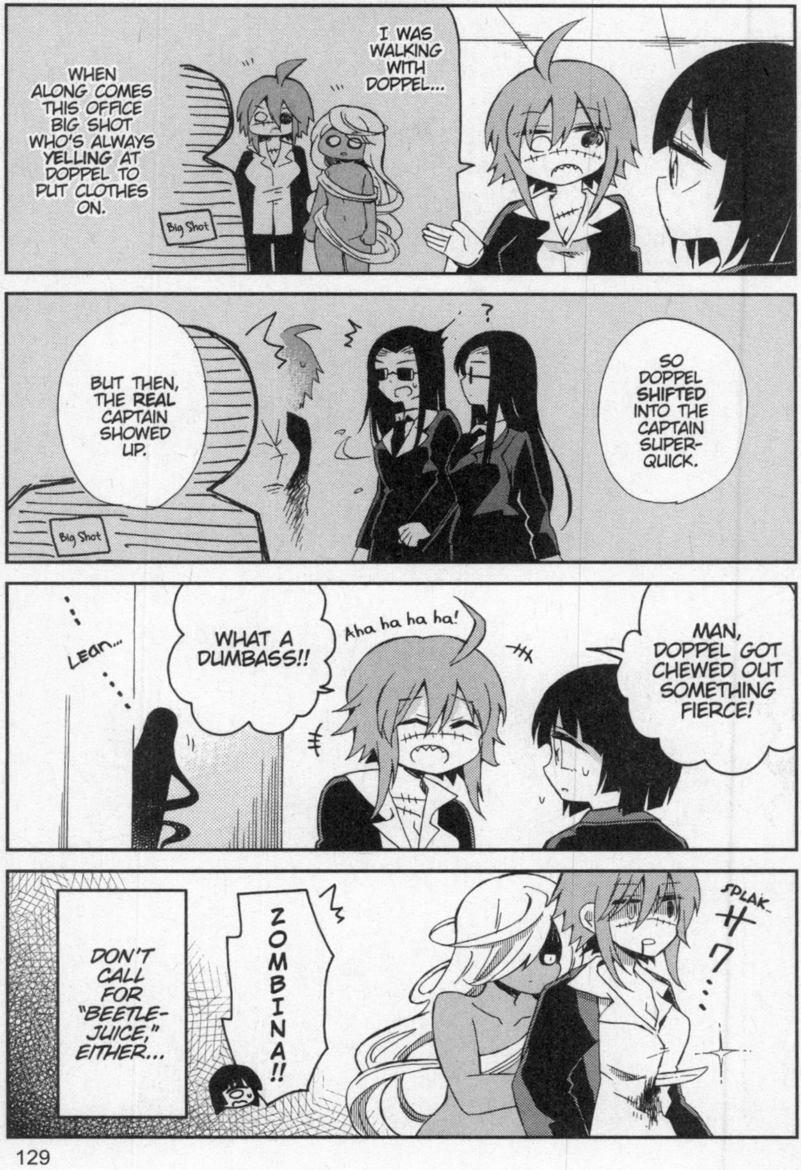
I WAS WALKING WITH DOPPEL...
WHEN ALONG COMES THIS OFFICE BIG SHOT WHO'S ALWAYS YELLING AT DOPPEL TO PUT CLOTHES ON.
Big Shot
BUT THEN, THE REAL CAPTAIN SHOWED UP.
SO DOPPEL SHIFTED INTO THE CAPTAIN SUPER-QUICK.
Big Shot
MAN, DOPPEL GOT CHEWED OUT SOMETHING FIERCE!
Aha ha ha ha!
WHAT A DUMBASS!!
...Lean...
SPLAK
ZOMBINA!!
DON'T CALL FOR "BEETLE-JUICE," EITHER...

When the Cat's Away, the Mice Will Play.

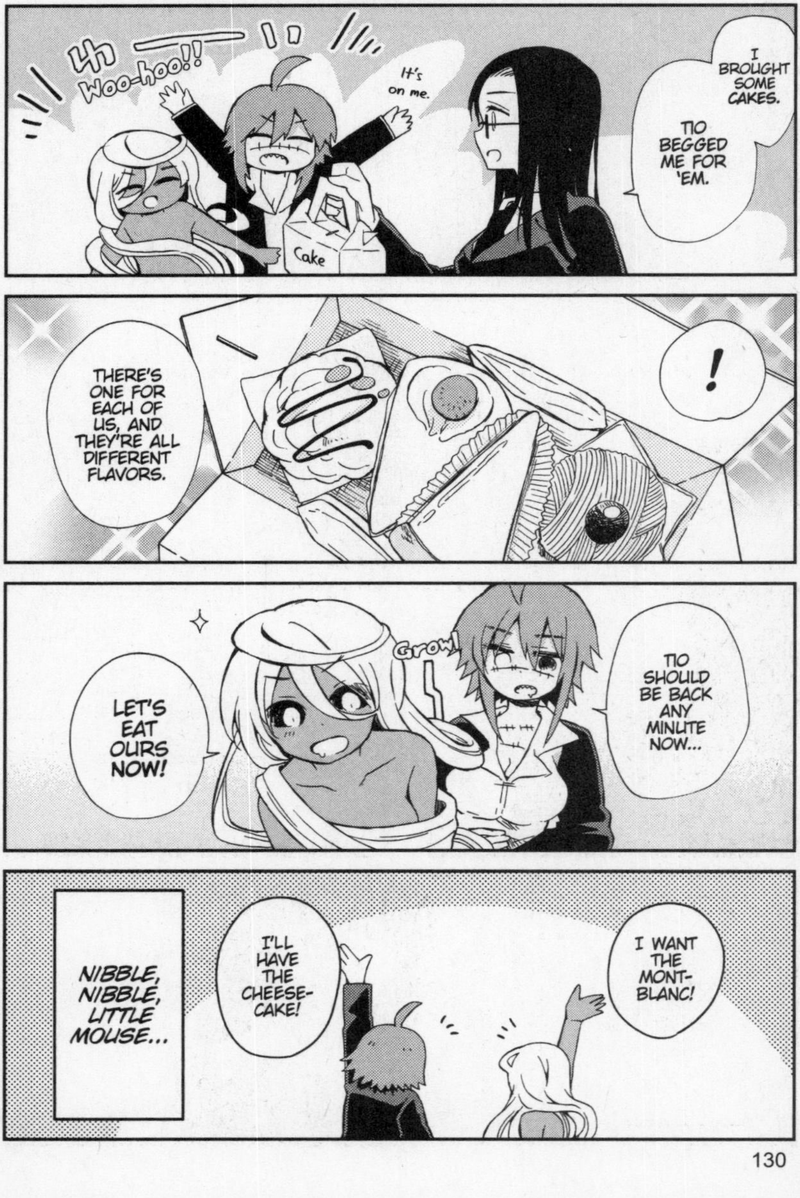

I BROUGHT SOME CAKES.
TIO BEGGED ME FOR 'EM.
It's on me.
Woo-hoo!!
!
THERE'S ONE FOR EACH OF US, AND THEY'RE ALL DIFFERENT FLAVORS.
TIO SHOULD BE BACK ANY MINUTE NOW...
Grow!
LET'S EAT OURS NOW!
I WANT THE MONT-BLANC!
I'LL HAVE THE CHEESE-CAKE!
NIBBLE, NIBBLE, LITTLE MOUSE...

An Eye For An Eye

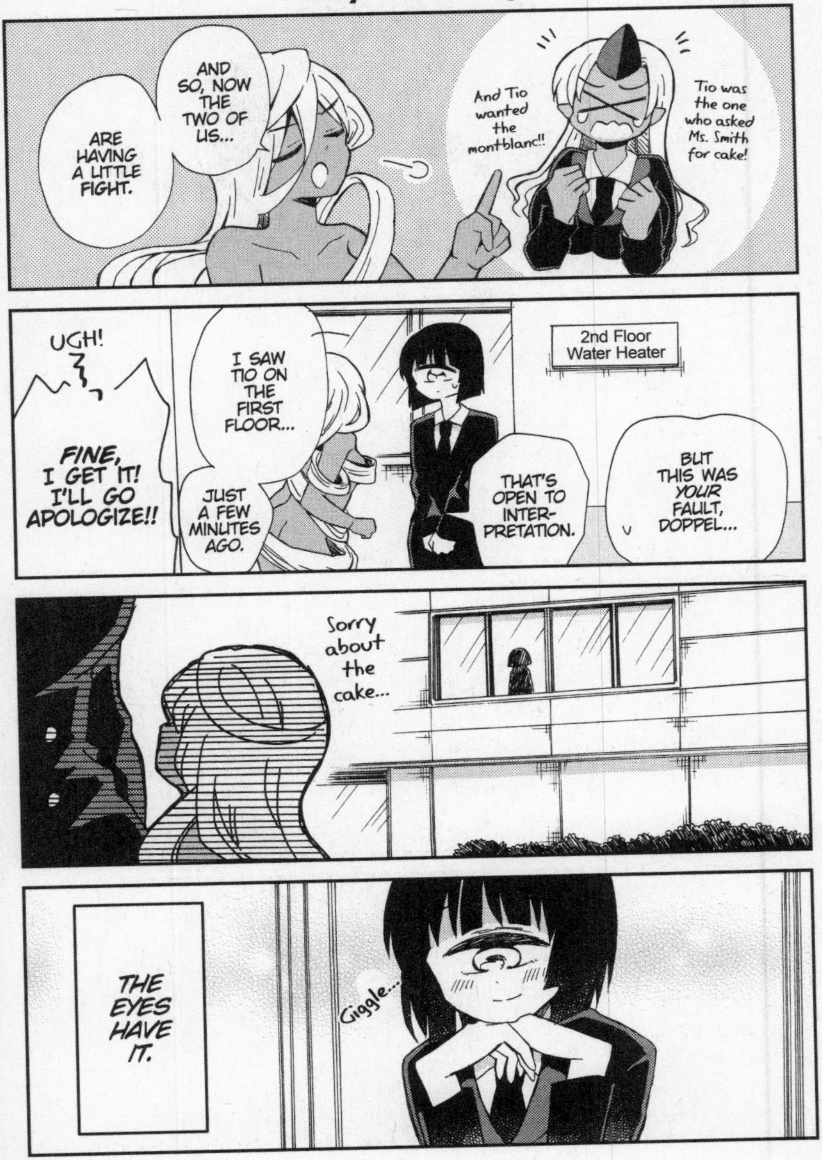
Tio was the one who asked Ms. Smith for cake!
And Tio wanted the montblanc!!
AND SO, NOW THE TWO OF US...
ARE HAVING A LITTLE FIGHT.
2nd Floor Water Heater
BUT THIS WAS *YOUR* FAULT, DOPPEL...
THAT'S OPEN TO INTERPRETATION.
I SAW TIO ON THE FIRST FLOOR...
JUST A FEW MINUTES AGO.
UGH!
FINE, I GET IT! I'LL GO APOLOGIZE!!
Sorry about the cake...
Giggle...
THE EYES HAVE IT.

Pun-nee-san

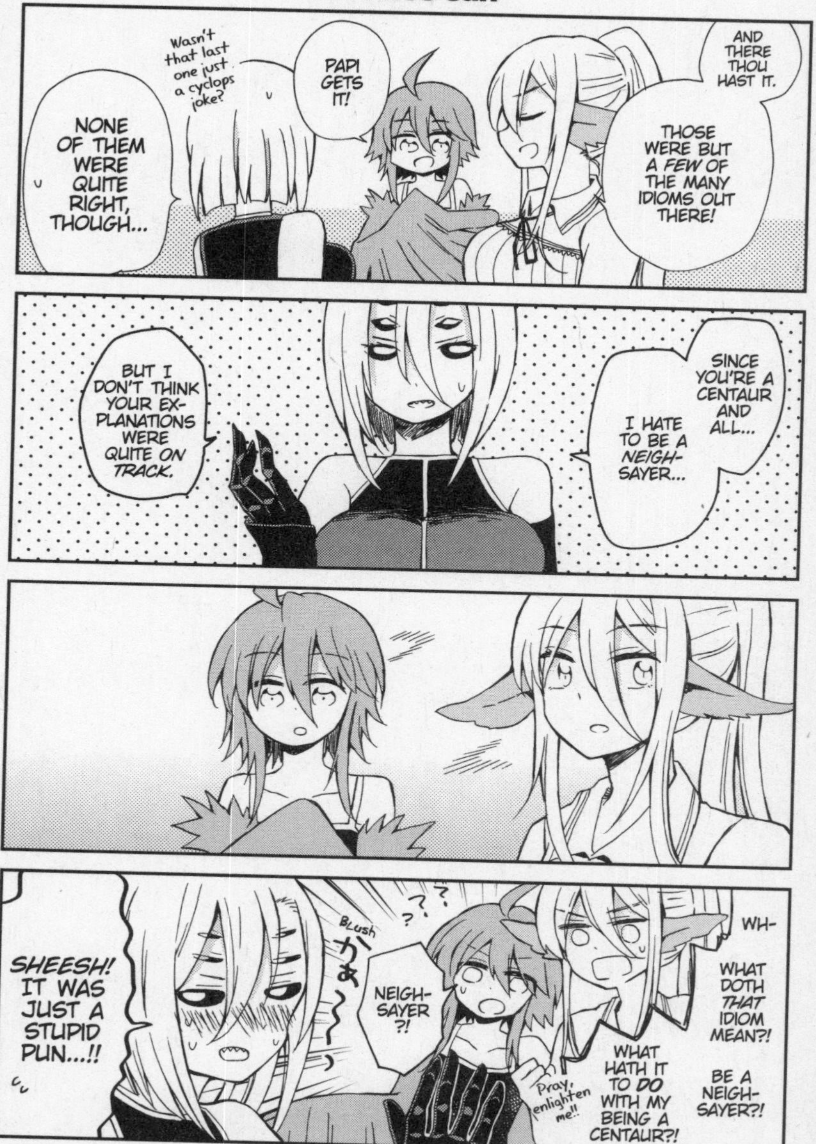
AND THERE THOU HAST IT.
THOSE WERE BUT A *FEW* OF THE MANY IDIOMS OUT THERE!
PAPI GETS IT!
Wasn't that last one just a cyclops joke?
NONE OF THEM WERE QUITE RIGHT, THOUGH...
SINCE YOU'RE A CENTAUR AND ALL...
I HATE TO BE A *NEIGH*-SAYER...
BUT I DON'T THINK YOUR EXPLANATIONS WERE QUITE ON *TRACK*.
WH-
WHAT DOTH *THAT* IDIOM MEAN?!
BE A NEIGH-SAYER?!
WHAT HATH IT TO *DO* WITH MY BEING A CENTAUR?!
Pray, enlighten me!!
NEIGH-SAYER?!
Blush
SHEESH! IT WAS JUST A STUPID PUN...!!

モンスター娘のいる日常
4コマアンソロジー

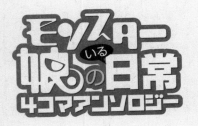

Monster Musume

I ❤ MONSTER GIRLS

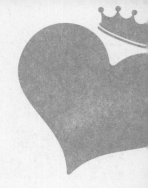

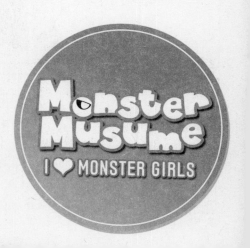

Remembering

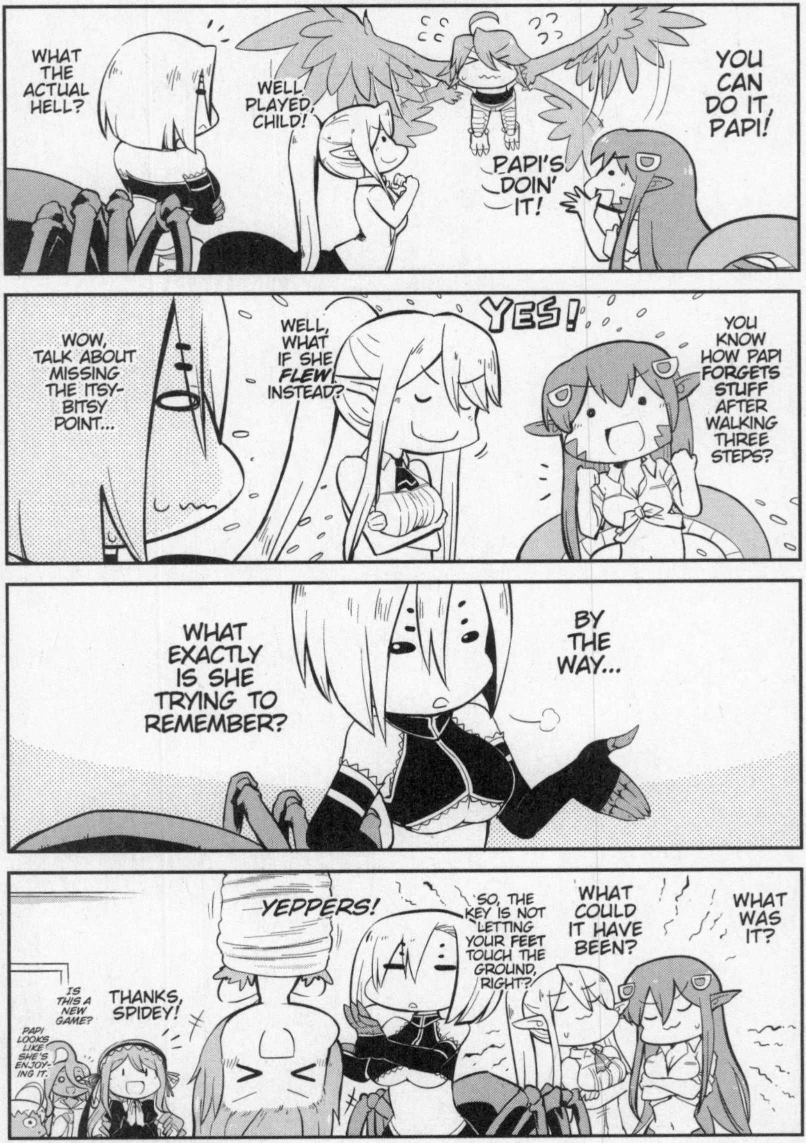
YOU CAN DO IT, PAPI!
PAPI'S DOIN' IT!
WELL PLAYED, CHILD!
WHAT THE ACTUAL HELL?
YOU KNOW HOW PAPI FORGETS STUFF AFTER WALKING THREE STEPS?
YES!
WELL, WHAT IF SHE FLEW INSTEAD?
WOW, TALK ABOUT MISSING THE ITSY-BITSY POINT...
BY THE WAY...
WHAT EXACTLY IS SHE TRYING TO REMEMBER?
WHAT WAS IT?
WHAT COULD IT HAVE BEEN?
SO, THE KEY IS NOT LETTING YOUR FEET TOUCH THE GROUND, RIGHT?
YEPPERS!
THANKS, SPIDEY!
IS THIS A NEW GAME?
PAPI LOOKS LIKE SHE'S ENJOYING IT.

By Nobuyoshi Zamurai

Message

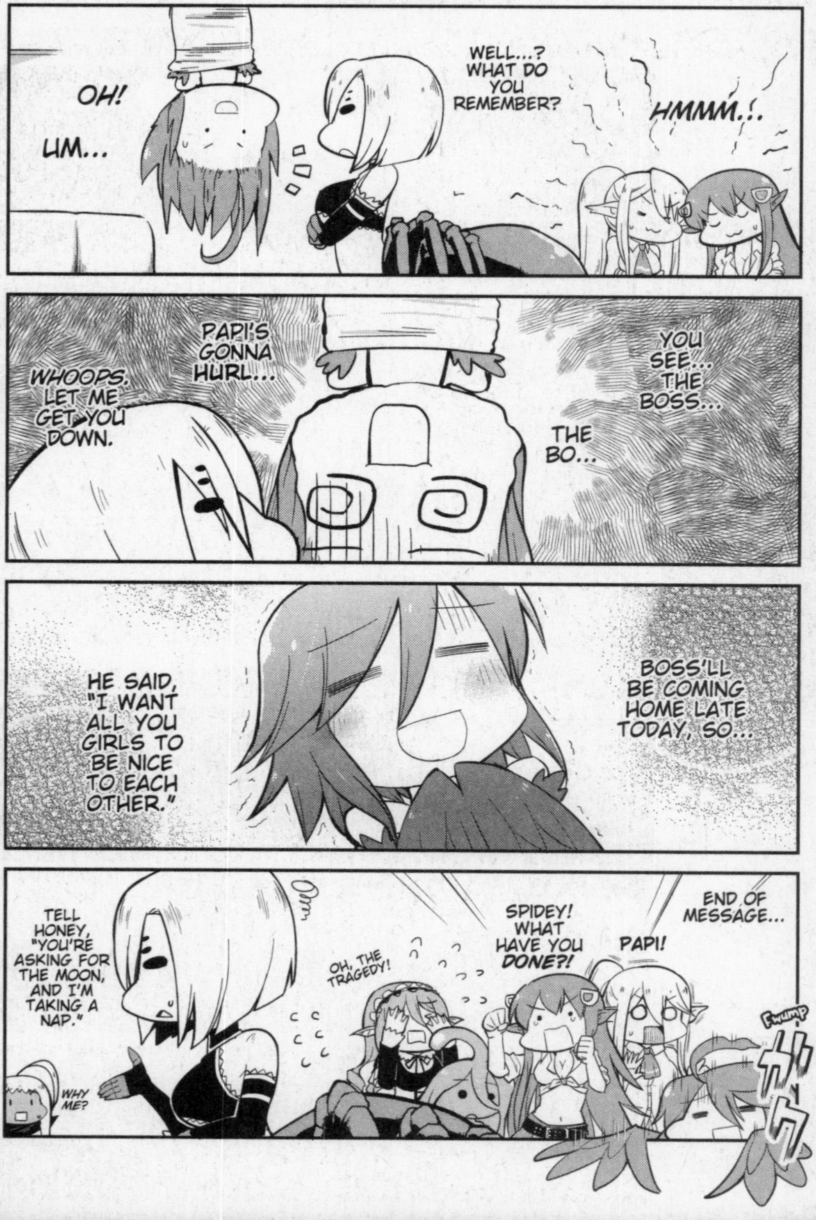
HMMM..!..
WELL...? WHAT DO YOU REMEMBER?
OH!
UM...
YOU SEE... THE BOSS...
THE BO...
PAPI'S GONNA HURL...
WHOOPS. LET ME GET YOU DOWN.
BOSS'LL BE COMING HOME LATE TODAY, SO...
HE SAID, "I WANT ALL YOU GIRLS TO BE NICE TO EACH OTHER."
FWUMP
END OF MESSAGE...
PAPI!
SPIDEY! WHAT HAVE YOU DONE?!
OH, THE TRAGEDY!
TELL HONEY, "YOU'RE ASKING FOR THE MOON, AND I'M TAKING A NAP."
WHY ME?

ILLUSTRATION

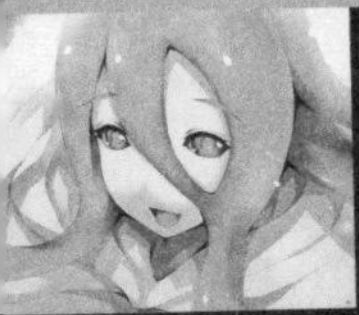

P01 **tsukasawa**

Serializes a story in a seinen manga magazine and participates in doujinshi sale events through the "Matsuri Gensou" circle.

I got hooked on the *Monster Musume* anime and I though Suu was cute, so I drew her. Then I got an email from Tokuma Shoten asking me if I'd like to work on an official *Monster Musume* book. So I was excited to draw my beloved Suu-chan.

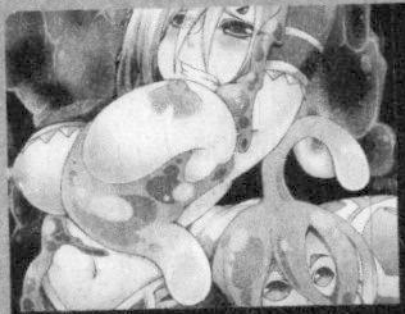

P02 **akahito**

Participates in doujinshi sale events though the "kemoyuru" circle.

Hello, my name is akahito. I thought for a long time about who I should draw, but in the end I decided to wield my pen to draw my two favorites. They seem like they went out of control, but I'm happy with how it turned out. (´ω`*

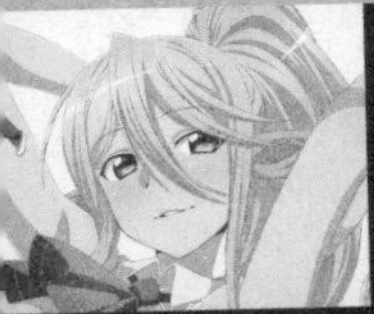

P03 **loliconder**

Sells seinen-oriented dojin CG collections through the "Condaya" circle.

I just think Cerea is great with her dignified face, unwavering loyalty, and her tendency to sometimes let her mind stray in dangerous ways! I love you, Cerea!

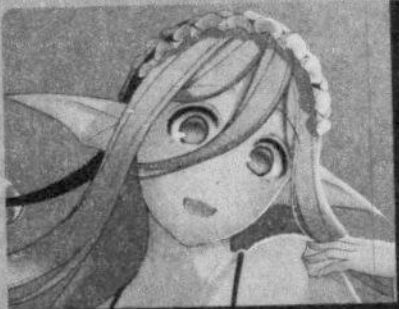

P04 **mog**

Uploads lots of monster girl illustrations to Pixiv.

I'm honored to be able to work on a *Monster Musume* anthology. I've always admired mermaids ever since I was little, so I was very happy to come across a mermaid as cute as Mero. Thank you so much.

COMIC

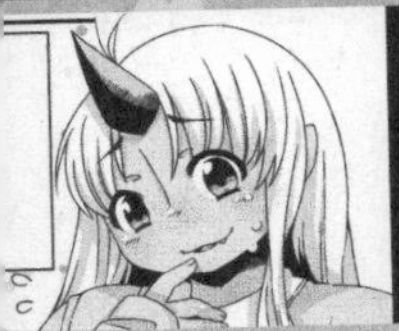

P05 **muroku**

Mainly uploads illustrations to Pixiv and Twitter. Works on clip art for several tankoubon for his main work.

Hello, I'm muroku. My manga focused on Tio and Manako! Tio's cute! Cute because she's huge! Thanks for reading!

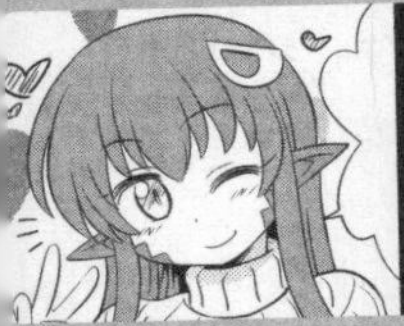

P11 **SHIRAHA MATO**

Serializes a story in a seinen manga magazine and participates in doujinshi sale events though the "Hagane no Tsurugi" circle. Representative work: Loveraune *-IDOL MONSTER GIRLS-* (Kill Time Communications).

I'm hoping for a second season of the anime!

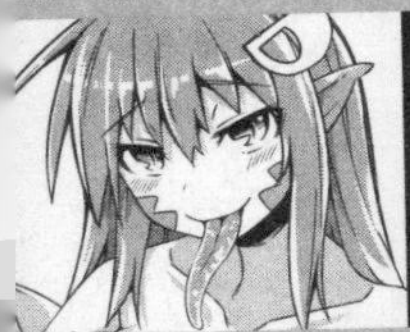

P25 **stealth kaigyou**

Participates in doujinshi sale events though the "SlapStickStrike" circle.

This is the second time I've worked on a Monster Musume anthology! Yay! I felt like my last comic wasn't sexy enough, so I upped the eroticism this time. I'd love to live in boob heaven like this!

❤ Afterword ❤

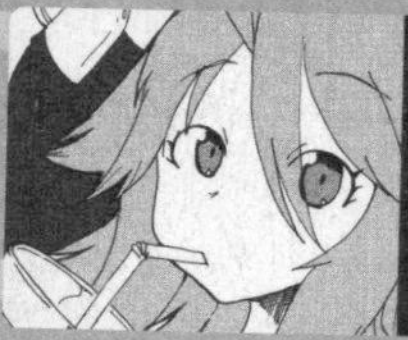

P29 **setouchi**

Participates in doujinshi sale events though the "setouchi pharma-ceuticals" circle. Draws illustrations for doujin games among other things.

setouchi here. Thanks so much for calling on me again. I moved to the countryside a few years back and was amazed by their culture of setting up buildings alongside the highway, so I incorporated that into this manga along with my beloved monster girls.

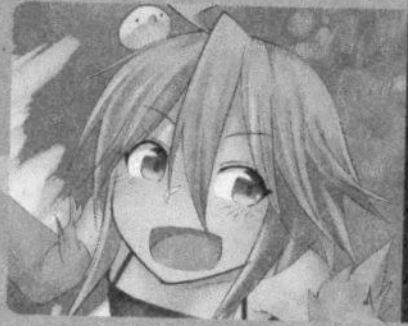

P37 **kasaijushi**

Participates in posting to web comic sites and doujinshi sale events though the "Kasai Kougyou" circle.

I was influenced by Okayado-sensei's one-page Monster Musume manga and fell in love with monster girls, so I was surprised and delighted when I was invited to participate in this anthology. I was a little intimidated after hearing about the others involved in this production, but worked my hard-est, so I hope you enjoy my comic.

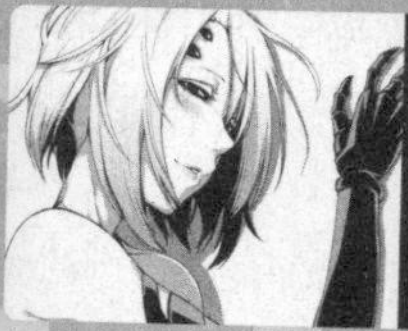

P49 **nakamura regura**

Serializes a series in a seinen manga magazine and participates in doujinshi sale events through the "Nanpou Hitogakushiki" circle.

I prefer insect monster girls, so of course I'm a Rachnera man. I chose her to be the main character of my manga, but ultimately Kurusu-kun wound up with the most lines. That's the protagonist for you.

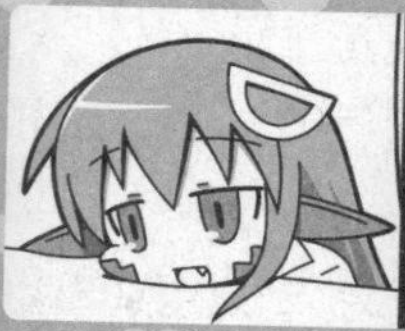

P57 **rolf**

Participates in doujinshi sales events through the circle "Kiiroiro."

It's strange for me to be working on the creative side of *Monster Musume* since I've been a fan of this title for a while now. It makes me so glad that monster girls exist.

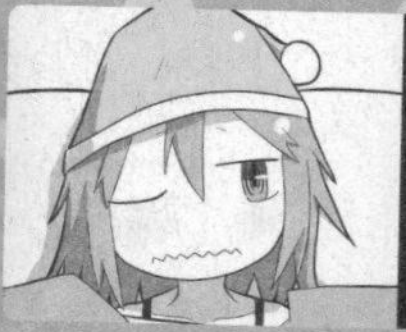

P67 **ikao**

Participates in doujinshi sales events through the circle "30 Little Pet Bottles."

I especially love Papi-chan and Suu-chan!

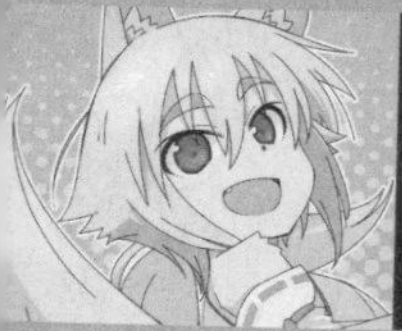

P71 **Tottori-saQ**

Participates in doujinshi sale events though the "Kimyoudou" circle. Representative work: *Oukokuchou Sorasore* (Kadokawa Shoten)

I drew this while eating some inarizushi from a nearby sushi restaurant. I'd love to snuggle with Ils-san's tails!

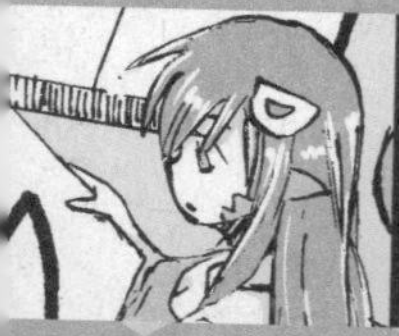

P79 **kanemaki thomas**

Serializes a story in a seinen manga magazine and participates in doujinshi sale events through the "Niku Drill" circle.

I only realized after the fact that I forgot to draw Lala on the frontispiece. By the way, my favorite puzzles are cryptograms.

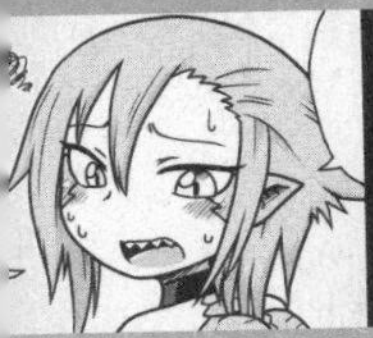

P91 **aruse yuushi**

Participates in doujinshi sale events though the "Chapedizo 2" circle.

I'm honored to be called back again for this! I was happy to draw Polt since she had such a minor role in the anime. I'd love to keep coming back to draw for *Monster Musume!*

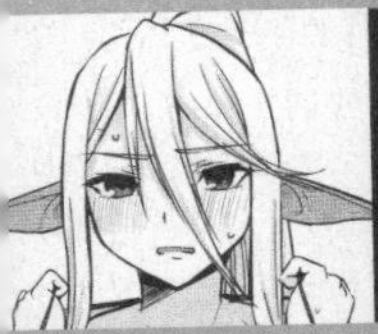

P101 **kurokawa otogi**

Serializes a story in a seinen manga magazine and participates in doujinshi sale events through the "Otogi no Kuni no Soapland" circle.

I like mermaids, so I'm happy to draw Mero, but because I'm always drawing giant boobs I was excited to draw Centorea. By the way, my first tankoubon is scheduled to be release in March! I'd love it if the 18+ crowd took a look at it.

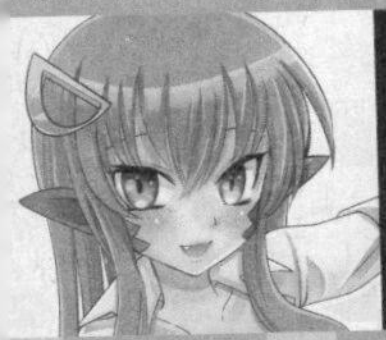

P105 **Tamon Hinoshika**

His manga *Shinigami-san ga Toorimasu!* is serialized in Shunin ga Yuku! Special (Bunkasha). Participates in doujinshi sale events though the "Smith of Shadeers" circle.

It's a pleasure to meet you! I'm Hinosika, sticking out like a sore thumb. I became interested in *Monster Musume* after seeing the anime, and then started reading the original manga. I'll never forget the impact those boobs had on me! If you enjoy my comic, I couldn't ask for anything that'd make me happier. It was fun to do the coloring! Thank you so much.

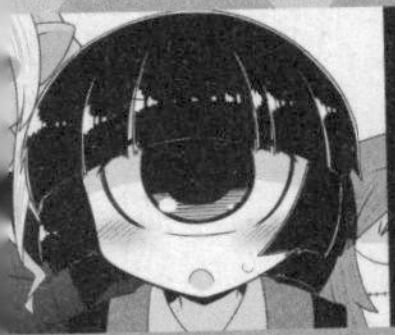

P109 **221 (tsutsuichi)**

Active in the "Karibanizumu" circle through which 221 participates in live Niconico broadcasts and doujinshi sale events. Representative work: *Mako-san and Hashisuka-kun* (Micro Magazine)

I was very excited to dress up Manako-san.

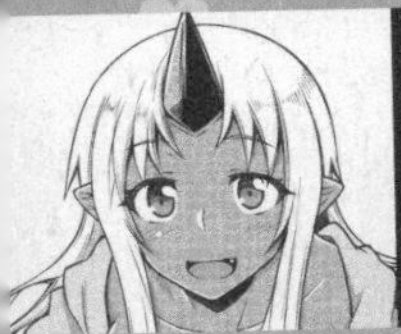

P119 **zank**

Participates in doujinshi sale events through the "shirakabadori" circle.

Tionishia-chan!!! She's *HUUUUUUUUGE!* No need for explanations. She's 2m 27cm tall! Bust 160cm! So I decided to draw Tio-chan and Polt-chan since she didn't have a lot of screen time in the anime.

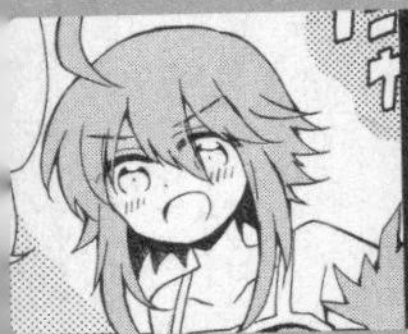

P125 **u-temo**

Participates in doujinshi sale events though the "Technostress" circle. Representative work: *Mononokesou no Neet Domo* (Holp Shuppan).

I went a little overboard with the puns... Monster girls are all so cute, they're fun to draw no matter which one I choose!

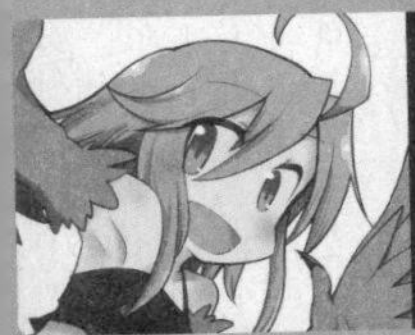

P137 **Nobuyoshi Zamurai**

Serializes his representative work *"Torikissa!"*(Bird Café!) in *Monthly Comic Ryu*. Participates in doujinshi sale events through the "Co-Op Samurai 203" circle.

Thank you for letting me draw Papi for the cover...Hooray! It seems like *Monster Musume* has just kept picking up steam ever since the pilot strips debuted online! I'm looking forward to seeing where it goes from here, Okayado-sensei!

By Okayado

ASSOCIATION FOR THE VICTIMS OF OKAYADO 2

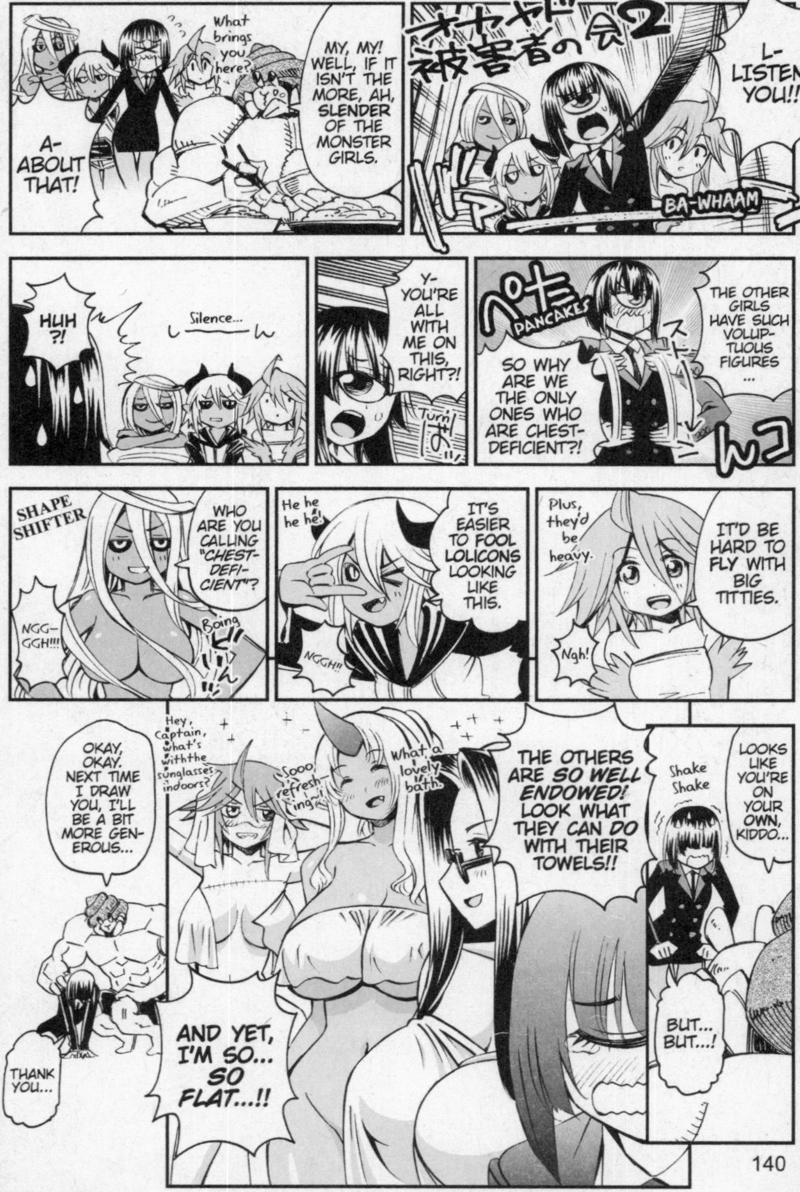
オカヤド被害者の会2
L- LISTEN, YOU!!
BA-WHAAM
MY, MY! WELL, IF IT ISN'T THE MORE, AH, SLENDER OF THE MONSTER GIRLS.
What brings you here?
A- ABOUT THAT!
THE OTHER GIRLS HAVE SUCH VOLUP-TUOUS FIGURES ...
PANCAKES
SO WHY ARE WE THE ONLY ONES WHO ARE CHEST-DEFICIENT?!
Y-YOU'RE ALL WITH ME ON THIS, RIGHT?!
Turn!
Silence...
HUH?!
IT'D BE HARD TO FLY WITH BIG TITTIES.
Plus, they'd be heavy.
Ngh!
IT'S EASIER TO FOOL LOLICONS LOOKING LIKE THIS.
He he he he!
NGGH!!
SHAPE SHIFTER
WHO ARE YOU CALLING "CHEST-DEFICIENT"?
Boing
NGG-GGH!!!
LOOKS LIKE YOU'RE ON YOUR OWN, KIDDO...
Shake Shake
BUT... BUT...!
THE OTHERS ARE SO WELL ENDOWED! LOOK WHAT THEY CAN DO WITH THEIR TOWELS!!
What a lovely bath.
Sooo refresh-ing!
Hey, Captain, what's with the sunglasses indoors?
AND YET, I'M SO... SO FLAT...!!
OKAY, OKAY. NEXT TIME I DRAW YOU, I'LL BE A BIT MORE GEN-EROUS...
THANK YOU...

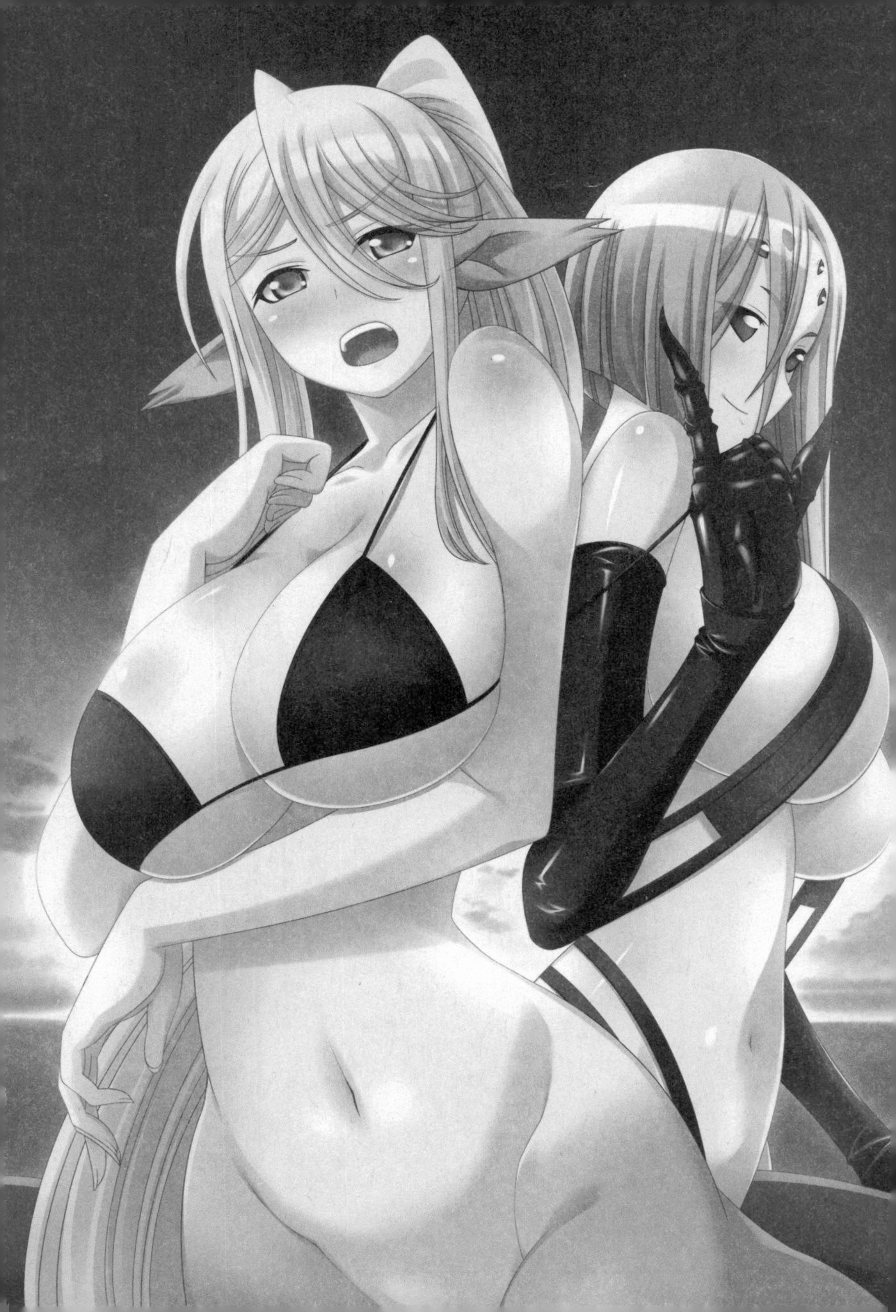

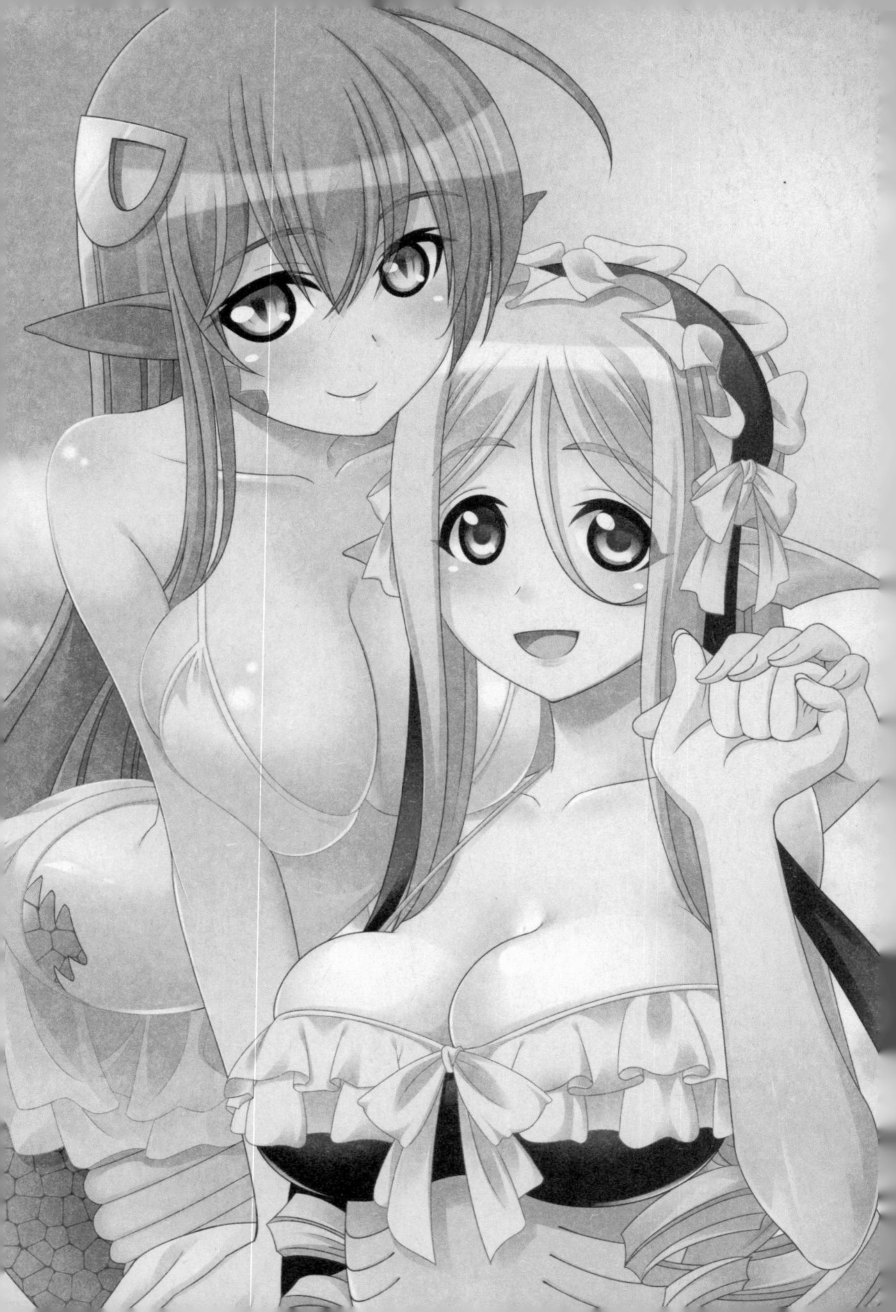

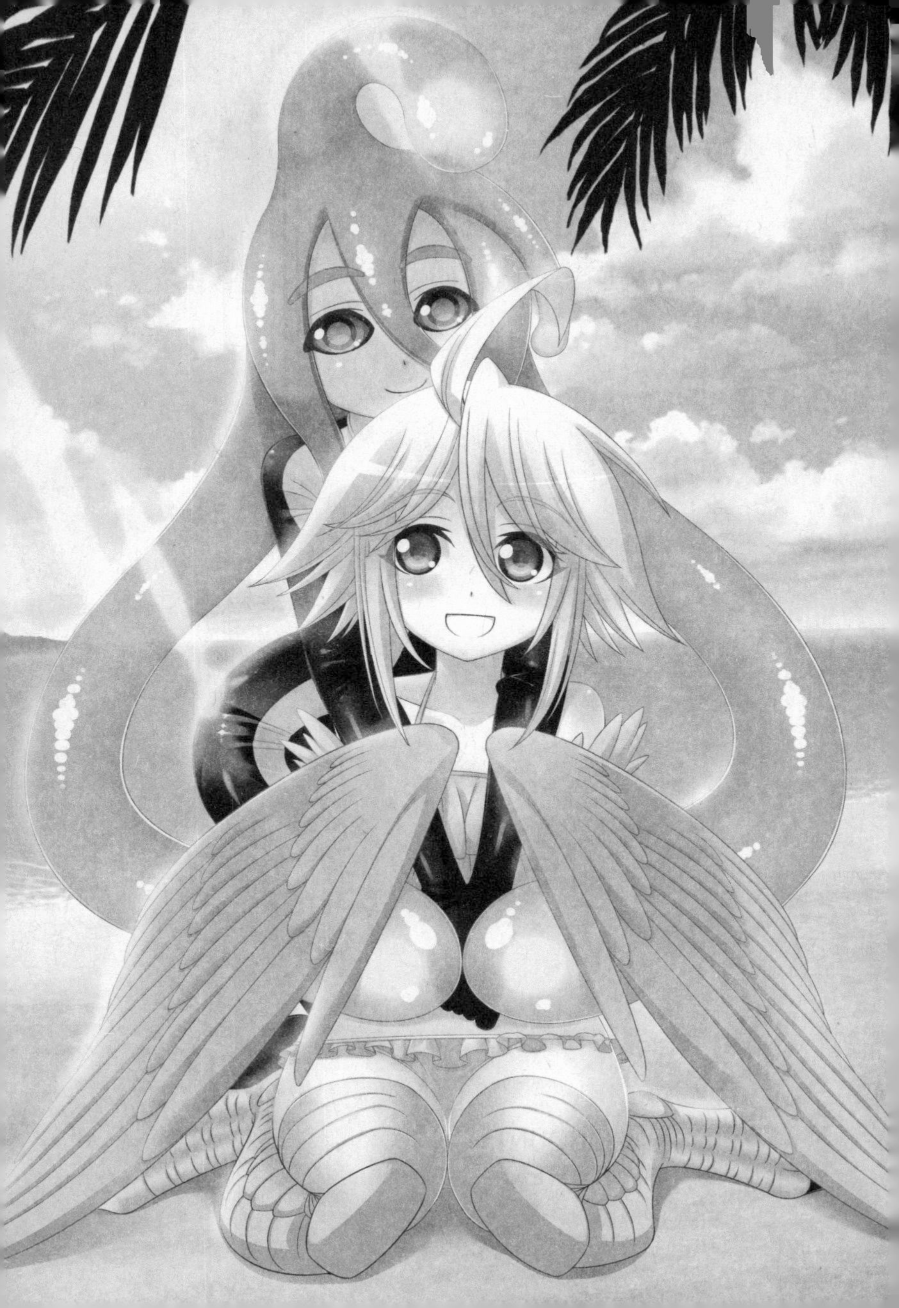

Monster
Musume
I ♥ MONSTER GIRLS